When
the Dog speaks,
the Philosopher
listens

When the Dog speaks, the Philosopher listens

A guide to the greatness of Pythagoras
&
his curious Age.

Nigel McGilchrist

First published in 2022
by
Genius Loci Publications,
71 Queensway, London W2

email:geniusloci.publications@gmail.com

ISBN 978-1-3999-2242-5

Maps by Nicholas Hill,
Nick Hill Design.

Book Design by David Gillingwater,
Herring Bone Design Ltd.

Printed in the United Kingdom,
By Short Run Press Ltd.,
Exeter, Devon.

This book is dedicated
to the memory of the woman
who made me flesh and bones, and bore me into this world.

These pages are the fulfilment of a promise made to her
on her death-bed more than thirty years ago.
I am truly sorry that it has taken so long:
but she knows no time now and will not have fretted, I hope.

INTRODUCTION

ASIA, AFRICA & GREECE

QUALITIES OF GREEKNESS

PYTHAGORAS DISTILLED

PROBLEMS
WITH PYTHAGORAS

PYTHAGORAS TODAY

AFTER-THOUGHTS
& APPENDICES

MAPS & ILLUSTRATIONS

INTRODUCTION

About This Book

East and West. We like to think of them as very different, and of their philosophies as separate. Yet their origins are one. Without the East there would have been no Western philosophy as we now know it. There would never have been what we understand today as the tradition of "Western thinking", had someone not brought a handful of profound observations and ideas from the East into the Mediterranean world at the dawn of Classical Antiquity. That person was Pythagoras.

In doing this, he deeply influenced the mind of Plato, who, more than any ancient philosopher, has shaped the structure of later Western thinking. In doing this, he also created for the West a particular spiritual awareness – a fertile soil in which it was possible, five hundred years later, for the revolutionary ideas of a Middle Eastern charismatic teacher called Jesus of Nazareth to take root and flourish widely, changing the life and thought of the West for ever. And, perhaps most important of all, Pythagoras was prominent among a group of philosophers who laid the foundations for that method of thinking which we now call science, and of which the West is justifiably proud. All of these things he made possible – for better, and for worse. Like a botanist who takes a spur from a delicate and precious plant and then grafts it to a vigorous root-stock so that it may grow with renewed strength and finer nature, Pythagoras was there at the right moment and in the right place to effect this extraordinary transformation. He married the mind of the East into the family of the West.

These are big claims. Yet, if anything, Pythagoras has tended to be regarded with condescension and a roll of the eyes by mainstream philosophers and historians. This is because of the incongruity of so much of the trivia of his reported legacy, which was preserved and written by a myriad lesser minds than his. History has not been kind to him, and the garbled and improbable things that were said about him in the centuries after his death do no justice at all to his true importance. The fault – if there is any – lies with Pythagoras himself, simply because he wrote nothing down and appears to have taken little thought for posterity, leaving it to hearsay instead to tell his story.

Pushing through the crowd of critics, admirers, commentators, historians, followers, disciples and interpreters who mill around him, in the hope of reaching Pythagoras himself, we find he almost invariably slips from our grasp. He is no easy subject. But his presence is unmistakable. In his thought there is an openness of perspective towards every kind of thinking; there is a humaneness of heart; a calmness of character; and an ability not just to move freely between scientific and spiritual search, but to understand their ultimate inseparability. Above all, there is an ever-present intuition that where beauty is, lies meaning. There are lessons and qualities here that we should take heed of in our own broken times.

The subject here is not just Pythagoras: it is also the world and the age in which he lived. The first few chapters of this book are a portrait of the unusually creative world in which he had the fortune to be born and of the geography across which he moved. Only after that, does the focus turn to the man himself – to try to understand who he may have been, and what he was at pains to show us. It could have been written, and still can be read, in a different order. The reader who wishes to engage with the thinking of Pythagoras right away, may want to begin with Section Three ('*Pythagoras Distilled*'), and later return to the earlier chapters. But my instinct is that we understand Pythagoras and his thought better, by first taking a journey around his world and his times. It is through the exploration of his remarkable and profoundly inter-connected age, that we begin to see how it was possible that one man's journeys could open a door in the Western mind onto a new and immeasurably productive territory.

These pages were written for the simple joy of exploring what we can reconstruct of the thought of a great mind, and of trying to cut through the confusion that has clouded it over the time-span of the twenty five centuries that separate us from it. They are about music, about sound, about the sky at night, the waters of the Mediterranean, the discovery of the world around us, harmony, the courtesy and respect we should show to others, to animals and to nature – many things, which, although it may not be apparent at first sight, are at a profound level crucially connected. Above all, they are about the discovery of an unexpected beauty in the design of the universe we inhabit, and how all these things came together in the mind of one man who left not a written word behind.

———————— ～ ————————

The Maze Within and Around us

The walls of green rise high on either side. We are caught in a labyrinth and cannot easily see how it works. If only we could just get to a slightly higher viewpoint and see it from above, then we could understand the pattern of it and perhaps eventually find a solution. Life is a labyrinth; and the labyrinth, since its first conception, has always been a powerful metaphor for our existence. Each turn we make in ignorance seems to determine what happens further down the line. We need a hill from which to understand it better.

Such a hill was found in the sixth century BC. It was a remarkable period of transforming awareness, not just in the West but across the whole breadth

*Pathways within the largest green maze in the world, 'Il Labirinto della Masone',
created at Fontanellato near Parma in Italy
by Franco Maria Ricci in the early years of this century.*

of Asia as well. This slight rise gave the human mind the possibility to view the labyrinth from a crucially higher perspective, at which point it began, unexpectedly, to reveal itself as a structure that was whole and coherent.

In our own development out of infancy and into early adulthood, we all encounter this same hill. We shed the spirit-filled narratives of our childhood and start to be aware that things appear to have an existence which is integrated and is quite separate from our own imagination. The child's world is filled with magic; the adult's is full of ideas instead. It is a radical change – not necessarily for the better or for the worse: it is just a change that happens. Fortunately, the adult never completely replaces the child in us: we keep, to the end, a yearning for that unknowingness we once had within the labyrinth.

These pages look at the moment in history when this hill was first discovered, the period in human intellectual development when ideas and perspectives began to replace stories. It is about the emergence for the first time of a coherent idea of what our universe – seen as a whole – might be: and for once it was not to be a mythical narrative. This is a book not *of* philosophy, but about how philosophy is born and what it was like to think the first scientific concepts in human history.

The story centres on the curious figure of Pythagoras, someone remembered by us today mostly as a mathematician and geometer. In reality he was far more than that. Mathematics for him were just one aspect of a quality that he had come to recognise in everything around him. He appears to have had a particular aptitude as an observer and a listener. It is claimed that he travelled widely in Egypt and Asia and gathered knowledge wherever he went, amassing a body of learning which his younger contemporary Heracleitus viewed with disdain. He possessed the open and uncommitted mind of the Greek mercantile environment from which he emerged. He listened and absorbed in a manner unlike others, and seems to have had an instinct for understanding intuitively the vaster significance of what he heard and observed. The other thing he did supremely well was to see connections between quite different areas of thinking and of human experience. It is his mind and his world which hold this whole story together. More than any, he grasped the significance of the hill which had been found and of the view it offered across the labyrinth.

Through all this Pythagoras himself remains almost invisible to us. The few recorded details of his life are frequently contradicted somewhere else, and there is scarcely a single thing he is said to have said whose authenticity cannot been brought into question for one reason or another. He is perhaps the most elusive of all the great figures of Antiquity. Like some curious subatomic particle, we can observe him only through the effect he has on others around him: we hardly ever see him directly. But also like a subatomic particle, his existence is fundamental to ours because the way in which he learnt to think was to shape, very significantly, the course of our later thinking in the West. One great philosopher-historian of the last century, Bertrand Russell, said of him in his sweeping survey of Western philosophy: "I do not know of any other man who has been as influential as he was in the sphere of thought." [1] And Russell was not a man given to rash overstatement.

Central to his thinking is something that tends to be overlooked in the wide range of commentary about him. It is the primordial value which Pythagoras attributes to beauty – and the significance which it holds, not just for the world of the spirit but also for what we have come to call science. We shall see how the idea of beauty is embedded deep within the very word Pythagoras chose to define our universe.   But it is also the flame within his thinking. It was a perception so fruitful in all that it signifies for us, that we need to understand how it came about – and how its importance was then lost from sight in the later development of mainstream Western thinking.

The labyrinth, by its superficially serendipitous nature, asks us to turn and turn, and explore in every direction first, before we arrive at the hill or tower at its centre. It gives us no alternative if we want to enjoy and to benefit from that wider view from the vantage point. One particular historical curiosity which took place just before the life-time of Pythagoras may help us to understand the strange way in which the process of exploration can lead us unexpectedly towards our goal. Let us begin with that curiosity.

The Maze of the Villa Pisani, Strà, Italy

---

[1] Bertrand Russell: *A History of Western Philosophy*, Part I, chap. 3.

ASIA, AFRICA & GREECE

The Constellation of Orion, the Hunter,
as seen in the Southern Hemisphere

A Turning World

Somewhere around the year 600 BC, an expedition set out from the warm, familiar waters of the Red Sea on a journey that would radically change the ideas that humanity had about the world in which it lived.

The handful of mariners and ships involved in the enterprise were Phoenician[1], from the coasts of the Levant; but their paymaster was the Pharaoh of Egypt, Necho II. The Phoenicians knew Necho to be a restless and ambitious monarch, blessed with extraordinary energy and inspiration. He had embarked on ambitious projects, and was entangled in an expensive war against Nebuchadnezzar, King of Babylon. These activities were a strain on Egypt's exchequer and so, seeking to have greater access to gold and minerals in the surrounding lands to finance his expense, he encouraged the Phoenician expedition to prospect the coasts of Africa. His orders would probably have been to follow the shore and to find points of access to whatever markets (preferably supplying gold) there were on or near to the coast, or at least accessible by navigable river if they proved to be in the interior. That, at least, was the spoken reason for their journey; but the Phoenicians knew that there were other unspoken objectives as well. They were being sent to explore the limits of the world and to return with information about its size and nature. They also knew well that they were embarking on a journey from which some of their number – perhaps all of them – might never return.

Hostages from the Phoenician community would have been detained in Egypt, as was the custom, and in exchange the expedition would have been provided amply with supplies and the Pharaoh's military escort for the first part of the journey.

And so this remarkable adventure began. Once the official Egyptian escort had returned home through the mouth of the Red Sea at the straits of Deire – called the Bab el Mandeb or 'Gate of Tears' by Arabs today – the Phoenician ships continued on alone, making probably good progress in the early months of the voyage. They may have survived more on the water of coconut fruit than on fresh drinking water, even though the ships were designed in such a way as to collect and store the rainwater which fell, often torrentially, in those strange climes to which they were little accustomed. They must also have carried a substantial cargo of commodities such as lamp-oil, bronze implements, cottons, and bees-wax, since their orders were to explore every possibility for trading goods. In their contacts with local communities they needed to be circumspect at all times and would have proceeded with that caution and meticulousness which was typical of the Phoenician character.

Hoping never to lose sight of the land which was to remain visible on their right-hand side throughout the journey, they would have sailed mostly by day, but on occasions also by night if the sky was clear, so as to avoid the stifling heat as the sun grew higher and higher in the firmament. The stars with which they were familiar sank ever lower in the sky, and new configurations of stars rushed to take their place in unfamiliar patterns that rendered nocturnal navigation with confidence much more difficult.

The world around them changed; yet, most perplexingly, the night sky which should have been their principal constant, had now changed, too, out of all recognition. The seasons, the weather patterns, the star patterns, the behaviour of the seas – everything altered. They had no idea how far they would have to go or how many months and years they would be away from home – if indeed they were ever to return home. They ran the risk of coming to the edge of the world, of dying from exhaustion, of encountering hostility or creatures who could use magic on them, or had strange coloured skins, strange bodies, or were part animal and part human, whose noises and language they could never hope to understand. They were making this journey in just the same period in which the *Odyssey* was first being recited to enthralled audiences: but theirs was no Mediterranean odyssey in familiar waters, with an occasional courteous princess, like Nausicaä, to take up their cause and help them out. For them no potential encounter would happen in any language that they could understand. They contended instead with the sometimes mountainous seas of the Indian and Atlantic Oceans, whose swells drew on thousands of miles of blank water behind them and mingled dangerously as they approached the very furthest point of their trajectory.

After how many months of rowing and sailing and navigating and provisioning on unknown and potentially dangerous shores, does a group of sailors say "enough!", and decide to turn back for home? Did they have women with them? Were there moments of joy amid the fear and apprehension and blank ignorance of where and how far they were going? How many illnesses, mutinies and deaths along the way would it take to break their spirit?

As they proceeded into cooler temperatures at the end of their first season of travel, strange things began to happen: the sun moved behind them in the sky at noon, inclining incomprehensibly towards the north – a disturbing phenomenon never seen before, even though some of the mariners may earlier have penetrated into tropical and equatorial waters. The constants remained: the land was still steadfastly to their right and the stars, though unfamiliar now, still swept through the sky from East to West. The sun itself rose impeccably on the same side as always, and set over the land. Everything told them they were still sailing southwards, and yet the sun was not ahead of them, and the shadow of the mast fell forward towards the prow of their ships. The world, it seemed, had turned on its head.

After nearly three full years away, the mariners – a portion of them at least – returned to Egypt from the West, across the Mediterranean. They had shown

Table Mountain, Cape Town, South Africa

that the lands of Egypt, Libya and Ethiopia, which they previously believed comprised all of Africa, were in fact only part of an island in the ocean – yet an island of such immense size that it was hard for any of them to comprehend. The world had grown suddenly much bigger after their expedition; but it had acquired, by the same token, a more knowable logic. They themselves must have been astonished and unbelieving of what it meant, when, after perhaps the most exhausting part of the whole journey, pressing against powerful swells and winds, pushing northwards along the Atlantic seaboard of North Africa in the third year of their expedition, they headed for the refuge of an off-shore island [2] and found to their amazement that fellow countrymen of theirs, speaking Phoenician and working in the smelting of iron, greeted them and told them that they were some way to the south of the Pillars of Hercules and therefore little more than one month's journey from entering the Straits of Gibraltar and the familiar waters of the Inland Sea, their home and their journey's final act.

The story makes a deep impression on us today, but we would never even have known that the journey had taken place, were it not for the fact that one Greek writer, Herodotus, a century and a half later thought it worthy of recording. He mentioned it primarily because he wanted to show that he did not really believe that it had happened. The claim that the sun, according to the accounts of the mariners, should have tilted into the northern hemisphere of the sky at noon, made the whole story highly suspect to his critical mind:

> They [the mariners] spoke of something which I do not believe, although others may, that when they were sailing around Libya [i.e. Africa] they had the sun on their right [North] side as they went.[3]

Herodotus's understandable scepticism of this part of the story, becomes ironically, for us, with our greater knowledge of the form of our planet, the very reason for which we most believe that the expedition *did* actually happen. The observation could hardly have been invented.

Sometimes, when we set out to look for one thing, we are astonished to come across something else quite different and unexpected. The Phoenician mariners were experienced enough to know that, where they were going, they would encounter strange peoples, strange creatures and strange seas; but they had no idea that the invisible structure of their world would alter so dramatically and that they would witness its most sacred and fixed points turn on their head: a firmament at night that bore no resemblance to the familiar one that they knew and by which they navigated; those few constellations that *had* stayed with them, now upside down and reversed – Orion, the hunter, standing on his head; the light moving across the moon in quite the opposite direction as it waxed and waned; and a sun which, by day, rose up into the North of the sky. The elements remained the same, but their behaviour confounded the mind. Or was it just that they were looking at them from a different point of view? And if it were their point of view that had changed, how could it be explained? and where did it mean they were?

For Pythagoras it was not dissimilar. Like the mariners, he was a journeyer to distant places. He, too, was an explorer, but of a rather different kind – an adventurer of mind. And in his journeys and explorations he, too, encountered things that were quite unexpected and which prompted him to re-imagine the world in a quite different way – chance observations about acoustics or geometry coming from Babylon or from the priests of Egypt; ideas about life and death which he heard, or thought he heard, coming from India. And then when he returned again to his home in Greece, he found that the heated debate was still running, half a century later, about where those Phoenician mariners had been, what they had seen, and how it could possibly be explained.

Before we come to what this gifted mind was to make of all these various things and of how they subtly related each to the other, let us begin our own journey with a look, first of all, at the world into which he was born and across which he moved. This is important in order to understand how his philosophy came about. His was a remarkable century: it witnessed the appearance on the world's stage of Buddhism, Confucianism and Taoism in Asia, and the laying of the first foundations of scientific thought and method in Greece. It was a remarkable world in which the deep interconnection of Asia, Egypt and Europe, permitted one such as Pythagoras to move freely in mind and person among its centres. A world in which the constant trade of goods and the unseen movement of people – merchants, minstrels, magi, mercenaries, diplomatic deputations, doctors, jesters, engineers and wandering gurus, whoever they might be – were the engine of its civilisation. The exchange of ideas and beliefs they brought about between one centre and another, between one culture and another, did more to further the well-being and wisdom of humanity in general, than all the wars and conflicts (which dominate our picture of history) were ever able to undo.

---

[1] The Phoenicians were a Semitic people, known to us through the Old Testament as the Canaanites.

[2] The Island of Mogador, at Essaouira in Morocco, became a centre of the production of Tyrian purple from at least as far back as the 5th century BC when Hanno, the Carthaginian navigator, established a trade entrepôt there; but the first Phoenician presence on the island for metallurgic activity is attested from the 7th century BC (see Car men Aranegui Gascó, C./C. Gómez Bellard/S. Jodin 2000: *Los Fenicios en Atlántico, Perspectivas de nuevas excavaciones en Marruecos: Revista de Arqueología* 223, 26-35.)

[3] Herodotus, *Histories*, Book IV, 42. [καὶ ἔλεγον ἐμοὶ μὲν οὐ πιστά, ἄλλῳ δὲ δή τέῳ, ὡς περιπλώοντες τὴν Λιβύην τὸν ἥλιον ἔσχον ἐς τὰ δεξιά]

'Oranges and Green Oranges' - Song Dynasty silk fan painted in ink and colour:
(?) Lin Chun, early 12th century:
National Palace Museum, Taipei.

The Gift of the East

The story of the West begins with our debt to the East. Even as the day starts the East is at our breakfast table: the orange – prince of hybrids, from the foothills of the Himalaya, known in China for two and a half millennia and brought by Portuguese merchants into Europe in the late 15th century; the tea and porcelain likewise originally from China; the glassware, first perfected in Mesopotamia and Egypt; the coffee from the Horn of Africa, via Arabia and Turkey, and the sugar first brought from South East Asia by the Arabs into Europe through Sicily. Through the window where the morning sunlight enters are gardens: cultivated tulips, magnolias, peonies, rhododendrons, camellias, dozens of varieties of plants, all life-enhancing, all with ancient origins deep in the mountains or plains of Anatolia, Central Asia or China. Our cotton and linen clothes, made from plants first cultivated and fabrics first woven in ancient Egypt and Mesopotamia, and the silk which has given its name to the arteries that connected the West with China. Yet more comes to mind in looking around the room: wine, made from an exuberant, fruiting climber first brought to the Mediterranean from the Caucasus and Persia in Neolithic times. Olive oil and olives, from the Middle East in the same period. The generous chicken and her eggs from India and Southeast Asia. In later history, the first lemons and citrus fruits, rice, aubergines, even pasta – almost all brought by the Arabs into Sicily from Persia. Almonds, pistachios, pepper, a thousand spices and flavours. Yoghurt, yoga; precious stones and jewels; the sound of the flute and the music of stringed instruments… If we take them all away, what is left?

It is hard to conceive of our lives, our clothes and the food we eat without feeling chastened by our millennia-long debt to Asia. But it is not solely a story of luxuries, spices and perfumes; it is about the essential and commonest things which we take for granted in our lives, even the religious affiliations we may have – Jewish, Christian, Moslem, Buddhist, Hindu, whatever – all of which are Asian in origin. Without the things that it has taken from the East, the whole nature of our existence in the West would be unthinkably different.

In ways both obvious and subtle, Western culture has been sustained and shaped by the East – by the abundance, the imagination, and also by the awareness of beauty which has flowed out of Asia. But the relationship is not just one of giving and taking alone: it is more complex. The West has crucially processed whatever it has taken from Asia over the centuries, transforming it and often humanising it profoundly. We will observe this very same process in how Pythagoras transforms what he learns from the East.

From earliest history through to the time of the Industrial Revolution, however, the movement of trade between the European Mediterranean and Asia has been characterised by a systemic imbalance. The fruits of civilisation, material and invisible, flowed predominantly from East into West. The West meanwhile did its best to plug the deficit with a supply of raw materials and basic necessities – metal ores, leathers, wool, pots, and many of the less glamorous things of life. Yet the imbalance persisted, and at the time of Ancient Rome's greatest influence in the West, the situation was perceived to have spiralled out of control. Pliny the Elder, writing around 70 AD, complained that the wealth of Ancient Rome was draining away in its pursuit of Eastern produce and its economy had become dependent on the East to an unhealthy degree: he conservatively estimated the deficit sum as an annual expenditure of one hundred million sesterces [1]. But, in writing this, Pliny had touched on a much wider phenomenon of cultural change: a profound and irreversible 'orientalisation' that had by then taken hold of his world. Less than two centuries later, when, in the year 248, Rome reached one thousand years of age since its

Marcus Julius Philippus – the Syrian Emperor of Rome 244-249 AD
who celebrated the millennium of the founding of the city of Rome in 248 –
believed by some to have been a Christian.

founding, the Emperor who celebrated this momentous anniversary was in fact an Arab from Syria. Less than a century after that, one of his successors did the most remarkable thing of all: Constantine the Great took the decision to move his capital from Rome to the shores of the Bosphorus. Nothing gives a clearer sign of the West's dependence on, and obsession with, the East than the emperor's decision to uproot what had been for generations the successful and widely acknowledged centre of Western civilisation on the banks of the Tiber and move it to a small Greek colony called Byzantion, which he re-named 'Nova Roma'. This move opened an avenue between the two hemispheres, along which – thanks also to the liberalisation of religious laws promulgated by Constantine – Christianity could now pass smoothly into the West, changing the character and the bloodstream of the continent for ever. European history became suffused for the next millennium and beyond with the colour of a messianic cult from Asia.

The contents of our kitchens, our clothing and our gardens tell the story of this flow of materials, plants and artefacts from East to West. It is a rich and fascinating story. But the traffic was not only stuff that could be packed into caravans of camels or into the holds of ships: religious creeds, technologies, whole ways of thinking, kinds of song and music, also hitched a lift on these journeys. Ideas travel with merchants; methods of building, measuring, writing, sculpting and painting also. The roads and seaways to the East are in one sense the parameters of early Western history.

Physical geography plays an important role in this movement. And Greece – by all accounts a curious country in that it is scarcely a land but more a sea scattered with islands – became a crucial player. The Aegean Sea is the shore both of Europe and of Asia; the place where their worlds and their waters intermingle. It is the slender diaphragm between two different continents and is the lens of change in the eye of both East and West. When the East's knowledge and skills crossed this shore or passed through this lens, facilitated by a sensitive and attentive thinker and traveller such as Pythagoras, they were transformed and became something significantly different.

The profound nature of this transformation is seen clearly in the art and artefacts produced in this geographical area of overlap. The Greeks learnt how to sculpt and build on a monumental scale from the Egyptians. This was only natural: Egypt was an impressively ancient and developed culture by the time what we now call 'Greece' was just appearing on the scene. This is not to say that Crete and the Aegean area in general did not have their own long history and even a distinguished painting and sculptural tradition in the Neolithic period: but all of that had fallen into confusion around the time of the Trojan War at the end of the Bronze Age and, after what appears to have been a cataclysmic implosion of society, several centuries of 're-grouping' followed – a period from about 1150 to 750 BC, often referred to as a Dark Age. When Greece awoke from this fallow period, it was natural, because of its geographical position and its growing trade with Egypt, that it should turn to the great monuments and buildings of the Nile Valley for inspiration and instruction.

Like an attentive child Greece learnt very fast: the sheer quantity of its production in sculpture and architecture in those early centuries between 600 and 450 BC is phenomenal. Although they survive only in ruins and fragments for the most part, these works still clearly reveal the nature of the transformation that is under way as the artistic ideas move west from Egypt into Greece. A couple of concrete examples of this phenomenon may help to illustrate it.

The well-preserved fragment of sculpture known as the *Moschophoros*, or 'Calf-bearer' (*see over*), is one of the most familiar emblems of early sculpture from the time of Pythagoras. Its scale is noticeably human: it would have been a little over 5ft tall when complete. It is stylised, and yet has a naturalism which we sense is bursting to break out. It is symmetrical in concept, yet it also has a deliberate and life-enhancing asymmetry. It is calm and poised, yet somehow radiating an inner energy – an intensity which would have been yet more commanding if the black and white stone insets defining the eyes and pupils had survived. This figure presents itself to us as a young man simply bringing an animal to the altar for dedication and sacrifice: we know from the inscription on the base that the piece was commissioned by a certain Rhombos, son of Palos, and was placed on the Acropolis of Athens somewhere around the year 560 BC – when Pythagoras would have been no more than a young child.

A first glimpse immediately reveals how the artist is working with forms remembered from Egyptian art. The 'X' created across the chest by the arms of the man and the legs of the calf is reminiscent of the crossed arms of Pharaonic statuary. The sarcophagi of Tutankhamun may come first to our minds; but more visible to Greek eyes at that time would have been something like the colossal statue of Ramses II in the Temple of Karnak (*see over*), created more than six hundred years before the *Moschophoros*. Names incised on the statue of Ramses II at Abu Simbel in Nubia as early as 591 BC tell us that Greeks were not uncommon visitors to the Nile Valley in those early times.

In design, the two pieces are superficially similar, and the later is a memory of the earlier. The Greek sculptor has quickly absorbed from Egyptian sculpture that love of clear and sensual volumes in the body. There is a similarly assured perfection of pure lines in the Calf-Bearer which define the edge of the garment, the borders of the hair and the outlines in the face. But there are a number of things that are quite new: the careful observation of the abdomen of the young man and of the musculature of the haunch and fore-legs of the calf he is carrying, both of which are beautifully evoked. These are interesting

The Moschophoros or 'Calf-Bearer', mid 6th century BC.
(Acropolis Museum, Athens)

considerations, but they relate largely to form. If we step back from the sculpture a little, however, we see the real gulf that divides these two pieces.

First, the scale: it was courageous of the artist of the *Moschophoros* to take a design, associated up until then with the representation on a colossal scale of divinity in a monarch, and to reduce it to human proportions, applying it to the figure of an Athenian citizen: the calf-bearer becomes, thereby, one of us. By doing this, rather than exalting the majesty of a monarch, the artist sanctifies the humanity of the individual. He humanises the figure before our eyes.

Next, the geometry: take the calf away and the piece dies because it loses that life-giving play between symmetry and asymmetry. Our eye takes pleasure in the perfect order and symmetry of the man, but then our pulse rate changes when we take in the contrast of the calf on the shoulders, lop-sided yet perfectly stable nonetheless. A shaft of surprise catches us, as when a familiar melody suddenly moves into a distant minor key or a contrasting rhythm.

Last, the idea. Gone are the insignia of Pharaoh's majesty, the crook and

Ramses II, 13th century BC
Temple of Karnak

flail which he holds in his crossed arms. In the 'Calf-Bearer' these are deliberately recalled, but they are transformed into an image which speaks instead of the inseparable bond uniting humankind with the animals of its husbandry, the mutual interdependence of man and beast at the most fundamental level. The juxtaposition of the two heads – animal and human – so close to one another, further emphasises this. It is an image which is hard to forget. The 'Calf-Bearer' steps straight out into our world as a human being – no longer an object of religious devotion, but rather an evocative philosophical observation.

The 'Calf-Bearer' (detail)

We know that the *Moschophoros* was dedicated on the Acropolis of Athens in the vicinity of a temple of Athena which no longer exists and which preceded the Parthenon that survives on the Athenian acropolis today. Just as we have seen with the sculpture, there looms behind the design and form of that subsequent Parthenon, which dates from a century later, the example of Egypt once again. It is from the hypostyle buildings of the Nile Valley that the Greeks picked up the concept of the temple-structure composed from columns and architraves. Here again the awe-inspiring religious 'interiority' and monumentality of the Egyptian buildings, has been replaced by a lighter, simpler, exterior clarity. The Parthenon is not merely human in scale as a building, but also profoundly human in design. Its columns are not perfectly cylindrical but swell very slightly in the middle, like the muscles of an arm; they are distanced varyingly from one another according to their position in the building and how the human eye perceives them interact with the light and shadow; they all lean slightly in to give a sense of a compact gathering of strength and tension; the base on which they stand is not flat but slightly bowed upwards so as to give it, too, the necessary

The Acropolis of Athens, viewed from the Hill of the Pnyx

tension to counteract any unwanted flatness that the eye might perceive. All this makes the building a vibrant and living organism, conceived as something human and not solely to be seen as a beautifully proportioned idea.

Yet exquisitely proportioned idea it undoubtedly is — once we step back from it. To look at the Parthenon in Athens from a distance and to see it rising above the plain of the city framed by mountains and sea is also to experience a profound symbol. Its apparently small human size sits calmly on top of a gnarled, wild outcrop of rock. The temple's poised form and balanced orderliness have the effect of taming the rude rock beneath. The very sight of it quells anxiety. Like the 'Calf Bearer', it is both a human creation and one which at the same time presents itself to our eye and our mind as a philosophical proposition. This life-giving duality lies at the heart of the Greek aesthetic.

The Parthenon and the Acropolis seen together constitute an immediately graspable image of the dynamic relationship between wild nature and order, harmony and clarity. The image of the building is one of the most reassuring statements in the history of architecture – reassuring to the citizens of Athens over whose lives it presided and to whom it was always present and always visible; reassuring also to us who see in its image (and in variants of it reproduced a thousand times in different places) that same expression of the influence of clarity and order. It is this eloquent dialogue between setting and building which gives power to many of the temples of the Greek world: the temple of Poseidon on the cape at Sounion; the temples along the ridge below Agrigento; or the sanctuary of Apollo *Epikourios* ('the Helper') at Bassae, high in the mountains of the Peloponnese.

Ruins of the 5th century BC temple at the mountain-top sanctuary of Apollo Epikourios at Bassae in Ancient Arcadia. (Photographed in 1972.)

The *Moschophoros* and the Parthenon are only two examples we could take out of many. But they show the way in which the accumulated technical knowledge of sculpture and building of the East becomes something quite different as it moves West and reaches the cooler waters and sharper light of the Aegean world. It becomes transformed in nature. It appears to be touched by an impulse both to *humanise*, and at the same time to *abstract*; to bring things to the heart of what it means to be human, and at the same time to see them as something universal. This is the particular genius of the early Greek mind. And it is this same transformation that we find with Pythagoras. In his travels he becomes acquainted with diverse techniques of calculation, observations about the stars, music, animals or the movement of water, the destiny of our souls or the diet of our bodies – all kinds of ideas that were current in different parts of Asia and in Egypt and which were already of considerable antiquity. But in his receptive mind new connections between these disparate ideas evolve and come into focus. Their nature is transformed.

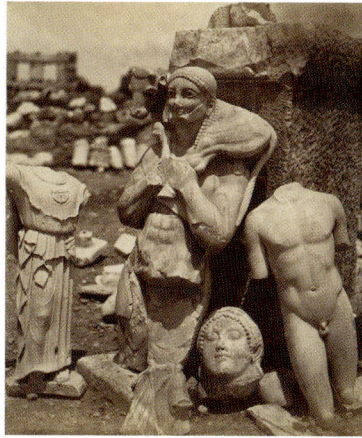

Early excavations on the Acropolis of Athens, c. 1865, reveal evidence of the Persian destruction during the summer of 480 BC when Xerxes the Great invaded mainland Greece and devastated anything that stood on the plateau of the Acropolis.

---

[1] Pliny, *Naturalis Historia* XII 41/84

Watercolour impression of the façade of the Ishtar Gate in Babylon, c.575 BC,
by the German Art Historian, Friedrich Wachtsmuth, c 1912.

The worlds that Pythagoras saw

To be born in the 6th century BC was, in so many ways, a stroke of great fortune. It was a period of astonishing intellectual fecundity and artistic development – an extraordinary moment in human history right across the arc of Europe and Asia. The already very ancient tradition of spiritual thinking in India was on the verge of being transformed by the appearance of Siddhartha Gautama and of what came to be known as Buddhism; the teachings ascribed to Zoroaster in Persia, to the Hebrew Prophets of Judaea, and to Lao Tzu and to Confucius in China, were at different stages of evolution or inception; and Greek philosophy and science were in their highly influential infancy. Through the wide travels he is claimed to have made and through his intelligence and sensitivity, Pythagoras was well positioned to transmit ideas and methods between cultures and to cross-pollinate the world's cosmological thinking at the very outset of its expansion.

Greece was at one extremity of this 'fertile crescent' of intellectual ferment; and because her fractured civilisation was in the process of reinventing itself after the fallow interlude which followed the sudden and violent demise of the Bronze Age cultures in the Aegean area, she possessed an identity and an energy quite different from her neighbours farther to the East. This took the form of what can only be described as the kind of 'youthfulness' and receptivity which is born out of renewal. Lacking the restraints and taboos imposed by venerated tradition in the royal courts of kings elsewhere in Asia, there was space for an openness to new ideas and technologies in the emerging Aegean world. For the same reason there was also an unmistakable intensity to its mentality. This expressed itself already in the preceding 7th century in the powerfully erotic sentiment and self-awareness to be found in the lyric poems of Sappho and Archilochus. The same intensity animates the thinking of the Ionian school of philosophers in the 6th century to which Pythagoras and Heracleitus belonged; and it carries through into the great tragedians and comedians of the following 5th century BC. It is an intensity that dwells in the Aegean landscape and seascape from which all these figures emerged. Even today its particular qualities of light and clarity can hold a spell over our imagination.

Ancient Greece was never a land-mass as we sometimes imagine it today. It was a sea, a network of scattered islands contained within an expanse of water which was bordered on all sides – taking Crete as the southern limit of the Aegean – by a coastline dotted with cities, ports and harbours, all belonging to a unifying Hellenic culture and language. The heart and spirit of Ancient Greece was the sea itself rather than the land whose mountainous interior was mostly looked upon with fear as intractable and hostile. Socrates acknowledges this fact about the Greeks when he says in the *Phaedo* dialogue: 'we [Greeks]... live like ants or frogs around a pond' [1] (*see over for map*).

For this reason the sea was to the Greek world what the land was to others. The islands in the Aegean 'pond' were rocky and poor in agriculture. That reality constrained the inhabitants to go out and trade, to master the seas, to study the stars for navigation, to explore other lands, to open their minds to

MACEDON

Abdera

THRACE

Byzantion•

PROPONTIS

Stagira•

Thasos

Samothrace

Olynthos•

•Dion

Imbros

•Abydos

Cyzicos

Lemnos

• Troy/Ilion

AEOLIS

Assos

Pagasae•

Skiathos

AEGEAN

Antissa

MYSIA

THESSALY

SEA

Eressos•

•Mytilene

Euboea

Lesbos

Skyros

•Phocaea

•Delphi

Chalkis

Eretria

Chios•

Smyrna

•Sardis

LYDIA

Corinth•

•Athens

Andros

Colophon• Ephesos

Argos•

Keos

Tenos

Samos•

Panionion

Troezen

Aegina

Ikaros

Modern
shoreline

—Ancient shoreline

Miletos

CARIA

•Sparta

Seriphos

Paros

Delos

Naxos

Leros

Kos•

•Halicarnassos

Milos

Ios

Astypalaia

Knidos

•Ialysos

Kythera

Thera

Kameiros•

Rhodes

Lindos

Antikythera

N

Karpathos

Crete

0   100km

MEDITERRANEAN SEA

The "frog-pond" of Socrates – the Aegean Sea

other languages, other cultures and other ways of thinking in order to take their goods for exchange in distant markets and to bring home the essentials for their existence. The sea, the weather, the winds were all unpredictable elements; they challenged, stretched and defied the mind to comprehend them fully. The Greek mentality, shaped by such needs and demanding realities, thrived on such challenge. It was inevitably a very different cast of mind from that of the inhabitant of Ancient Egypt, living in the calm valley or the delta of the Nile where the predictability of Nature's cycles was an article of faith.

The physical geography of a marine world of scattered islands favours political plurality. In its early history, the Aegean world was never effectively dominated by a single ruler because its geographical nature rendered such an idea virtually unachievable on a practical level. This was very different from the case in the tranquil domesticated river-valleys and the monarchical and bureaucratic structures to be found in the more ancient worlds of the Near East – Egypt, Assyria, Persia and Babylon – into whose long-sedimented cultures, Pythagoras brought his restless, island mind.

Nor was the island of Samos on the Asian side of the Aegean sea, where Pythagoras grew up, an island of negligible significance. It was in fact one of richest and most cultivated centres of the Greek world at that time, a full century before the 'golden age' of Athens. In the 6th century BC it dominated Aegean trade and boasted a metropolis which was equalled by few other Greek cities for its size and sophistication. Such islands prospered on mercantile economies: it should not surprise us therefore to learn from the philosopher, Porphyry, who wrote a dedicated life of Pythagoras almost eight centuries after his lifetime, that Pythagoras's father, Mnésarchos, was probably a merchant. We cannot be certain of this since some sources speak of him as a gem-engraver, and others as a merchant. Yet the two are not mutually exclusive: Mnésarchos may have

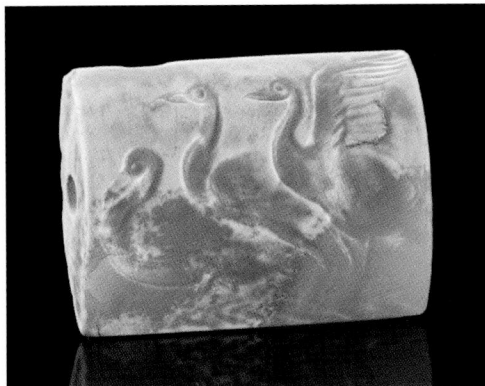

Exquisite Minoan engraved seal in blue chalcedony from the 17th century BC, figuring three swans, illustrating the timeless beauty of the gem-worker's art which was already very ancient by the time of Pythagoras's father.

begun his life working as an engraver of gemstones and then decided to turn his skills to trading in the materials on which he was used to work. We cannot say. But in any case Pythagoras's childhood and schooling, and his contemporaries in Samos, would have been deeply imbued with the prevailingly mercantile ethos for which the island was renowned. Merchants necessarily travel, they learn other languages, they have stories to tell back home about the curiosities and wonders and differences of the places they visit. They need not just to be acquisitive but also *in*quisitive, researching the sources for their products and becoming connoisseurs of quality. They need some quite specific habits of mind, too, such as a sure grasp of arithmetic and calculation, and preferably a good sense of the forms of solids in order to assess accurately the volumes of the different goods that can be packed into the holds of their cargo vessels. All of this fed Pythagoras's mind. I can only imagine that the reason why many more merchants have not been great mathematicians and philosophers in early history is because they were simply too busy and focused on their trade to pull back and contemplate the wider picture of all that they did and saw. Not so, Pythagoras, however.

Porphyry, who cites Neanthes of Cyzicus as his authority, tells us furthermore not just that Pythagoras's father, Mnésarchos, was a merchant, but that he was either a naturalised Phoenician, or else possibly of Etruscan/Lemnian [2] origin – adding thereby to the confusion regarding the origins of his son, Pythagoras. He goes on to suggest that Pythagoras was born and brought up at first in the city of Tyre (in modern-day Lebanon), the mercantile centre of the Phoenician homeland. This information should be accepted with some caution because Porphyry himself was from Tyre. There could be an understandable bias here; but there could equally well be good local knowledge. If what Porphyry says is true however, this would make Pythagoras, by upbringing, part Phoenician and part Greek, and therefore half-European and half-Asian in formation. Such 'differentness' might have distanced him to some extent from his fellow Greeks of the Aegean islands once he later settled in Samos and would go some way to explain that slight detachment we may detect in his relations both to the island and to his philosopher peers. By the same token, however, it would have made him more at home in the very different world of Asia, and would have given him another language to facilitate his journeys there. We must be careful not to give too much credence to Porphyry and his sources; but his claims, if correct,

Map of the Eastern Mediterranean

would undoubtedly be a help in explaining that unexpected ease and affinity with which Pythagoras absorbed the experiences and philosophies of Asia.

The Greeks and the Phoenicians between them dominated maritime trade right across that extraordinary expanse of inland water which separates, and at the same time unites, the continents of Africa, Asia and Europe, and which we call the Mediterranean Sea. The Phoenicians began their history of trading providing their native cedar and cypress wood from the mountains of the Lebanon to the virtually timber-less Egyptians. Later they were the middle-men in the trade between the centres of the Euphrates/Tigris river-

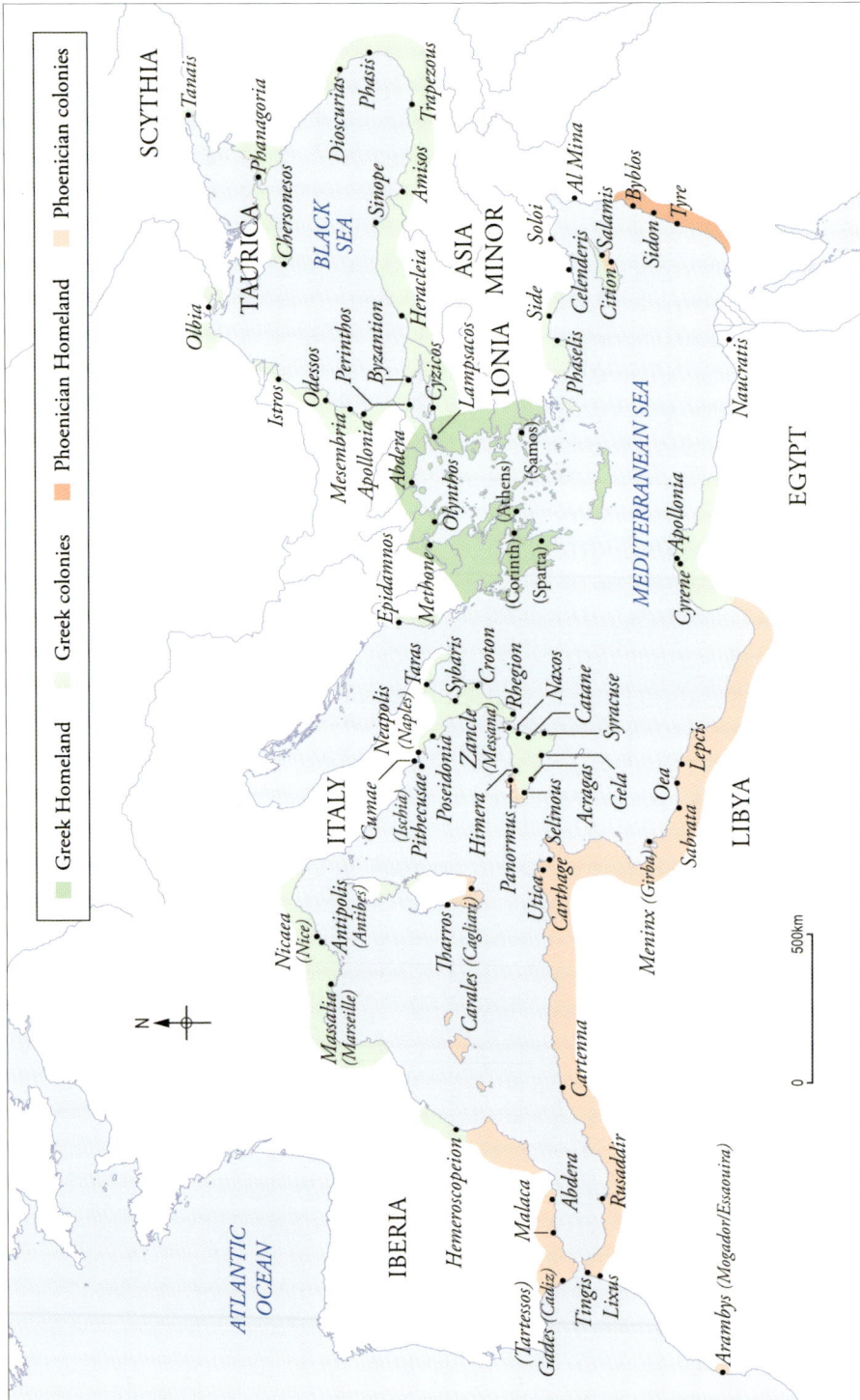

Map of the Mediterranean Sea showing 9th to 6th century Greek and Phoenician colonies and trading posts.

Legend:
- Greek Homeland
- Greek colonies
- Phoenician Homeland
- Phoenician colonies

Labels on map:

SCYTHIA

TAURICA

BLACK SEA

ASIA MINOR

IONIA

Tanais
Phanagoria
Chersonesos
Discurias
Phasis
Trapezous
Olbia
Sinope
Amisos
Istros
Odessos
Perinthos
Byzantion
Heracleia
Mesembria
Apollonia
Abdera
Cyzicos
Lampsacos
Al Mina
Byblos
Sidon
Tyre
Salamis
Citium
Celenderis
Soloi
Side
Phaselis
Naucratis

EGYPT

MEDITERRANEAN SEA

Epidamnos
Methone
Olynthos
(Athens)
(Samos)
(Corinth)
(Sparta)
Cyrene
Apollonia

ITALY

Neapolis
(Naples)
Cumae
(Ischia) Taras
Pithecusae
Poseidonia
Zancle
(Mesana)
Sybaris
Croton
Rhegion
Naxos
Catane
Syracuse
Himera
Panormus
Selinous
Acragas
Gela
Oea
Lepcis
Sabrata
Utica
Carthage
Meninx (Girba)

LIBYA

Tharros
Carales (Cagliari)
Nicaea
(Nice)
Antipolis
(Antibes)
Massalia
(Marseille)

Cartenna

IBERIA

Hemeroscopeion
Malaca
Abdera
Rusaddir
Tingis
Lixus
(Tartessos)
Gades (Cadiz)
Arambys (Mogador/Essaouira)

ATLANTIC OCEAN

N

0   500km

valley and Egypt. From this they expanded their mercantile activities further and further west along the southern shores of the Mediterranean, later to be called the 'Place of Sunset' or *Maghreb* by its Arab settlers, and out onto the Atlantic coast of northwest Africa: they also seeded settlements on Sardinia, the Balearic Islands, Malta and in the western part of Sicily. If Herodotus's sources are correct, it was only thirty years before the birth of Pythagoras that Necho, Pharaoh of Egypt, had sent his expedition of Phoenician mariners on their successful, three-year circumnavigation of Africa.

The Greeks in this same period expanded their trade network along the opposite, northern shores of the Mediterranean and far into the Black Sea, reinforcing it by the myriad coastal colonies and settlements which they founded during the 8th and 7th centuries BC all the way from Marseille in the West to the Crimea in the Northeast, including the southern portion of the Italian peninsula and the eastern half of Sicily, with a few settlements even on the Libyan coast. In this way, a consensual geopolitical equilibrium – Greeks largely along the northern, European shores of the Mediterranean and Phoenicians largely along the sea's southern and African shores – was established between the spheres of influence of these two peoples, even if in places it may have overlapped. Both were known for their formidable skills as mariners; and both had a keen sense of trade. Even though there were times when their different geographical areas of interest imposed political compromises and obligations on them that brought them into opposition and sometimes into conflict, it appears there was mostly cooperation and mutual respect between their merchants at the level of their meeting and working together in the same ports around the Mediterranean.

It is in the context of this encyclopaedic activity of trade, movement and exploration that we should understand the travels which Pythagoras may have undertaken. They are, in one sense, the single most important element of his life: yet we have little concrete evidence for either their extent or their frequency.

Where there is trade of material goods, there will also be trade of intellectual goods. And the role of Pythagoras as a merchant of ideas was pivotal for the development of the Greek, and of the later 'Western', mind. He is almost the very definition of a traveller-thinker. It is true that Thales, perhaps a generation earlier, may have travelled to Egypt also; and that, too, is of importance. But it is partly a question of degree. It is because the body of learning which is associated with the name of Pythagoras is so deeply infused with and indebted to Eastern learning and ways of thinking – those of Asia, more than of Egypt – that his travels, mental or otherwise, assume such historical significance.

No historian of ideas would seriously contest the close links that Pythagoras had with the learning of the East; but when it comes to where he went and how long he travelled and sojourned away from Greece, we have only the words of Porphyry and Iamblichus who were both writing a very long time after the age of Pythagoras. It could be claimed, at one extreme, that no long journeys were necessary at all, and that it was sufficient for Pythagoras merely to have crossed the narrow straits of Samos to the cities of the Asia Minor coast opposite – to Miletus, Ephesus, Smyrna, and to Sardis, the local Persian administrative centre further inland – for him to have met with plenty of ideas and mental skills coming from deep within Asia. But this is to miss the point. Knowledge is not just a parcel that can be passed from person to person. It is a wholly different kind of commodity from the textiles, gems and spices that were traded. A philosophy, a way of looking at the universe, is inseparable from the mental and physical geography that gives rise to it. The unique way in which the Ancient Egyptians envisioned their existence and conceived their very particular cosmogony cannot sensibly be separated from the unique physical world which they inhabited. The same is true of Babylon. And of India. For this reason, I find it hard to believe that Pythagoras never travelled to Africa or into Asia. In fact, it seems more likely that he may have stayed in these places for a considerable time, allowing the profound associations of culture and natural environment to infuse his own thinking.

The island of Samos, Pythagoras's early home, lies less than two kilometres from the Asia Minor coast at its closest point, and only thirty kilometres as the crow flies from the city of Miletus which was the centre of the area's intellectual activity. Thales and Anaximander, in the generation before Pythagoras, Xenophanes, in the same generation, and Anaximenes, Heracleitus and Hecataeus in the next generation, all came from the Asia Minor coast opposite Samos, and all of them from Miletus, except for Xenophanes who was from Colophon and Heracleitus from Ephesus – both cities in the same neighbourhood. The proximity of these ingenious minds to each other in time and space meant that they must have been well aware of what the others were saying or had said, and each probably knew personally at least one or two of the others in the group. Movement would have been easy and continuous between these cities and among the philosophers. The only exception was Heracleitus who was tenaciously unwilling to move from his base in Ephesus: in his case the mountain had to come to him, rather than vice versa, and even then, it seems, it would not have been particularly welcome. The influence, both direct and through competitive debate, that these individuals had upon one another's thinking cannot be overestimated, and it brings to mind the covert competitiveness and consequent artistic fertility of 15th century Florence, or of late 19th century Paris, where writers, painters, sculptors and thinkers were in similarly close contact and competition.

The coast of Asia Minor, and particularly the greater area of Miletus, had always been a slender diaphragm separating the Aegean Greek world from Persian-dominated, continental Asia. Through that porous diaphragm passed in both directions technologies, customs, musical modes and ideas. It is for this reason that those who like to hold that Pythagoras never travelled to the East, claim that he had only to go to the local Persian capital of Sardis, seventy kilometres inland of Smyrna along the Hermus Valley, in order to meet with all the oriental knowledge, and know-how, and mathematics and religious teaching he needed. I'm sure he did go to Sardis; but I doubt that that is the whole story. It was simply not possible for him to learn as much as he did, and as deeply as he did, without a more intimate acquaintance with the East and its learning. There was a period when it was likewise fashionable to claim that Marco Polo never went to Mongolia and China, and that he compiled his *Travels* from the stories of others whom he heard talk at the Rialto in Venice.

Like Marco Polo, whose travels were made possible by a rare moment of pan-Asian unification under the reign of Kublai, grandson of Genghis Khan, the generation of Pythagoras, eighteen hundred years earlier, could likewise contemplate a comparably unified Asia. "As I have said before, once Croesus was subjugated, Cyrus [King of Persia] ruled the whole of Asia" [3]. Herodotus's simple yet astonishing statement speaks volumes. For the formative decades of Pythagoras's adulthood, from 550-530 BC, what we might call 'Near-Asia' was under the rule of a single man — a great and intelligent leader, spoken of with deference in the Books of Ezra and Isaiah by the Jews, viewed as a liberator by the Babylonians, and profoundly admired by Alexander the Great. The stability and wide tolerance that the reign of Cyrus the Great brought, facilitated the movement of people and ideas across a large area of the world's surface. It constituted a rare window of opportunity and transparency in a region which had so often been subject to strife. It was this geopolitical reality that was the facilitator of whatever journeys Pythagoras made.

Yet, for the Greeks of Pythagoras's time it was Egypt that was the cynosure of civilisation and of all learning. It remained so through the 5th century BC, as is witness the unreserved admiration of Herodotus for all things Egyptian, and for whom the country possessed 'more marvels and monuments that defy description than any other' ⁴ . It is in the context of this same admiration that we should also see the impetus for the founding of the city of Alexandria in the 4th century BC by Alexander the Great, and of the city's supremacy in learning and science during the 3rd century BC. From the Greeks, the Romans later learnt this same, understandable awe for Egypt in the 2nd and 1st centuries BC. Egypt, it seems, was for ever the dignified and unchallenged dowager-queen of Mediterranean civilisation throughout Antiquity. Even her majestic geography seemed to express this: the massive tranquillity of the flowing Nile; the rich density of her riparian vegetation; the magnificence of her light both by day and by night, and the transient crepuscular stillness of the evenings which separated them. We feel its thrall even today. And it is good that we do, because it helps us to understand what Egypt signified for the Ancients, for Pythagoras, and for the generations of travellers who assiduously made their pilgrimages there throughout Antiquity.

It was the fullness of Egypt that cast a spell on their imagination – not fullness in the sense of its material wealth and gold, although that was certainly an aspect of its fascination, but the fullness of its very ancient and densely interwoven society, the fabric of unchanging ritual and social order, like a human apiary whose parameters were the walls of the desert, the arc of the sun, and the measured rise and fall of the Nile. Egypt was like some fruit that had achieved a perfect ripeness. It felt no need for change, no need for others. Its lore, it seemed, was perfectly adapted to every circumstance of life and of nature. It existed as a highly evolved organism, perfectly tuned to preserve itself and its wholeness, without regard for the individuality of its components. And, as such, it was the exact opposite, in almost every respect, of the restless Greek world with its vying city-states scattered around their turbulent sea.

And so to Babylon – the furthest destination which is mentioned by Iamblichus in his account of the philosopher's travels. A radically different atmosphere prevailed in Mesopotamia from that in Egypt. Babylon had for millennia been a nerve centre of the movement of people, goods and ideas within Asia, a receptacle of influences from East and West and a reservoir of knowledge both ancient and current, which was fed from many sides. Mixed, polyglot, multicoloured and open to a constant traffic of change, Babylon was a thoroughfare whereas Egypt was a mansion. Egypt fed on itself, closed off almost from the world outside by both its intractable desert and its mentality that instinctively resisted the influence of outsiders. It belonged on a different continent and believed itself – if we read between the lines of Herodotus's account – to be on a higher flight-path than that of the other cultures with which it came in contact.

From both Egypt directly, and from Babylon through the intermediary agency of the Persian Empire, Greece had long drawn deeply on the advanced knowledge of calculation and computation, and the superior technology of engineering, hydraulics and surveying of these already very ancient cultures. This was what they had to offer in abundance. But we have no clear evidence that either Egyptian or Babylonian thinkers had ever attempted to synthesise and integrate their impressive grasp of calculation, astronomic data, medical and musical practice into a philosophy which aspired to unify them. It was this synthesising capacity, in particular, which was the signal contribution of the Greek mind, as embodied particularly in the person of Pythagoras.

Greece had learnt her sculptural and architectural skills from Egypt; her geometry, arithmetic and calculation from Babylon; and, side-stepping Egyptian hieroglyphic script and Babylonian cuneiform, had sensibly adopted the flexible, phonetic alphabet of the Phoenicians, increasing its potential notably by the addition of vowel symbols. All three of these cultures stand as godparents to the new, emerging Greece. But there was one thing that – because of its strategic position in Asia – only Babylon could offer: and that was a conduit for the thinking that came from deeper within the East, namely from India. We would be only picking up half the story of Pre-Socratic and early Greek philosophy, if we were to neglect the powerful influences that are entering the West from India.

How is this possible? India is a very long way away from the islands and ports of the Aegean Sea. This is true: yet it lies at the other end of a vast arc of territory, stretching from Asia Minor through to the borders of today's

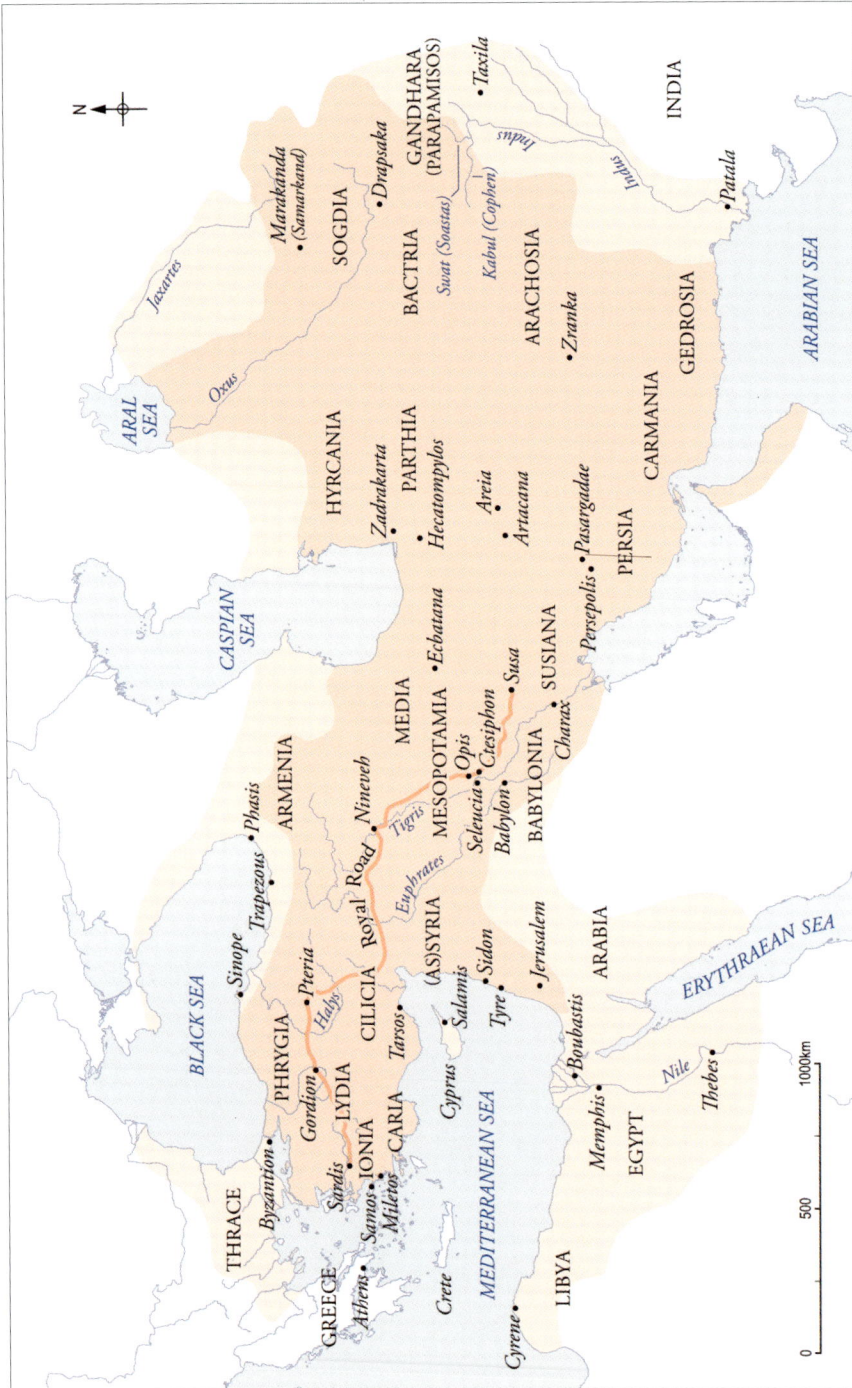

Extent of the Persian Achaemenid Empire under Darius I (500 BC) – from Libya to the Indus Valley and Western Himalaya, and from the (former) Aral Sea to the Straits of Hormuz.

Afghanistan and the Indus Valley, most of which the Persian emperor, Cyrus the Great, as Herodotus related, brought under his own single control, while his successors, Cambyses II and Darius I, annexed the remainder. Both Hellenic Asia Minor (which included Miletus, Ephesus and Sardis, the former capital of the kingdom of Lydia) and the borderlands of the Indian sub-continent found themselves all of a sudden held within the same political entity, and this remarkable situation lasted for a crucial half-century, from the early campaigns of Cyrus in the 540s through to Darius's ill-fated invasion of Greece in 490, which culminated in his defeat at Marathon. The court of these three Persian emperors – Cyrus, Cambyses and Darius – was, by design, highly multi-cultural; and so it was that, in both the Persian imperial capital itself and in the regional capital of Babylon, the intellectual and spiritual worlds of Greeks and Indians met and enjoyed contact, half way between their two geographically very distant poles.

Two millennia earlier, it seems that those who were later to become the Greeks and those who were to become the Indo-Aryans, lived in the same steppe-lands of Central Asia, sharing a common, Proto-Indo-European linguistic and cultural space. The latter, it is thought, moved east into the Indus Valley borderlands of the subcontinent, the former into the Balkan peninsula, although the dates, reasons and extent of these migrations – even their occurrence – are still debated by historians. When they met again many centuries later it was natural that there existed common and innate mental characteristics on which to build. In the 1st millennium BC it is only in these two cultures, and in China, that what we call philosophical and speculative thought is recorded and recognised as one of the defining characteristics of civilisation.

Persia and her *pax persica* facilitated commerce, cultural exchange and exploration across the wide arc of Western Asia, the Red Sea and Egypt. Her emperor, Darius, commissioned a Carian-Greek captain, Scylax of Caryanda, to organise an expedition to explore the Indus river to its mouth and then to return through open seas around the Arabian peninsula to the Red Sea. Scylax's account of what he found in his periplus written at the end of the 6th century BC survives only in a handful of quotations in other writers; but the journey appears to have been successful and on the strength of the reconnaissance gathered, Darius ordered the cutting of a canal from the Red Sea through to the Nile at Boubastis so as to consolidate the economic and military unification of his empire. Military projects and reconnaissance fed into improved trade, and improved trade brought closer cultural contacts. Up until the collapse of the Roman Empire in the 5th century of this era, there was constant contact between India and the West. Eusebius, quoting Aristotle's pupil Aristoxenus, even cites a conversation which is said to have taken place between Socrates and a visiting Indian guru [5]. Maybe fanciful; but not impossible. The contacts were closer than we might imagine; and they were later given huge impetus by Alexander's conquest of Persia in the 4th century BC. The cities which were founded in Bactria and in the upper Indus Valley following his campaigns there, were free to form mixed Hellenic-Buddhist communities; and it was this that helped to create the earliest visual and plastic arts of Buddhist culture (*see p.230*).

The picture which emerges is one of profound cultural interpenetration over a considerable area of the surface of the globe. For much of this commerce of ideas Persia was the intermediary, and even though Greece and Persia were at times implacable foes, their cultures were nonetheless deeply linked. There were many Greeks who worked for the court of the Persian emperors in positions of trust: engineers (Mandrocles of Samos), military advisors (Histiaeus of Miletus), explorers (Scylax of Caryanda), sculptors (Telephanes of Phocaea) and physicians (Democedes of Croton). And these are just the ones we know by name. The syncretism that evolved was not just oxygen for the awakening intellectual culture of Greece in Pythagoras's time, it was a force that shaped its content through the meeting of ideas and minds between Persia's far West and its far East, which now stretched even into India.

The journeys Pythagoras undertook – to whatever extent we wish to accept they happened – are a metaphor for the discovery of the encompassing world by the human mind, and of the search for a structure underlying our existence in it. In him, the journeys become the thinking. His person is, in the most literal meaning of the word, a 'metaphor' – a meaning that is still preserved in Modern Greek where '*metaphorá* ' refers to the business of 'transportation'. In his openness to and fascination with Egypt, Mesopotamia, Persia and India, Pythagoras transported ideas and knowledge that were of ancient and distant origins out of the Orient and carried them back to the Greek world. At the same time – in a process that resulted in a cross-fertilisation that would gladden the heart of any botanist – he brought into contact with the East a quite new cast of mind, moulded by the evolving Western world from which he came.

Let us turn now to the more immediate surroundings in which Pythagoras grew up – the coastline of Aegean Asia Minor and its scattered islands. It is hard to imagine a more naturally benign corner of the world than Ancient Ionia, with its reassuring vegetation, its protected and majestic shores, its pleasing climate, abundant produce and unforgettable light. And Samos, the island of his maternal ancestors, which rides like a ship at anchor just off this coast at a distance of only a couple of kilometres, was witnessing a quite extraordinary flowering of creativity in precisely the years which saw Pythagoras grow into adulthood.

The closing lines of Nebuchadnezzar's foundation inscription from the Ishtar Gate in Ancient Babylon, written in Akkadian cuneiform on blue glazed tiles: early 6th Century BC.

[1] *Phaedo*, 109b

[2] The origins of the Etruscan people and their culture are still debated today. In Antiquity, the similarity of the language spoken by the natives of the island of Lemnos, close to the mouth of the Dardanelles, with that of the Etruscans of Italy, led to several theories that the Etruscans had originally migrated into Italy from the Aegean area. It is to this idea that the comments of Neanthes and Porphyry are referring.

[3] Herodotus, *The Histories,* I.130.3

[4] Herodotus, *The Histories,* II.35.1

[5] Eusebius, *Preparatio Evangelica* XI.3.8

The Samos Kouros, early 6th C. BC
(Archaeological Museum, Vathi, Samos)

Samos

To stand in front of the *Kouros* of Samos is a revelation. In spite of his immense size as a sculpture (nearly three times life-size) and his two and a half tons of marble, he is still a wholly benign revelation. His presence makes a profound impression upon the beholder. He energises the space around him and enters willingly into an optimistic, and far from oppressive, dialogue with the viewer. If ever a single work justifies that evocative word which the Ancient Greeks used for sculpture – *'agálma'* – which means 'something that gives pleasure and respect', it is this. Few other works of art radiate a more tangible sense of the vigour, optimism and humanity of this 6th century BC world. He is the incarnation of the vibrant cultural landscape from which Pythagoras emerged.

The *Kouros* stood originally beside the Sacred Way that led to the Sanctuary of Hera on Samos. He may represent a divinity, a young hero or an athlete, or he may simply be an ideal embodiment of youthfulness and divine beauty. That very ambiguity of subject is itself eloquent. There are other *kouroi* of substantially larger-than-life dimensions which have survived from this early period elsewhere in Greece: but they are few in number and, apart from the *kouros* from Sounion, most are either in more fragmentary form (Delos) or are unfinished pieces (Naxos, Thasos). None of them evokes a comparable balance between elegant stylisation and naturalism, nor possesses the sophistication of technique which we see here in the mesmerising cavity between the arms and the flanks, shaped with the precision that an instrument-maker would dedicate to the sound-holes of a cello or a violin. It takes a moment, too, before we notice the quietly enlightened smile. We find such smiles again appearing in later figures from Buddhist and Hindu sculpture.

Any citizen of ancient Samos would have been familiar with the workshops where such a huge and prestigious sculpture was being created. The principal craftsmen themselves would also have been well-known figures. Beyond merely knowing of the creation of these pieces, Pythagoras, though still young at the time, would also have been aware of the method by which they were designed – the simple canon of integral proportions which determined their primary structure, mapped out as a scheme on the surface of the rough-hewn block of stone before cutting began. For human figures a unit of measurement of approximately 33 cm (the length of a forearm from fist-knuckle to elbow) was established and a central point on the block of the marble chosen as the point of departure which corresponded to the navel. Different sculptural workshops used different canons, but a number of them seem to have operated something like the following: one unit in either direction laterally from the navel determined the extremity of the flanks at the waist, two units perpendicular to that downwards marked the point of separation of the legs; two further units from there to the knees; and three again from there to the soles of the feet. Two units upwards from the navel marked the sternum; one further, the mouth; and another further, the crown of the head. From the sternum, one unit laterally each way determined the extent of the clavicles which constituted an important horizontal. And so forth. Fractions of the unit measurement then guided further refinement, and from these cardinal points a network of diagonals also positioned the eyes, elbows, nipples, toes and fingers. In this way all the

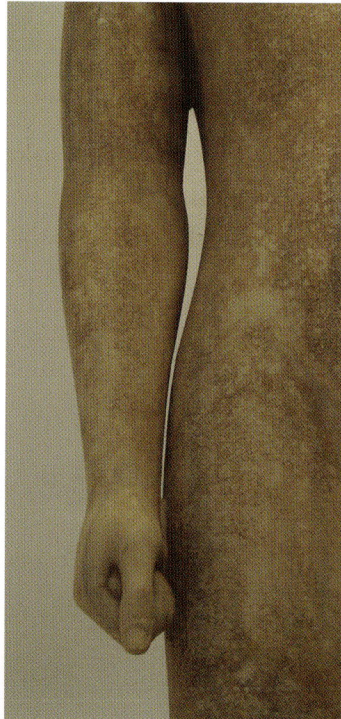

Samos Kouros, detail of right arm and flank

individual features and the whole pleasingly proportioned form of the figure, were confidently realised in preparation for cutting to begin. Then, with the carving, began the miraculous process of humanising the scheme into a figure of profound sensual and spiritual appeal.

These simple integral measurements and proportions underpinned the form of the sculpture, and were – although latterly invisible – always present to the inner eye in the balance and elegance of the finished piece. The sculpture had an armature of number, but was finished with a surface and appearance that was highly evocative to the senses. This was a phenomenon that had a profound significance for Pythagoras: it reflected what he would later observe more generally about the universe around him. The unconscious aim of the craftsmen was that same unifying superimposition of structure and aesthetic appeal. Nor does this apply just to the great figurative sculptures of male *kouroi* and female *korai*, but even to abstract architectural elements such as the Ionic capitals which were made for the temple of Hera – carved and scrolled with a sensitivity which makes them seem to our eyes as soft as cushions, even though made from solid limestone. These images and techniques fed Pythagoras's imagination; and the recognition, in particular, of the deep cooperation of abstract and sensual in the creation of beauty, would lie in waiting in his mind until the time that he first became aware of the arithmetic ratios which underpinned musical harmonies – at which point it became something of wide significance to him.

The unity of structure and sensuality: a capital from the Temple of Hera, Samos; 6th century BC.
(Archaeological Museum, Vathi, Samos)

Pythagoras's homeland of the Eastern seaboard of the Aegean was the home also of Homer, Sappho, Terpander, Thales, Anaximander, Anaximenes, Hecataeus, Heracleitus, Hippocrates, Herodotus, Aristarchus, and a hundred other thinkers and writers. All of those mentioned by name were remarkable innovators and seven of them are also commonly referred to as a kind of progenitor: 'the father of Western Literature' (Homer), 'the mother of Lyric poetry' (Sappho), 'the father of Music' (Terpander), 'the father of Science' (Thales), 'the father of Geography' (Hecataeus), 'the father of Medicine' (Hippocrates) and 'the father of History' (Herodotus). All were Ionian, except for Sappho who was from Aeolian Lesbos a little further to the north, and Herodotus and Hippocrates who were from the Dorian-populated coast to the south. What was it about this area that made it so culturally fertile?

There are at least four considerations that come to mind which help us in understanding the signal importance of Ionia and its neighbourhood: first, the works of Homer and the language he used; second, Ionia's frontier geography on the border of Europe and Asia; third, the introduction of coinage for the first time in history in neighbouring Lydia in the 6th century BC which led to the evolution of a monetarised economy; and, last of all, something we might term the 'energy of rebound' from several lost centuries which followed the destruction of a whole society of civilisations in the Aegean area at the end of the Bronze Age. In addition, the Ionian Greeks were, to much of the outside world in this early period, the archetypal Greeks – the ones who were seen and who travelled and traded abroad. The Turkish and Arabic word for Greece today is still 'Yunan', a variant of 'Ionian': and in ancient Sanskrit, the Greeks were known in the Subcontinent as *'yuvana'* or *'yavana'*. Ionia is not a closed territory, but rather an ill-defined stretch of the eastern Aegean seaboard inhabited by a Greek people who distinguished themselves by dialect, cult and culture from other Greek speakers, such as the Dorians or Aeolians (*see map opposite*). They settled after the end of the Bronze Age in the 11th and 10th centuries BC, mostly in the central part of the coast of Asia Minor (modern-day Turkey) and in the islands of Chios and Samos just off its shore.

Homer's origins – leaving aside for now the thorny question of how many Homers there may have been and of whether the author of the *Odyssey* may have been a woman from Drepanon (modern-day Trapani in Sicily) as Samuel Butler intriguingly proposed at the end of the 19th century [1] – were by tradition

The Aegean Sea, Samos and Ionia

linked to this particular area of the Aegean coast, either to the Ionian city of Smyrna or to the Ionian island of Chios just opposite to it. The Homeric epics passed on two gifts of primary importance to early Greek thinking: the first was a fully mature language of great flexibility and fine syntactic architecture. That thrilling sense of clarity and spaciousness in Homer's sentences is important, and it contrasts markedly with the compact terseness of the Latin of Virgil's *Aeneid*, written seven hundred years later, highlighting how profoundly different were the Roman and Greek minds. The second gift was a deepened understanding of the individual and of individual responsibility. The Homeric epics are the awakening of a new kind of humanism. They speak for the first time in Western literature, and very early on the world stage, about what it means to be human and to live with existential dilemmas and human failings. This was a powerful legacy to the area.

Next, there is the importance of the geographical position of Ionia. We have already referred to this coastal area before as a kind of permeable diaphragm between the maritime Aegean world on one side and the ancient land-Empire of Persia on the other. The roots of the Persian Empire ran deep across Western Asia, drawing sustenance both from its own long cultural history as well as that of the peoples of Anatolia, Assyria, Mesopotamia and the Indus Valley, whose territories it now dominated. The Royal Road, whose history substantially predates the improved form given to it by Darius the Great at the turn of the 5th Century BC, ran from the Persian capital of Susa, which lay beyond the Tigris, 2,700 kilometres away in the foothills of the Zagros Mountains, all the way to Sardis, near the Aegean coast. Herodotus was much impressed by the relays of couriers who could cover this distance in (a scarcely believable) seven days: otherwise it was normally a three-month journey, he says [2]. This was the main artery of communication through the western half of the Persian empire. It joined Europe to Asia – and its terminus was at the very border of Ionia. Along its length, in both directions, travelled goods, music, language, skills, fables – every kind of physical and cultural baggage.

On the Persian side of this 'permeable diaphragm' was a magnificent and unbroken cultural tradition going back deep into early human civilisation in Mesopotamia. That cultural heritage had adapted and metamorphosed repeatedly throughout the geopolitical and dynastic upheavals of the wide area which it infused; but it had remained a constant and unbroken tradition – not as pure or monothematic a heritage as that of Egypt, but equally ancient and equally continuous. On the other side was the Greek world with its tragically broken history. Here the cultural heritage of prehistoric Greece – the sophisticated civilisation of Minoan Crete and the powerful but much rougher, martial culture of Mycenaean Greece – had been snapped off in a meltdown and destruction in the twelfth century BC, whose origins and nature still remain unclear today. This contrast of histories created a considerable imbalance between the Asian and the European sides. For almost four hundred years between approximately 1150 and 750 BC, the Aegean and Hellenic worlds had known only political insecurity, economic poverty and a lack of cultural confidence by contrast with the unbroken wealth, both material and spiritual, of Asia.

In that half millennium of ethnic and cultural re-setting in the Aegean area, a collective subconscious memory of the collapse of the brilliant Bronze Age world which had preceded it continued to resonate. It was incarnate in Homer's epic poetry, which constituted a nostalgic and impassioned evocation of its values that echoed through all of later Hellenic culture, carrying forward the image and myth of this former greatness. But those same lost centuries also gave space for a process which is much harder to define and which arose out of a vital genetic re-grouping. When eventually a new and youthful mind emerged from this fallow period it was to be something radically different from what it had been at the time of the collapse of the Bronze Age centres of civilisation. It possessed the reflex, rebound energy of something that had been long restrained by poverty of opportunity. It was hard-headed, almost aggressively inquisitive, and unfettered by priestly lore or the parameters of a state religion and royal courts. Yet, at the same time, it was also remarkably humane and open without prejudice towards the learning it encountered in the older civilisations of Asia and Egypt.

Trade tends always to lead history by the nose. The commercial ports of the Ionian coast which were close to Sardis – namely Miletus, Ephesus, Smyrna and Samos – became wealthy because they were, in one sense, Persia's window onto the continent of Europe, an area potentially rich in raw materials and manpower. By the same token they became Europe's window onto the East; and through this window, the Hellenic world saw a wealth of wisdom and cultural sophistication which brought back to their minds all that had been lost in their own ancestral world, whose shadow had been kept alive by Homer. It was this, more than anything, that caused the East and its knowledge and culture to cast such a spell on the minds of Pythagoras and the other Ionians of his age.

As the mercantile network of these cities expanded, the new phenomenon of a monetarised economy also began to evolve with the introduction of coinage for the first time in history at the turn of the 6th century BC, under king Alyattes of Lydia – a kingdom that stretched inland from Ionia into Asia Minor, and is perhaps more commonly associated with the name of his son, Croesus, who was so fabled for his wealth. This, by any account, was a revolution. The simple bartering of familiar goods in the market-place could now be abstracted, quantified, logged and carried through space and time in the new medium of consensually valued forms of precious metal: at first these coins were made of electrum, a rare alloy of gold and silver found locally in the Pactolus river in Lydia, but later pure silver became the principal metal. Although coinage may have been slow to take off at first, it nonetheless brought with it demands for important new skills both in calculation and in the manipulation of abstract concepts. It explains the particular attention to mathematics which Thales,

Anaximander and Pythagoras all shared; and it may also explain their urge to conceptualise in quite other fields of thinking. All three philosophers had continuous exposure to the technical-mental skills of Asia both in their home cities and in their travels either near or far.

Familiarity with skills can soon give rise to a comfortable complacency; the well-oiled and controlled machinery of the ancient states of Mesopotamia, Persia and Egypt fostered a literate scribe-class who may have been technical experts in writing, calculation, surveying and astronomy, but their independence of thought was always in thrall to the State – its worship, its ritual calendar and its priesthood. The Greek borderlands such as Ionia, on the other side of the diaphragm, had access to this raw material of technical know-how, but were unconstrained in the uses to which they could apply it. When Thales or Anaximander, proposed radically new concepts of our world and its functioning, there was no High Priest or Royal Court before whom they could be summoned in order to explain themselves.

Samos lay at the heart of this rapidly evolving world. It was a small island, but it was anything but a provincial backwater. It harboured probably the largest standing fleet of ships in the Aegean in the 6th century BC, and operated a trade network that stretched from the Black Sea to Egypt, and from Syria to the Straits of Gibraltar. Much of our knowledge of early Samos comes from Herodotus who took a considerable interest in the island and greatly admired what he learnt about it. Herodotus lived approximately a century after Pythagoras, and travelled just as widely. Since he belonged to a later and more inherently literate generation, he wrote with a fluent thoughtfulness about all that he saw. The trajectory of his travels is uncannily similar to that of Pythagoras: he was born on the Eastern seaboard of the Aegean, travelled to Egypt and possibly to Mesopotamia, and then in later life emigrated west to mainland Italy – just as Pythagoras is said to have done in the second half of his life – subsequently dying it is thought in the Athenian colony of Thurii, less than a hundred kilometres to the north of Croton where Pythagoras had latterly lived. It is curious that Herodotus in his compendious writings mentions Pythagoras only once and in passing, referring to him as "certainly not the most negligible thinker among the Greeks" [3].

The *Histories* of Herodotus mention Samos and its people frequently and in several contexts, recounting their achievements. The engineer who built

Samos: the remains of the podium of the 6th century Temple of Hera, which was, in its time, one of the three largest temples of the Hellenic world.

a pontoon bridge across the strong currents of the Bosphorus for Darius the Great, king of Persia, during his expedition against the Scythians in 513 BC, was, he tells us, a Samian by the name of Mandrocles. Mandrocles proudly commissioned a painting of his achievement and had it sent as a dedication to the Temple of Hera on Samos [4]. Hera, Queen of the Heavens and consort of Zeus, was herself also a native of Samos, born according to legend among the osiers beside the Imbrasos stream. Her cult and her sanctuary, full of marvellous dedications and populated with regal peacocks and their plaintive cries, brought huge prestige and wealth to the island. Among the sights of the sanctuary Herodotus makes mention of a lavish monument dedicated by a merchant from Samos, named Colaios, in thanks for his safe return from a maritime mission which had generated for him exceptional wealth from trade in metals [5] . His journey had taken him through the Straits of Gibraltar out into Atlantic coastal waters where he appears to have passed the winter. Colaios's journey was completed, it is thought, some time around 630 BC. Samos had a long tradition of courageous mercantile and engineering enterprise.

But above all these, Herodotus noted in particular three things on the island which he cited as the greatest technical achievements he knew of in the Hellenic world. These were an aqueduct more than one kilometre in length which passed straight through the base of a small mountain behind the city of Samos; a protective mole for the city's harbour which was built out into a depth of twenty fathoms of water – no mean feat in an age before diving gear; and the construction, in the Sanctuary of Hera, of one of the largest and most magnificent temples, in Herodotus's opinion, of the whole Greek world. It was a building whose base-dimensions gave it a footprint approximately two and a half times that of the Parthenon which now stands in Athens and which was built a century later. This great temple was the work of a Samian architect called Rhoikos, son of Phileos, together with Theodoros of Samos who was either his son or brother or colleague (according to which historian we most trust). All of this gives a sense of the sheer scale of ambition with which tiny Samos sought to emulate its great trading partner, Egypt, and to bring the material spirit of Egypt into Greece. Samos may have been a small island, but it had large aspirations and wide horizons.

Of all these remarkable things mentioned by Herodotus, it is the rather prosaic-sounding aqueduct tunnel, perforated through the mountain behind Samos in order to carry fresh water safely into the heart of the city, which unexpectedly brings us close to the thinking of Pythagoras. It must be said, straight off, that there is no evidence to say that Pythagoras was or was not involved in the planning of the tunnel; but given the nature of society in an ancient city, the likely prominence of Pythagoras even as a young man within that society, and the fact that the engineering of the tunnel was proceeding for several years within sight of everyone in Samos, there must inevitably have been some conversations at least between Pythagoras and the builders, the engineers and the chief architect of the project whom Herodotus names as Eupalinus of Megara. It is not really important – and we shall never know for sure – whether the project of the tunnel influenced the thinking of Pythagoras, or the other way round. The truth is probably a mixture both of influence and contribution. It is the connection alone that is important.

The digging of a tunnel over a thousand metres in length right through a mountain may seem like a difficult but routine matter, involving only tenacity and manpower; but in this case it was much more than that, because Eupalinus,

The tunnel of Eupalinus, Samos c. 540/530 BC

the chief engineer, had for several reasons – and at considerable risk of failure – decided that the tunnel should be excavated simultaneously from both ends, by two separate groups of workers. In doing so he had turned the project into one of those challenges in which the early Greek mind delighted: how could he guarantee that his two digging teams, beginning from two points on opposite sides of the mountain and progressing into the darkness of the rock, would be sure to meet, half a kilometre and many months of digging later, at precisely the same point in the centre of the mountain where, with diminishing oxygen and failing light, they were about 500 feet below the surface of the earth above? How could he ensure that they did not just pass one another like ships in the night? In fact we should more correctly say "like aircraft in the night" because the problem did not just involve a meeting on a two dimensional surface, but in three dimensional dark and solid space. By all accounts it was an extraordinary feat; and it involved some considerable mental gymnastics.

The tunnel is still visible on Samos today. It remains one of the most remarkable, extant, material testimonies to early Greek ingenuity. At this point, it would take us far from our subject to go into the complex detail both of the problems posed by the engineer's decision and the ingenious solutions he found to them: the interested reader may find the author's full account of the tunnel's construction in *Samos, with Ikaria and Fourni*, Volume 3 of *McGilchrist's Greek Islands* (2010, Genius Loci Publications, London). Here, however, what concerns us and what links the achievement to the thinking of Pythagoras, is that its construction came about through a thought-experiment, an extrapolated conceptual solution projected down into the body of the mountain which separated the city of Samos from its vital source of fresh water. Eupalinus successfully reconciled the triangulation of elements he was dealing with: the physical topography, the human workers, and the conceptual model.

Pythagoras, if he were not involved in the project, certainly had much to learn from it. The execution of the tunnel, along with the other remarkable projects of his native island, in sculpture, architecture and engineering, were going on under his eyes during his early adulthood, and they had a defining influence upon the way in which his mind evolved. From them he learnt a number of important mental habits.

First, he assimilated the habit of standing back from situations and from phenomena in order to try to see them conceptually in their entirety. This is a lesson that can be taken away from the construction of the tunnel – that when we stand back from an endeavour and conceive it as an *idea*, we can manipulate it with greater ease and can refine the outcome more closely to a perfect solution. But its implications for Pythagoras were wider than just that. He is, as we shall see, the first person of whom we know anything substantial who proposed that the whole cosmos we experience could be understood and explained through an idea, as opposed to a narrative or a fable or poem. And the idea which he proposed was the most quintessential of ideas – namely the realm of number which we call 'mathematics', which has since become the basis of our scientific understanding of the world.

Second, the remarkable pieces emerging from the sculpture workshops with which he was familiar, intimated to him that there existed a profound connection between two quite distinct levels in their creation: on the one hand, the simple numerical and geometric schemes which mapped their structure; on the other, the finished artistic forms, with all their ability to beguile the senses. Neither had meaning without the other. He would later recur to this most significantly in his thinking about acoustic harmony. But from the very start it suggested to him the complex interdependence of the abstract (or numerical) with the sensual in our experience of beauty.

Third, all of this, together with the cultural and economic character of Samos, predisposed him to recognise without prejudice the richness and wisdom of the arts and sciences that had developed to the East of his own world. It was because Pythagoras approached them with respect and open-mindedness that they revealed so much significance to him.

"I have given a lengthy account of the Samians", Herodotus concludes towards the end of his discussion of the island, justifying its detail by his admiration for their extraordinary achievements. This, too, has been a lengthy account of Samos, and it is justified by the belief that this ferment of activity and ingenuity within the compass of his small island, provisioned Pythagoras's mind and launched it, prepared, into a wider world.

---

[1] See Samuel Butler, *The Authoress of the Odyssey*, (Jonathan Cape, London 1897)

[2] *Histories*, V 52-54; & VIII. 98

[3] *Histories*, IV. 95.2

[4] *Histories*, IV. 88

[5] *Histories*, IV. 152.4

[6] *Histories*, III. 60

QUALITIES OF GREEKNESS

The Temple of Hephaistos (or 'Theseion'), Athens, mid 5th century BC;
drawn by James Stuart and Nicholas Revett, 1794.

Architecture of mind

Perhaps the most enduring gift of all those bequeathed to posterity by the early Greek mind was the gift of simplification – a cutting away of the irrelevant and the illogical, and a seeking out of the universal and essential instead. A pursuit of structure. A Doric or Ionic temple is the physical embodiment of that spirit. Orderly, unpretentious and immediately comprehensible, it is fundamentally a simple idea – even though its eventual refinements may possess considerable subtlety. The temple structure has no complex forms: its interior is plain and subdued; its exterior is a paradigm of unity, clarity and symmetry. Its success throughout all of history as an architectural model to be copied reflects the success of the Greek way of thinking both about the cosmos and about the proper functioning of society. Structure, clarity and balance are pre-eminent in both.

Architecture is the visible and material expression of a way of thinking: yet at the same time it also actively shapes our thinking. It is in a constant and living dialogue with the mind. We create the outdoor and indoor spaces we inhabit, and those spaces in turn create ways of being and thinking in us. Buildings themselves have helped to fashion our attitudes towards the divine, to death and to the exercise of power. They also illustrate how thought structures vary fundamentally between different cultures and different periods. John Ruskin observed that, unlike the written histories of a particular age, buildings never fail to tell the truth about the epochs and the minds which created them [1].

Bold projects of architecture dominated the horizon of Pythagoras's native Samos during his lifetime, as we have seen, and it is not merely coincidental that, among his peers, Pythagoras is perhaps the most 'architectural' thinker in the way he envisions his cosmos as a geometric and harmonised structure. In the period in which he was a child in Samos, the grandest temple of the Greek world was being constructed on the edge of his city, soon to be followed by competing projects at Ephesus and at the Oracle of Apollo at Didyma on the mainland of Asia Minor opposite. These buildings were to change the course of Western architecture, just as his own observations were to alter the thinking of those who came after him. In seemingly very little time, the conception of a temple-building had evolved out of all recognition from its clumsy predecessors, transforming itself from chrysalis to butterfly – mirroring the rapidity of development in thinking and philosophy under way in the same geographic area. It is not easy to explain the speed and degree of such architectural development: much has to do with Samos's close commercial and political ties with Egypt, and what the island's merchants had seen there. There was also the ingenuous desire simply to emulate, or even outdo, the greater and older culture of the Egyptians. But, once again, it is the transformation that Egyptian ideas of building design undergo when they take root in the Aegean world that is so significant.

The enduring and widespread influence of the design of the classic Greek temple through history is testimony to the power of its simplicity and clarity; its success far exceeds its rather limited practicality as a building type. The temple's emphasis is much more on appearance and harmony than on usefulness. It is many hundreds of years since anyone dedicated a sacrifice or last shared a sacred banquet in front of a Greek temple; yet the pedimented colonnade and the familiar form of the building itself have lived on, and on, and on in the history of architecture – in Ancient Rome, in Renaissance Italy, in Adam's Edinburgh, in Jefferson's capital on the Potomac River, in Napoleonic Paris, and in countless other cities around the globe. We find it put to a remarkable variety of uses also, in contexts, climates and ages quite different from those in which it was conceived: in Roman Africa, or in the bayous of Louisiana; as an adornment to an English landscape garden, or the expression of Bavarian royal pretensions; as a civic or symbolic building in Scotland or Tennessee; as a cathedral in Buenos Aires, and as home to the legislature in Manila and Belfast. Its presence in these far flung places in recent centuries tells a political and historical story, both good and bad, of the colonising push of a particular way of thinking which appropriated the temple-design as its symbol. But, most commonly and at its best, it merely expresses certain innate values of order and clarity – values that are arguably universal and without harm.

The Greek Temple in a rural context:
Henry Howard's Madewood Plantation, Louisiana, 1846.

In aesthetic terms, the temple functions optically as a simple cage of light and dark – solid and still, yet dynamic in its rhythmically broken surfaces, its succession of fluted columns and regular juxtapositions of flat and curved surfaces, rectangles, triangles and cylinders. Although abstract in conception, it is never cerebral and dull because it possesses a plasticity akin to sculpture.

Yet this alone does not explain its immense success as an architectural model: the answer lies in a deeper, psychological effect. Whether in an urban setting where it rose reassuringly above the cluttered mass of habitations and crowded squares, as in the Temple of Hephaistos in Athens, or in an isolated setting where it seemed to tame the power of a rugged, natural landscape, as in the Temple of Poseidon at Cape Sounion, the effect of the temple's simple and symmetrical form has always been the same: to focus the mind and to quell human anxiety.

In a quite different way, the ziggurat speaks of the more centralising and aggregating cast of the Babylonian mind, and that genius for urbanisation which was the earliest gift of Babylon to human history. Similarly, a Jain or Hindu temple – with its very different proportions and spaces, its interior penumbra and its often pullulating exterior decoration – is a vital key to understanding the nature of Indian thought processes. It favours the rich and intricate detail of surface over apparent structure. Such buildings impress by their imposing size or complexity and intrigue with their suggestive hidden spaces. The Greek temple, on the other hand – in particular the Doric temple – hides nothing: its form is clear from the first glance. We do not have to 'explore' a Greek temple, or penetrate a myriad chambers protecting the holy of holies as we need to with an Egyptian temple. We behold it always in its immediate entirety,

A photograph of 1885 of Jain temples from the 10th & 11th centuries, in Khajuraho, Madhya Pradesh.

either from afar or from near. It may possess interesting narratives of relief sculpture in certain areas; but the role of these is secondary, and we come to them once we have already absorbed the immediate impact of the wholeness of the building. Greek temples dedicated to the Olympian deities are nearly always free-standing objects, similar in general appearance from all sides. They are not excavated into a hillside, or contiguous with other buildings: they stand alone, independent and complete, in the midst of their sacred enclosures.

It was in the nature of the Greek mind to give priority to structure over substance. The preference of early Egyptian monumental architecture was either for constructions of solid mass or else excavated spaces within the rock; and its later temple structures with their dark and densely filled hypostyle halls were a compromise between these two instincts to create mass and to preserve the subterranean gloom with its accompanying sense of protection. The Greek temple, by contrast, arises from an impulse to balance solidity with open space, to alternate light with shadow continually, and, where possible, to leaven the substance while enhancing the structure.

To value structure over substance is not intrinsically better or more natural; it was just the way that the Greek mind thought. John Ruskin, a person of the greatest aesthetic sensibility, had little time for classical architecture and abhorred its revival in the work of Andrea Palladio and his followers during and after the European Renaissance. For Ruskin it was the plastic forms that took their inspiration directly from nature, the colourful organic decoration and the textured sculptural qualities which a building possessed, that truly gave it life. The dominance of idea in the classical temple design, he felt, was simply deadening. His point is a valid one, and it reminds us that harmony is not merely about symmetry and mathematical order but something much more intricate. Clarity and internal logic may be a successful way of looking at the world, but they are not everything. How could we pretend to understand, say, the art and culture of the Celtic world if we were not open to the hidden, the mysterious and the unobvious? And what would we make of the beauty of the often lopsided symmetry of a Byzantine chapel, or the strangely irregular forms of Gothic architecture?

Pythagoras himself, his native region, Ionia, and his epoch, the 6th century BC, occupy an interesting position in relation to this ceaseless tension between the rational and the organic. Two things which have been alluded to already impinge on this: first, the fact that Ionia constituted a kind of geographical shoreline or fluid border between the reviving Greek world and the ancient cultures of Asia to its East; second, that Pythagoras and his contemporary philosophers of the 6th century BC also constituted a 'temporal shoreline' which separated an earlier way of thinking dense with animistic habits and powerful deities, from the more objective, conceptual vision of nature and of the firmament which they had begun to bring into being. They were the fulcrum between these two realities, old and new, East and West. The great temples being raised in Samos, Ephesus and Didyma in this same area and period reflected this. They had a similarly ambivalent character partaking of both of these worlds: they possessed a particularly fruitful ambiguity which

Imagined reconstruction of a part of the portico of the
Temple of Artemis at Ephesus.

intertwines the latent animism of the beliefs of the East, with the emerging predominance of a 'Western' structural order.

Almost nothing of these great, early Ionic temples has survived, beyond their buried foundations. Later structures were built over them. But, when conjuring an image of them to our minds, we must put aside the more familiar purity of a Doric temple, such as the Athenian Parthenon, which belongs to the mind of a different age and world, further to the West and freer of oriental influence. In the huge Ionic temples of the age of Pythagoras, the proportioned structure of design was fast emerging, yet their porticos were still like dense forests alive with sounds and mythical creatures – reflecting and perpetuating the idea of the sacred grove of trees which often surrounded the earliest places of cult. The cornices, door-frames and the base-drums of their columns – like decorative socks – were sculpted, coloured and finely carved with male and female figures, foliage, birds, gorgons and other fantastic beasts that would have cheered the heart of Ruskin. The space would have been vibrating with an animism and animation quite different from the cultivated simplicity and sober lines of the great Doric temples of the Western Greek world and Magna Graecia.

The few exquisite fragments that remain from the sculptural decoration of these temples breathe a spontaneous and unstudied refinement, and belong to a very different world from that depicted in the carefully segregated narrative reliefs of the Athenian Parthenon, built a century later. These sculptural figures would have looked out unaffectedly towards the visitor at every turn and from every column. It is interesting, too, how they speak of a markedly different status of the female. There is an absence of that patriarchal perception of women which was to close in swiftly over the course of the next century and to alter the nature of Greek society for ever: its chill is already felt in the Parthenon reliefs. These marvellous early Archaic faces, by contrast, still breathe the air of a different world. They belong to the world of Sappho, which was still close to them in space and time – but even closer to them in spirit.

It is these same differences between East and West, historic and innovative, organic and rational, that are the key to understanding the mind of Pythagoras. They are also what constitute his fascination. In this way the art and the architecture help us to understand his milieu and his mind. They make us aware of the emphasis on structure in his thought and the value he gave above all to proportion, number and geometry; but at the same time they help us understand his interest, fascination, nostalgia, weakness – however we wish to call it – for the more ancient and mystical knowledge of the East. It was this curious propensity towards the mystical which came to be transmitted in garbled form by his followers and which caused such problems in the attempts of later centuries to understand what Pythagoras himself may have wished to say.

Two fragments of female faces from Ionic architectural decoration (column drums)
of the mid-6th century BC:
left – from the Archaic Temple of Apollo, Didyma (Antikensammlung, Berlin);
right – from the Archaic temple of Artemis, Ephesus (British Museum, London).

---

[1]   John Ruskin, *St Mark's Rest: The History of Venice*, 1877; Preface, page 1

Freedom from Sacred Texts

To possess sacred texts may be a marvellous thing: but the Greeks were blessed in having none. They were fascinated by those who did have them – which meant almost everyone else of importance with whom they came in direct contact: the Egyptians, Persians, Israelites, Babylonians and Indians. The only ancient and overarching body of words which the Greeks possessed were the works of Homer and Hesiod; and even though Hesiod, in particular, touches on matters of cosmology, their works cannot remotely be considered sacred texts in the obvious meaning of those words.

The Greeks did possess Mystery Cults which were ancient and important to them, the two most significant being the cult of Demeter and Persephone at Eleusis, near Athens, and the cult of the nameless 'Great Gods' on the small, North Aegean island of Samothrace. Even a 'mainstream' intellectual such as Herodotus had been initiated into the latter: so their relevance cannot be considered negligible. But they appear to have been specific in their scope and did not represent any kind of universal cult, religion or teaching, certainly not something that defined the Greeks as a people. And if these cults did possess sacred texts as well as the 'Sacred Objects' that formed part of their rites, we know nothing of them because they were secret and the initiates were bound not to divulge any of their contents, ever.

What therefore might it mean to possess no sacred texts? Two things stand out. First, in the absence of a voice that tells you where you come from or how the universe was created or what happens to you after death or what your relationship to the divine should be and what your relationship to temporal power should be, what is good, what is bad, whom you can marry, what you should eat, how you should dress and behave – in the absence of any such instructions coming from God or from the Wisdom of Ages, all these very important matters need to be formulated independently. The particular importance which the Greeks accorded to philosophy and their need to master logic, cosmology, politics and ethics – all Greek creations as concepts – derive from this simple fact that they possessed no revelatory book or tradition that told them what to do. Their existence and survival as a culture that was to be taken seriously came to depend, therefore, on their efficacy in philosophy. Second, if there exists no revered, sacred text to refer to, those who hold power in a society do not have the possibility to manipulate the sacred word to their own ends in the relentless and all too familiar games of dominance, subjugation and inculcation of fear. As a consequence of this there could be no divine ruler nor powerful priesthood in the Greek world as was the case in Egypt, Persia and Mesopotamia.

In this context, we can begin to understand what exactly it was that drove Pythagoras out on his long journeys and motivated his curiosity. We can understand the urgency of philosophical reflection for him and his contemporaries, and for their intellectual descendants; we understand the often high temperature of the debates in which new ideas were proposed and contested. It was not like the easeful and recondite exercise of philosophy today: the early Greek thinkers were engaged in a mission of pressing importance, because they had to create for their own culture something with which to match the many sacred teachings which the other great peoples of the world at that time possessed. The early Greeks had only vaguely defined ideas of what happened after death – amongst them the gloomy limbo intimated in Homer, which offered ultimately so little hope – while, on the other hand, Egypt possessed detailed *Books of the Dead* providing for every eventuality *post mortem*, and India had its growing body of Vedic literature based on the development of self-knowledge and the idea of the transmigration of the soul.

The possession of divine or sacred texts – whether they claimed to be sempiternally existent or delivered in an epiphany out of the mouth of the Divine – bestowed authority; and their manipulation by a priestly caste and a royal dynasty who had sole rights on the interpretation of the divine word, was the basis of the cohesion and control of a society such as that of Egypt. Sacred texts rapidly become instruments of power and have been, throughout history, the often irrational rallying standard of causes and peoples.

How then did it come to pass that a culture as vibrant as Greece could hold together and evolve without any sacred texts? It did so partly as a result of *not* having them. In an important sense, as we have seen, it was a liberation to have no sacred texts; but it also left a vacuum. Into that vacuum went not only the speculation of the early philosophers, such as that of Pythagoras and his contemporaries, but also the important corpus of ancient drama which was to emerge most significantly in the following century with the works in particular of Aeschylus, Sophocles, Euripides and – with rather different purpose – of Aristophanes. These great poetic works were smithies in which ideas about destiny, ethics and human relationships were forged into a kind of many-sided corpus of sacred texts for the Greek world – quite different in nature from the canonical sacred texts of other cultures, but no less valid. The most significant difference was that they were not a top-down transmission of wisdom, but rather a sort of existential workshop in which moral and psychological issues were made incarnate on a stage before the eyes of an enrapt audience. When, under the open skies and in the magnificent settings of the many ancient theatres of the Greek world, whole communities sat for hours, and sometimes over several consecutive days, transfixed by the relentless unfolding of these dramas, every spectator was made a philosopher, a participant in the pursuit of knowledge and *philosophía*, not merely a passive receptacle for received wisdom.

The ancient Theatre at Delphi

This participation functioned also as a vital preparation because, on some occasions, the very same spectators might have been required the next day to participate in a council of the citizenry in order to pass judgement on the life of a fellow citizen, or to decide communally to take up arms in a war for the sake of their survival and freedom or to redress a perceived wrong. Although neatly compartmentalised in our own times, the various realms of philosophical debate, drama, politics, justice and warfare were, in Ancient Greece, woven together into an inseparable fabric of direct relevance to the daily life of the citizen. What is so remarkable is the seriousness with which the Greeks busied themselves with giving birth to this alternative kind of wisdom, which was both empirical and theoretical, but never passively received or divinely delivered.

The principal effect of this was not just to foster a flexibility and independence of thought, but to impart a profound sense of responsibility to the pursuit of science, ethics and philosophy. It also gave rise to a quite different vocabulary of thought and to a philosophical grammar which still cuts at a different angle from the one with which we are familiar. In the West and the Near East, the thought-routes we use and the ways in which we frame metaphysical questions and answers are so entrenched that we lose sight of the extent to which our minds have been structured by two millennia of a dominant mental model – namely that of monotheism as projected by Judaism, Christianity and Islam. The decisive imprint of monotheism has endowed us with the 'hard-wiring' of our thought processes. It has given us the predominating language of judgement and of legal process which we use in matters of ethics and religion. It has enforced within us the idea itself of "religion". It has fostered the overly binary emphasis of our morality. It has favoured the one-directional, linear concept of time, and of the individual life. And, through all this, it has consistently tended to diminish and devalue the body and its senses. These are powerful shadows to live beneath. And they are not of necessity the only way of looking at our existence in this world. As a result of this, it has become hard for us to conceive of a kind of divinity that might be *other than* all-powerful, all-seeing and all-judging, or of there being a life-giving plurality within divinity itself, above all one which might even include ourselves as creating participants. Or to understand the geometry of time and history as cyclical rather than linear. Or to conceive of beauty as lying at the very core of the meaning and self-manifestation of our universe. Over the centuries these impulses have been silenced within us. Even today it can come to us as a surprise to rediscover them alive in all that the thinking of Pythagoras implies. It can be a liberation. It can feel like a renaissance.

It is for this reason that the act of *philo-sophía* – the love of awareness and knowledge – assumes such importance with Pythagoras. It was an exploration, a choosing of paths, directions and mental landscapes. The sacred text, on the other hand, discouraged all of that. It imposed borders; serendipity was its enemy; and it drew lines that were not to be crossed and built gates that were not to be passed through. There were questions that could never be asked of the gate-keepers, because the sacred text had already justified everything. For Pythagoras, who predated this curious spasm of monotheism, there was no requirement for any complicated and sophistical justification of our existence: no requirement for divine judgement or for salvation either. Our consciousness alone of beauty and of harmony between things, wherever around us we should find them, was what gave value and meaning to our universe. Nothing more. The importance of beauty can neither be justified nor explained; it can only be intuited. And without it, our human existence has no meaning.

The Strait of Telendos, looking South from the Hellenistic fort of Kastri above Emboreio on Kalymnos.

Clarity, Poverty
& Nakedness

The sea shapes Greece, its spirit and its thought. The astringent, iodized air, the clear horizon and the uncompromising light, are not merely the physical parameters of its thinking, but rather its very essence. The philosophy of Pythagoras and of his contemporaries does not merely spring from the head, it belongs also to the physical landscape in which they lived. It is the philosophy of their natural environment. We cannot fully understand Greek thinking without sensing the landscape from which it arose, just as we cannot understand what made Ancient Egypt so irreducibly itself without knowing the reality of its own particular and extraordinary natural environment. I have not lived in

Central America, but I would not pretend to have any true understanding of Mayan culture without witnessing first-hand the physical reality of the densely forested natural world from which it emerged. Even today, someone wishing to understand what makes America America would be wise, as a start, to travel its breadth from coast to coast. The same applies for India or for China. Greece, by contrast with these huge realms, is very small; and its smallness and concentrated intensity are a part of its identity.

Greece's compressed size was what gave impetus to the expansiveness of its imagination. This was first expressed quite materially in the pushing out of its people and culture from Aegean shores to found a multitude of new Greek coastal trading colonies, in the 8th and 7th centuries BC, in places as distant as the Crimea, the North Coast of Africa, Southern Italy and the Gulf of Marseille. This urge to explore and to spread out gave to Greek culture the character of a diaspora. Its heart, the Aegean Sea, was a profoundly fragmented landscape in any case; and now, with the creation of dozens of far-flung colonies, the fragmentariness was perpetuated on a greater scale. And this fact, in turn, helped the Hellenic world to preserve its independence.

A fractured landscape of rocky shores and scattered islands by its nature resists possession and political agglomeration. With the exception of its very fine building marble, potter's clay and olive oil which Greece possessed in abundance, it was a territory that was poor in both the quantity and quality of its resources, and comparatively weak in primary productivity. These two things made it neither easy to unite nor particularly worthwhile to dominate. The capricious seas and the de-centralised scatter of the islands made it hard simply at a practical level for a state, a navy or an army to bind together and hold. It was not a geography able to accommodate an embracing monarchy. And the Hellenic world's only serious invaders before the era of Roman expansion – the Persian Emperors, Darius and Xerxes – launched their doomed and expensive expeditions in the early 5th century BC not out of any pressing need to possess this unproductive area at their borders, but in order to redress a perceived insolence and sleight to their royal power. Although Macedonia later united much of the Aegean Sea under Philip II and his son Alexander the Great, Greece in Antiquity effectively knew no central monarchy, no imperial court, no rigid hierarchy, no priestly castes, no stultifying bureaucracy nor common divine liturgy right up until the time of Byzantine centralisation in the 4th century of this era, when all of these, at one swoop, became her lot. There were always rich merchant families in Ancient Greece, clans who dominated priesthoods, and frequent tyrants and autocrats; but that is not the same thing as having the solid core of a quasi-divine monarch, a central court, a national army, an orthodox priesthood and a state bureaucracy at the axis of your turning world.

This fact is important for our understanding of both the liberty of thinking as well as the spare simplicity of the poetry and visual art that emerged from the Greek world in early Antiquity. It aspired to a proportioned humanity rather than to a rich and sophisticated complexity. A comprehensive cultural history of the world could be written through a study solely of its imperial and royal courts – the courts of the Egyptian Pharaohs and of the Emperors of China, of Persia, of Japan, of Ancient Rome, of Byzantium, of the kingdoms of Mesopotamia, Assyria, India, Africa, Europe and pre-Colombian America. Because of the combined wealth and sophistication of these courts, such a history would encompass most of the finest artefacts produced by human civilisation. But in such a history, the Greeks and their art would be notable absentees. There was never anything we could call 'court art' in the Ancient Hellenic world.

Royal courts are like apiaries: sophisticated, conservative, profoundly regulated and organised for self-perpetuation. Like apiaries they are also adhesive and they produce their own kind of honey – a remarkable elixir which is a quintessence of accumulated tradition and exquisite craftsmanship – in quantities often way in excess of necessity and demand. Ancient Egypt and China in particular, and later Japan, were all realms with a high degree of self-sufficiency in materials, technology and foods. All flirted with or aspired to closure from the outside world. All developed complicated hierarchies in which status was expressed through modes of costume, registers of language and symbols of office; all were sustained by state creeds and weighty bureaucracies. All evolved an aesthetic sophistication and societal complexity of a kind which Greece never had, never dreamt of, and never would have wanted to possess. Even today, Greeks are innately suspicious of, and resistant to, any kind of centralised authority.

In an epoch of great monarchies, early Greece stands out as an artistic culture very rapidly evolving towards a full maturity, yet by nature free of the structures of courts and creeds – its sculpture proudly naked, its gods unashamedly human, its architecture clear and confident, its poetry profoundly humane, and its thought pregnant with the power to enlighten in a manner that none of her far wealthier peers could share. It is this that makes the solitary journeys of Pythagoras into the world of Eastern thought so significant as a meeting, and ultimately a fusion, of very different mental worlds.

Geography is the force that shapes political identity. A comparison between Greece and Egypt helps to illustrate this. It is no coincidence that the relationship between the two countries was particularly close and fertile for so much of their history, in part because of their marked difference from one another. Greece admired and was fascinated by Egypt, and their worlds became ever closer with time, especially after the founding of Alexandria. The rich syncretism of their cultures begins with the early lessons that Greece took from Egypt in technology and art in the age of Pythagoras; deepens through the remarkable portraits of Faiyum in the Roman era – which are in effect our only glimpse of the extraordinary quality and humanity of painted portraiture in the Greek world – and continues right up to the time of Constantine Cavafis in the last century, whose clear poetry, though quintessentially Greek, is nonetheless deeply accented with a timeless Egyptian stillness.

As the Egyptians rightly sensed, the design of their country was like a beneficent incarnation of divine providence. A great river flowed through the granite desert from South to North, creating a corridor of improbable fertility. When seen from the air, it is an unforgettable sight – a thin band of vivid green moving relentlessly up to the Mediterranean across an expanse of solid, buff-coloured void (*see over*). The river flooded regularly as a result of the summer monsoon rains in the highlands of Ethiopia, enriching the soil along the hundreds of miles of its banks every year, bearing harvests out of the constantly renewed fertility. Its delta was a haven for cultivation and livestock, the embodiment of tranquil protection. The river itself was perhaps the greatest artery of the Ancient World, easier to navigate than the Indus, the Euphrates/Tigris complex, or the Yangtze and Yellow Rivers. The Nile has a clear trajectory, a constant current from South to North, and an almost equally constant breeze from North to South which facilitates travel upstream once you have hoisted a sail. Like a girdle around it, the path of the sun circles perpendicular to its flow, rising and setting in two separate oceans of yellow-pink granite which hem the river on both sides with an intractable *cordon sanitaire* of continental proportions. No damp to destroy things; almost no rain to erode walls made

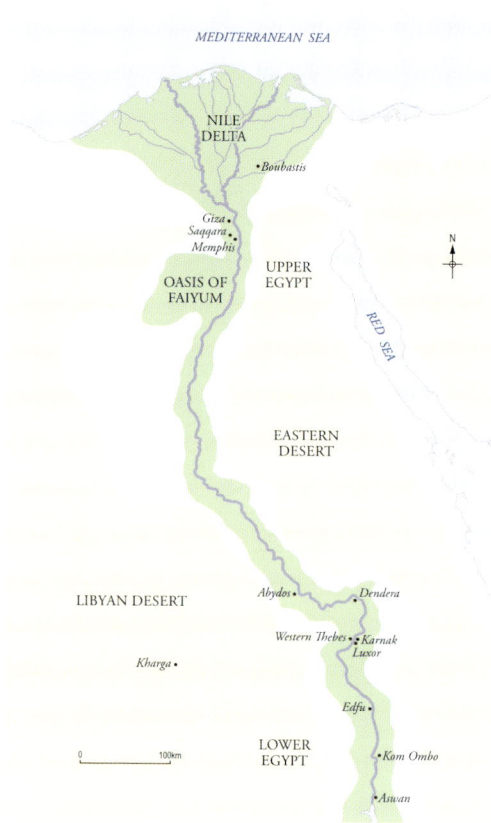

The Nile Valley

with mud bricks, yet an abundance of stone for construction when required. Grains, greens, beans, fish and foul in plenty. Everything humanity might want – except perhaps good timber. Egypt's surpassing richness in produce at times built surpluses that sustained and swelled the coffers of its monarchy, funding, as John Maynard Keynes aptly observed, the manifest superfluity of its pharaonic building projects. The river all the while facilitated control and allowed swift communications to hold the kingdom together once it was united. The Pharaoh guaranteed the fertility, and the fertility guaranteed the Pharaoh. It was, above all else, the unchanging regularity and constancy of everything – the flow, the floods, the winds, the sun, the silent walls of the deserts, the very steadiness of nature – that gave Egypt its monumental character: enduring, self-protective, involuted and resistant to change. Egypt was one stable and perfectly articulated structure, where Greece was a mass of fractious, competing centres.

Nature in Greece is unpredictable by contrast. Its seventy or so habitable islands are scattered across an often turbulent sea. Its shores are rocky and dangerous. Its winds are unruly. Its few pockets of fertility are small and seasonal; its land incapable of sustaining more than subsistence. Much of its mountainous interior is inhospitable. Yet, in spite of all that, it is a nature that is sublime, invigorating and always changing. Nothing is stable in the Greek geography, nothing predictable – not even its volcanic and seismically active bedrock. Greece, in short, was everything that Egypt was not: a treasure-house of transience and broken variety, rather than a monolith of long sedimented culture.

The bay of Ancient Brykous (Vrykounda), Karpathos

Aegean geography necessarily focused the mind on competition and self-reliance. The sea was not a hostile boundary as it appeared to the Egyptians, to be embarked on only reluctantly and out of necessity, but rather something which the Greeks embraced as the very incarnation of opportunity. The sea facilitated their life and their movement in a positive manner, and connected them with a much wider world which, even before the age of Pythagoras, was already pan-Mediterranean in compass. The Aegean Sea became just the main square or *plateia* of the Greek world. Yet crucially that same facilitating sea also enforced a 'closed season' – the winter months in which navigation was mostly suspended and little could be cultivated. Egypt had no closed season; its human machinery continued relentlessly. But when, on the other hand, the winter storms hit the Aegean world and its coastal settlements, what was there to do but repair boats, mend nets, plan strategies for the next season of trade and – most important of all – debate, talk, discuss, hypothesise, speculate, compose and versify? It is not an exaggeration to say that the richness of the literature and speculative philosophy of Greece is inseparable from the seasonal 'down-time' which its climate and geography enforced.

In this way, the restlessness of the sea which surrounded them became a quality of mind for the Greeks, just as the clear marine horizons and unambiguous light which it reflected shaped the character of their thinking. Greek thought had no fat to it. It remained influential and beautiful for so many centuries primarily because of its elemental clarity.

Clarity.
Poverty.
Nakedness.

These are the formative qualities of the Ancient Greek spirit.

Perhaps because of its visuality, the last of these three words is the one that captures our imagination. It is the particular signature of much Greek sculpture and drawing, and it distinguishes their culture from that of most of their neighbours and successors. Nakedness was something that possessed symbolic and ritual significance for the Greeks, especially in the contexts of athletics and art. But in a deeper and metaphorical sense it is also the primary quality of early Greek thought whose character still strikes us today as remarkably unencumbered by otiose verbal and symbolic clothing. Whether it is the searing perceptions of Heracleitus, the roving spaciousness of Homer, or the passion of Sappho, there is always a directness which awakens us with its intensity.

The middle word of the three shocks us, however, because to our own materially-oriented age it has associations that are almost always pejorative or shameful. It did not have those connotations for Saint Francis; nor did it for the ancient Greeks. There exists a liberating, positive kind of poverty, which the Greeks learnt from their spare landscape and which they espoused in the material simplicity of their daily life. This is something that can be seen by setting their culture alongside that of the Romans who, with the sophisticated luxury of their urban life, cultivated the art of living better than any. By contrast, it was the lean poverty of the natural world of the Aegean which was Greece's truest blessing in Antiquity.

Clarity comes first and last. It follows from the previous two and it also precedes them, giving them meaning. It is the Archaic and Classical Greek quality above all others, imparting an 'essential-ness' to its architecture and sculpture, a radiance to its thought and poetry, and reflecting the unmistakable intensity of Greece's light.

Looking south from the Western extremity of Ikaria,
with Patmos, Amorgos and Naxos (from left to right) just visible along the horizon.

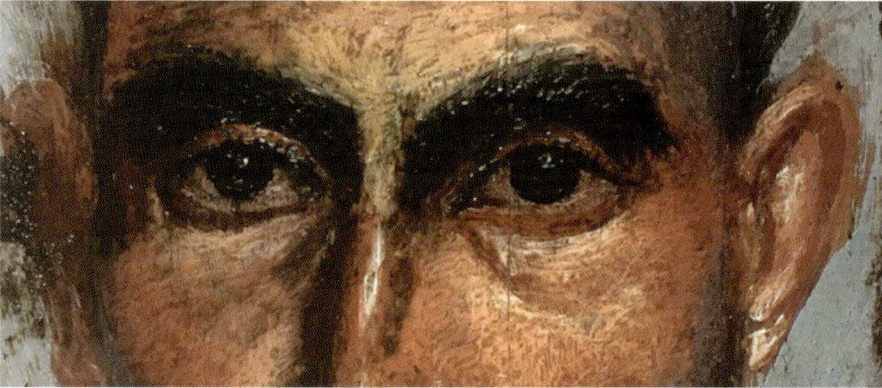

PYTHAGORAS DISTILLED

'His Master's Voice', oil painting by Francis Barraud, 1898.

Catching the Voice

Now let us turn from the world he inhabited, to the man himself.

W hat Pythagoras has to say is disarmingly simple. There is nothing innately obscure about him: he has been made obscure by those who came after him. His voice is quiet: he never shouts. Our problem just lies in trying to hear it above the background noise.

Trying to catch what might be his true voice is like tuning into a faint radio signal on an old-fashioned short-wave radio: we are able just about to hear the words, but only with a great deal of whistling and buzzing interference in the way. The signal comes and goes, and we can only catch snatches of what he is saying. The biggest problem, however, is that there is another station very close to the same frequency called 'Radio Pythagoreanism': its signal is much clearer and it has many listeners. It is a rambling pot-pourri of a station with lots of comment and opinion, broadcasting twenty four hours a day; and it purports to talk all about Pythagoras. What we need for our purposes, however, and what we want to capture is the master's voice. We must try to tune out the interference and the more dominant stations as much as is possible. We need to listen as intently as we can.

Detail from Michelangelo's 'Last Judgement', 1536-1541,
on the west (altar) wall of the Sistine Chapel, Rome.

The problem with 'Pythagorean*ism*' as opposed to Pythagoras is one that may be familiar to us. Imagine that you grew up in a small village in, say, rural Indonesia or Thailand and were raised with a good education probably as a Muslim in the first case, or as a Buddhist in the second. One day you had the opportunity to come to Europe for the first time in your life and someone took you to see the Sistine Chapel in Rome. You were interested to know something about Christianity simply because it was the prevailing religion in the area you were now visiting, and you knew that the chapel was one of its most important and venerable sites. You looked at the great cycle of paintings by the early Florentine painters and by Michelangelo. Your host or a guide perhaps explained some things about them. But what would you really understand from looking at these paintings about the person known to us as Jesus of Nazareth and who lived in Judaea in the period of Roman occupation? For a start you would see in the images of the story of his life a quite different world, and a figure – who certainly did not appear to be a Middle Eastern Jew – moving among strange buildings and settings that also had little to do with Roman Judaea.

Michelangelo's great vision in his *Last Judgement* might also profoundly impress you; but whatever would it actually tell you about the figure at its centre? Even after many hours of thought and explanation you would have only the remotest sense from these works of art of who Jesus of Nazareth really was, what he said, and what he wanted for the world to understand. Nonetheless you would have understood that he and his words were considered of great significance. And you might also have had an intimation of the extent to which religious faiths are themselves huge and highly structured works of art.

Our problem with Pythagoras is comparable: a kind of theology called 'Pythagoreanism' – a creation of later times around the central figure of the philosopher, and something full of strange and marvellous stories and ideas from different periods, has got between us and Pythagoras himself. In some way we need to take leave of the '-ism' and try to see our way back to the individual who inspired it all and gave it its name.

In setting out to do this we are like someone sifting or panning for traces of gold in a large body of water. We will need, therefore, a pan, a sieve, a filter – anything that will separate out what is close to Pythagoras himself from the accompanying accretions which we must set aside for the moment. This is all we can do since there is nothing – nor probably ever was – written by Pythagoras himself, and nothing equivalent to the gospel-writers of Christianity to speak from close knowledge about him.

Since the passage of time tends to be a corrupting influence on reliability, a first principle will be to keep anything that we can reasonably assume is of the same period as Pythagoras or immediately after: this way at least a small handful of words and references directly pertinent to him will be left in our pan. It is almost nothing. And yet for our purposes it is everything. The extraordinary thing about these few gold flakes that remain is their coherence. They may only be fragmentary glimpses, but they intimate a completeness nonetheless; they mutually reinforce one another in unexpected ways and together cohere into a picture that is compelling in its simplicity and clarity.

These are the items that remain in our pan:

- three words;
- an acoustic experiment;
- a precept that has a reasonably good chance of being original;
- an anecdote (about a dog);
- three comments from Heracleitus;
- and a geometrical theorem.

In the following pages, each one of these will have a section (Chapters Eleven to Sixteen) devoted to its consideration.

As regards all the later accreted material which we are setting aside for now, we will never be able to know for certain its status or authenticity. Many things within it might of course be recognisable to Pythagoras and he might be tempted to acknowledge their paternity. But most of it is the product of an industry that grew up around his name and his person in later times; and, although of considerable historical interest, it remains beyond the scope and the aim of this particular study.

The next problem we encounter is when we attempt to establish some kind of narrative for the life of Pythagoras in which to place the fragments of thinking we have carefully separated out. This in itself is a two-fold problem. It is not just that there is a disappointing paucity of verifiable information about him in general; it is also that there emerges an almost irreconcilable divergence between different parts of his presumed biography and the kind of thinking associated with them. On the one side, there are the far-reaching insights which he gives us and which seem to belong to his early years; and then on the other, a mass of sententious and often irrelevant material associated mostly with the later half of his life. It is as if there are two quite different people being talked about. We will return to the significance of this intimation in Chapters Twenty and Twenty-one.

Confusion is further compounded by the understandable vagueness of the ancient historians, biographers and philosophers who wrote about him, and also by their aptitude to be tendentious: some wish to idolise him, others to deprecate him, and most are writing so long after the time of Pythagoras that their biographies could really never be more than anthologies of second- and third- hand memories reverberating in an echo-chamber. Porphyry and Iamblichus, two later philosophers both from the area of ancient Syria and each the author of a biographical monograph dedicated to Pythagoras, wrote about him eight hundred years after he died: a comparable span of time separates us from the prominent figures of the 1200s. Another historian, Diogenes Laertius, writing in the third century, passes on a treasure-house of miscellaneous information but rarely pauses to think about the motives or the plausibility of the sources for his information, and he often seems even to relish reporting stories and versions that conflict. Then, a little closer to the time of Pythagoras, there is Diodorus of Sicily, a conscientious and serious-minded historian writing in the 1st century BC: he was similarly dependent on earlier historical works which are now lost to us and whose accuracy and authenticity of fact he too had little possibility to judge with objectivity. Yet another monograph was evidently written by Aristotle, entitled *"On the Pythagoreans"*; but unfortunately it is lost to us and only quoted fragments of it now survive. And then there is Plato who, more than anyone else, was profoundly indebted to Pythagoras's thinking: and yet he is strangely tight-lipped about him. It is tantalising to have someone in our thoughts as important as Pythagoras clearly is, but about whom we can know so little for certain. In the end, what we have remaining from his life and thought is something like a metaphorical dental impression – the negative imprint left by his presence on the soft inside of history.

We therefore have to do the best we can in the circumstances. What follows is just a brief sketch of Pythagoras's life, some of which will be familiar from what has already been said about his movements in earlier chapters. It is drawn both from the sources mentioned above and from a number of others, and is intended to give some idea of the possible shape of his life. It amounts to a summary of what we are told or can credibly deduce about his time in this world: yet, ultimately, little of it has more than the status of conjecture or hearsay. For now, however, let us allow it to stand as a guiding structure. In one paragraph, then, this is what his life may have looked like:

Pythagoras was born in the early 6th century BC: the general consensus is around the year 570 BC, on the Aegean island of Samos. His paternal family may have been merchants, even though his father, Mnésarchos, is also said to have worked as a gem-engraver on Samos. In his youth, Pythagoras almost certainly travelled to Asia Minor, possibly also to (Phoenician) Tyre in the Levant, and later, it is said, to Egypt perhaps even on several occasions; the belief among his followers that he went also to Babylon is strong, although ultimately impossible to verify. If he did go as far as Babylon, it is not impossible that he travelled to other centres in Mesopotamia, or even beyond, in that same period. He then returned to his native Samos in mid-life when the island was under the autocratic rule of Polycrates. It is hard to read the relationship between the two very different personalities of the ascetic Pythagoras and the worldly politician, Polycrates, who must have known one another and been of similar age. According to Diogenes Laertius [1], Polycrates had earlier given Pythagoras a letter of introduction to Amasis (Ahmose II), the Pharaoh of Egypt, with whom Polycrates was directly or indirectly acquainted. Nonetheless, finding perhaps the political environment in Samos little to his liking on his return, Pythagoras left the island again, this time for Southern Italy where he eventually settled in the Greek city of Croton on the Eastern side of the toe of the Italian peninsular. This is generally thought to have been around the year 530 BC. The city perhaps had been suggested to him by Democedes of Croton, who spent time in Samos as physician to Polycrates. In Croton, Pythagoras appears to have established a philosophical academy and there is a tradition that, willingly or not, he became involved in the governance of the city to the extent that he may have been instrumental in moderating or even directing the course of the dispute which arose between his adopted city of Croton and its neighbour, the wealthy city of Sybaris. The conflict resulted in the defeat, capture and virtual annihilation of Sybaris. Not long after, however, it appears there was some kind of popular uprising in Croton inflamed by the leadership of a political activist named Cylon. The Pythagorean followers, resented for their secrecy and perhaps perceived as an élite with too much influence, were evicted from the city and their meeting halls were burned. At some point, either before or after this crisis, Pythagoras himself left Croton and he may have died in refuge at Metapontum, a city further along the coast to the North of Croton, some time around the year 497 BC (*see map, p.188*).

So: we now have almost half a dozen philosophical fragments in our pan or sieve, as well as the faint outlines of a life-story in one paragraph. This is the degree of fragmentariness we are dealing with. Yet, for our purposes, these elements are sufficient, so long as we keep our eyes on the crucial relationship between the different pieces, rather than fix our attention on each one in isolation. We need to work like the archaeologist who seeks to place the destroyed fragments of an ancient wall-painting into a coherent and justifiable picture which the mind can grasp. It is an exercise in concentrating on the negative space between things, as much as on the things themselves. This helps us to understand the relationships that will ultimately define the whole. It is delicate work and requires patience: but it repays us amply because, in doing it, we experience the excitement of living through the thought-processes of the thinker himself afresh.

Armed lightly, then, with the meagre contents of our sieve together with the mere outlines of a biography, let us now move on to look at the elements we have sifted and see what they can tell us of the man and his thinking.

Grave stele from Tanagra in Boeotia; early 4th Century BC.
(National Museum of Archaeology, Athens)

A first Encounter with Pythagoras

The one and only glimpse we have of the person of Pythagoras through the eyes of his contemporaries is an incident with a dog. The philosopher intervenes on behalf of the dog which is being maltreated. No other sighting of Pythagoras recounted during his own lifetime has come down to us. Everything else we know about him was written long after his death – often centuries later – from handed-down memories and conflicting beliefs about what he may have said or done. The fact that this makes him the most shadowy figure of early Greek thought – the one whose true persona is the hardest to pin down – would in itself matter little were it not for the fact that, hidden in the mass of semi-fictitious material about him which we have received from later times, is a handful of extraordinary observations about our world which are of a wide and resonating significance. The unusual anecdote of the dog is among them, and it remains the first and oldest surviving reference we have to his existence on the surface of this planet.

It is a perfectly normal and generous act on the part of Pythagoras to try to rescue the dog from this treatment; but what is *not* normal is the reason which he is said to have given. "Stop beating the dog," he says, "because I recognise in its cry the voice of a deceased friend of mine." Whatever does he mean? A friend of his has died and become a dog? The cry of a dog can still carry the recognisable characteristics of a once living human being? Or is he speaking more metaphorically? Is he wanting us to understand that there is much more to a dog than meets the eye? That a dog is not merely a quadruped which scavenges from our tables, but might actually be a living soul of which we need to take cognisance? That it is a creature to whom we might even extend sympathy because (who knows?) we may one day become a dog ourselves?… and suffer the very beating which we are meting out… and then see of ourselves from this other, much less flattering, point of view…? This gives pause for thought.

Pythagoras implicitly raises such questions, not because he is being silly or because he wants to denigrate humanity or supercharge the significance of animal life: instead he is inviting us to reflect for a moment on what our relation to the rest of creation should be. It is a question that ramifies deep into the very capillaries of our existence. And it regards a relationship that, in the recent centuries of our human evolution on earth, has undergone many changes and much neglect, creating problems for us which now threaten to engulf our continued permanence in this world.

The incident with the dog is recounted in four short lines of verse from a lost work by Pythagoras's brilliant contemporary, Xenophanes. The lines have survived for us because they just happen to have been quoted by a later historian. We will return in greater detail and depth to this curious, but important, anecdote in Chapter Fourteen, which is on the subject of 'Animals and Souls'. There we will have more space to consider the wider question of what Pythagoras and his contemporaries may have thought about animals, about humans and about souls. But for now it is important to observe the way in which the mind of Pythagoras works: a simple and unremarkable scene becomes something rich with universal implications. It raises important questions about the kinship of living things in our world and what that signifies for us, both regarding how we relate to animals and to the natural world, and how we relate to one another, even to our own self. It touches on broader questions also: the possibility of our living other lives and other realities; the possibility that our actions, good and bad, might return to visit us, teach us, hurt us, haunt us or help us. Such considerations lead us back right across Ancient Asia to the roots of spiritual philosophy in India.

Notice, furthermore, the way in which these questions are raised by Pythagoras using no explanation and scarcely any words or dialogue. This is his method. We will see in a moment how his elementary demonstration of acoustics revealed that simple numbers and their proportions gave rise to the harmony of sound, thereby creating music out of mere noise. Here again, he uses no words: just sound and measurement. And then, of course, there is the theorem: it is what is remembered most about Pythagoras, and yet what is remembered worst. At school we all succumb to some degree of mystification as to why the relationship of the sides of a right-angled triangle should be of such importance as to be taught in classrooms all over the world. The triangle itself, of course, is not the primary consideration, but rather the fact that it revealed for the first time that there existed such things as 'laws of nature', relationships which were applicable universally. This is the fundamental assumption on which all scientific thinking is predicated. These were far-reaching issues: and yet no words were involved. The paradigm alone was sufficient.

This is philosophy working in a quite different way – in almost the opposite direction – from that of the great Greek and European thinkers of later generations. With Pythagoras there is no lengthy exegesis, no wordy explanation, none of the logical coercion and relentless cross-questioning of Plato's Socrates, moving stealthily towards his pre-figured conclusion. There is nothing even of Plato's implicit injunction (and that of so many later philosophers) to follow and admire the ingeniousness of the argument. With Pythagoras it is simply, 'see and understand'.

The supreme quality of Pythagoras's thinking is this purity. You might not think so to read what has been made of him in the writings of countless followers, commentators and historians in the centuries following his death: yet, of the handful of observations which may reasonably be attributed to him, each one is transcendently clear. This is what we have to hold fast to in the face of the mass of later writing and speculation and invention about him which leads in every possible direction away from that core purity.

It needs saying from the outset that Pythagoras isn't the bogeyman of the primary school maths class we generally consider him to be: yet neither is he either the demi-god wonder-worker that some of his later admirers seemed to want him to be. He is just a very human and humane soul. Nor is it even that he was an unmatched genius as a mathematician or astronomer or musician, or a superhuman ethical teacher or mystic. Not at all. The sixth century BC was no ordinary epoch in human history and there were those who were living in the world at the same time as he was alive who had much better claims than he did in each of those different fields – Gautama Buddha in India; Confucius, and the figure we know traditionally as Lao Tzu in China; Thales, Anaximander, Heracleitus and the semi-mythical Orpheus in Greece; Zoroaster in Persia, also, if we accept one of the later chronologies for his life. What is extraordinary about Pythagoras, however, is that he possessed, to some degree, *all* of these qualities in one person: the fascination of his mind lies in the way it moved between these different realms, human, abstract, material, social and spiritual, and saw better than any the ways in which at a deep level they related to one another.

He was more than anything a philosopher of the whole, and an explorer of the connections – often quite unexpected – that exist within that whole.

A close look at the ferment of intellectual activity of Antiquity in Europe and Asia, however, will reveal that many of the things which were long assumed to be the discoveries of Pythagoras and his Greek philosopher-contemporaries appear to have been already known to the literate and numerate worlds of India, Babylon and Egypt for many decades or centuries before the time of Pythagoras. A simplistic view would conclude that this substantially undermines the value of what he, or Thales, or others of their age were saying. In fact, quite the opposite. One of the recurrent themes that emerges from the study of this period is that the nascent Western mind, as embodied in the early Greek philosophers, had an extraordinary gift for perceiving the general and universal application of specific observations that had been lying unnoticed, in broad daylight, in Eastern thinking. The knowledge that was acquired and the concentrated observation that was practised in Egypt, Mesopotamia, Persia, India, as well as in China, are a marvel of early science: nothing will change that fact. But the controlled, monarchical and mostly theocratic cultures of these great civilisations had too often the effect of suffocating any real flexibility of thinking. This thwarted the evolution of a wider, simpler, more universal expansion of ideas and observations *sub specie aeternitatis*. By contrast, such independent thinking could thrive in the smaller, decentralised world of Greece, with its relative youthfulness, its fluid maritime culture, and its broken geography that defied any kind of centralised culture or power.

The wonder of Pythagoras, then, is what he makes of the observations that he took from the more mature cultures of Egypt, Mesopotamia and ultimately from India, and how he perceives their more universal significance. It is an extraordinary transformation which occurs when the knowledge of the East crosses the threshold and becomes the possession of a way of thinking we can finally begin to call 'Western'.

There is a lesson here not just about Pythagoras, but a wider and more significant insight into the way that Western civilisation consistently built upon the ancient experience of the East. So why should we single out Pythagoras? This migration and flow of ideas from the East into the West affects the whole Greek world and all of the innovative thinkers who jostled in the same small geographical area and narrow period of time as Pythagoras. Some of these brilliant minds – Thales and Xenophanes, who have been mentioned already – travelled extensively. Others, however, such as Heracleitus, stayed resolutely at home. This is an important consideration, because the geographical movement of ideas is fundamental to changes in cognition. Pythagoras is commonly said to have travelled more widely than any of them. But whatever the actual extent of his travels, we know that he somehow came into contact with ancient and very different traditions of thinking from the East; and as a Greek and a traveller, a listener and an observer, he had the opportunity to absorb what he saw and heard, blessedly free of the theological context and interference of the civilisations from which that knowledge emerged. He benefitted profoundly from the open-mindedness innate to the maritime and mercantile culture in which he moved, and to the luminous and airy Aegean landscape in which he grew into adulthood.

For this reason, it is important to see that Pythagoras was not so much a thinker who discovered, but rather one who transformed what he found, and who taught us to look at familiar things in wholly new ways. He altered the evolution of human consciousness: he nudged its trajectory onto a slightly different path. At a crucial moment in human history he made us aware of a quality which he defined as '*kósmos*', and this in turn led him to conceive of '*the* cosmos' – an entity which encompassed us and which was both comprehensible to our minds and appreciable to our senses through the beauty of its design. He did not resort to stories or myths, or to a colourful panoply of wilful deities to render it comprehensible to us. He used just two things instead to reveal its nature – mathematics and musical sound.

This was for its time – for any time, in fact – an extraordinary thing to do and it changed the boundaries of the playing-field of thought. In respectfully setting the gods and anthropomorphic deities aside from his picture and relieving them of their role as the movers and causers of things, Pythagoras helped give birth to something we might call a 'Divine Idea' instead – not human in form, but abstract in nature – which was the guiding principle of our world. For him this divine presence or immanence was *kósmos* – the meaningful 'arrangement' of things in nature.

'*Kósmos*' is a fascinating word which means in Ancient Greek not just 'order' alone, but the 'beauty-inherent-in-order' as well – an aspect which relates to its modern use in the word 'cosmetics'. What Pythagoras was saying by choosing this word was that the design of the universe which surrounded us had two distinct but related aspects: a profound unchanging order at its heart and an infinitely varying beauty in its appearance. Both arose from the 'arrangement' and inter-relation of things, which is the root concept of the word *'kósmos'*. There was the immutable structure of number and mathematics which everywhere underpinned the architecture of the universe as he saw it; yet at the same time there were the countless ways that *kósmos* appeared to our senses through the diversity of beauty. The two were inseparable. Each was as important as the other: each gave the other meaning. For the first time in history, a thinking human mind had implied that the concept of beauty played a vital role in the very meaning of our universe and of our existence within it.

---

[1] Diogenes Laertius, *Lives of the Philosophers*, VIII, 1. 36

John Craxton, Shepherd and Rocks, Crete 1943. Oil on board.

Three Words

Three Pythagorean words have remained in our sieve. To understand their significance, let us imagine for a moment a scene.

A shepherd rests beneath the firmament of stars. Gazing at the heavens in the early hours of a summer night, he sees their movement, the shapes of constellations, the differing colours and brilliance of the stars and the steadier lights of the wandering planets. Some of them are familiar to him: he distinguishes them from others out of the mass of lights, and acknowledges their strange and silent beauty. His sheep meanwhile ruminate their food in the fields beneath the self-same firmament; they see in the scattered stars neither order nor beauty. They do not share in what it means to be human.

What is order and why do we perceive it? What is beauty and why does it affect us? It is our consciousness of these two manifestations of our universe that makes us human. It is not necessary for the shepherd to understand what the particular workings are of the order which he senses – the different models of epicycles and orbits that might be used to explain the paths and sometimes retrograde movements of planets in the sky, or even the slow rotation of the whole firmament itself. That is fascinating, but it is secondary. It is simply the recognition that there is order at all that is important; that there exists such a thing as significant arrangement. To see order and to feel beauty is to be human and alive. A person who is blind to them both would be less than human even though he or she might possess legs, arms, eyes, a nose and all the bits that make up a human body. Where humans gaze, sheep prefer to graze.

Nor is order just a vital quality within the universe: it is the means through which we become aware of a universe in the first place. Order appears everywhere, from the functioning of our solar system to the shape of the room we are sitting in now, from the processes of the brain to the succession of waves breaking on the shore, from the forms of our human bodies to the way we prepare our food each day. Pythagoras intuited its primordial importance. What he did was to 'create' the universe for us in two ways: first by saying that order is what defines it; and second, by giving it a name – κόσμος, *'kósmos'* – whose primary meaning in early Ancient Greek was 'arrangement'. Inside our minds, words create realities, and every time we transfer a familiar word to a new context a new reality comes into being. If I am the first person to use the word *'kósmos'* to signify 'the universe' then I have created a universe according to that model: I have said to my fellow human beings that they can recognise the universe, if they want to, by its order and arrangement. And this universe which Pythagoras envisioned was no soup of anthropomorphic forces and battling deities, but was something as calm and congruent as a piece of music, sustained by a kind of order that was mathematical, musical, and spiritual, all at the same time.

In choosing *'kósmos'*, Pythagoras took a word which existed already in his language and which had been used by Homer two centuries before him to signify the rather more concrete idea of marshalling soldiers into their correct position or seating oarsmen in their appropriate place on a ship – in other words placing things in a rightful arrangement. By using this word he was saying, 'this is what the Universe which we experience is all about: we can begin to understand it because it is ordered and comes about through correct arrangement'. Our experience of existence is as a *'kósmos'* of phenomena.

To see the significance of what Pythagoras did we need to remember that before his time – at least among those languages which have survived into our own times – there was no practical, single word for what we would now understand as 'the universe'. There were countless anthropomorphic deities in the cosmogonies of Egypt and India and Mesopotamia, and different names given to the incarnations of primordial forces by peoples all over the world. There were words for 'everything' and words for the 'world', but not for what we now think of as 'the cosmos', which is something different. There was no word which referred both to a universe as the totality of what we know of, and at the same time referred to the particular quality of ordered arrangement that characterised its nature. Without a word there can be only the vaguest apprehension of a universe as we have since come to understand that concept. With time, however, a growing awareness creates the need for a word, and the word then sharpens and propagates the awareness. In this case, Pythagoras happened to be the one who gave us the word.

This humble disyllable, κόσμος, is crucial to our understanding of Pythagoras because it has come into our current language also as the root of the word 'cosmetics', implying those things which can make us more beautiful. Through a richness characteristic of the Greek language, κόσμος possessed from earliest times these two parallel significances, dissimilar yet – once Pythagoras shows us – crucially intertwined: on the one hand 'order' and 'orderliness', on the other 'ornament' and 'embellishment'. The first sense is used always with a positive connotation: it contrasts with that which is chaotic. It carries the additional overtone of 'rightful order': Homer implies this when he refers to the seating of the oarsmen, each in his right place, as they row the sleeping Odysseus away from the land of the Phaeacians [1], almost as if the benign and welcome repose of their captain somehow reinforces the *'kósmos'* – the innate rightness of arrangement – of his sailors as they ply their oars.

The second meaning, 'ornament', refers most commonly to the beautifying ornaments that women used – hence 'cosmetics'. Homer uses the word in this sense in the *Iliad* [2] to evoke the magical beauty with which Hera, the Queen of Heaven and consort of Zeus, would adorn herself before setting off on any mission in which she might need her majestic powers of seduction. In this way Pythagoras is using a word for the order that infuses the whole of creation which, at the same time, brings with it a clear sense of a divine elegance. He is saying that our cosmos is defined both by its order *and* by its beauty. He is speaking directly to the two sensations perceived by the shepherd.

In turning his attention to the beauty implied in his idea of 'cosmos', Pythagoras availed himself of another word which already existed in the Greek language and which possessed an explicitly concrete meaning. Once again through his choice of it he has given it a new life and meaning – a meaning which it still bears today. Instinctively Pythagoras sees that our awareness of beauty is not as a single static quality but rather is an organic sensation arising out of many elements and existing in the active dialogue between different things and between the object and the beholder. He did not use the word '*kálos*' which was the common word in his time for whatever gave pleasure through its goodness, but rather '*harmonía*' which implied something both more complex in origin and more dynamic and reflexive in nature.

The word, ἁρμονία, '*[h]armonía*', belonged originally to the wood-worker's art and it defined a snug, close-fitting joint. It is the root '*[h]ar-*' in Greek which gives the idea of joining and, on the evidence of even the earliest usages of its various forms, it seems to have had the connotation of a joining-together which is also right and gratifying in both a beautiful and a functional way. The most important derivatives of this root '*[h]ar-*' are the verb ἁρμόζω '*[h]armózo*', and its noun, ἁρμονία '*[h]armonía*', which describe this satisfactory joining and linking together of things. In Homer the noun first appears as a kind of carpenter's joint, relating to the wooden beams of the boat which Odysseus builds for himself on the island where he meets Calypso [3]. A few centuries later, however, it already begins to acquire a wider application implying the state of being well composed or combined. We find it applied to an arrangement of mind (or 'mind-set' as we would say today) in Euripides [4], or to the divine scheme of things in Aeschylus [5]. Meanwhile, like a snowball slowly picking up mass, the word seems also to be acquiring, even from as early as the time of the poet Pindar, a couple of generations after Pythagoras, the idea of a particular kind of musical arrangement, for example the Lydian mode to which Pindar is referring when he uses the word '*harmonía*' in his 4th Nemean Ode [6]. This shows us already the direction in which Pythagoras has launched the word.

Music and the way musical sound worked were at the heart of Pythagoras's thinking: it is one of the unusual things about his philosophy. But it is good not to lose sight of the practical, woodworking origins of the word 'harmony' even when considering what Pythagoras might actually have meant by a 'Harmony of the Spheres' – if indeed he did ever conceive such an idea. At first he may not have been talking exclusively about a sound, but more simply about the linked and well-designed relation of each of the paths of observed planetary movement to all the others. Later writers – most notably Johannes Kepler – thought he was talking about a celestial music, which is an exquisite idea, it must be said; but that was because they were writing later, by which time the word 'harmony' had acquired a preferentially musical meaning. With Pythagoras, however, we are perhaps on safer ground if we return to the meaning that the word had for Homer, and which he uses in the context of the building of a ship. This gives an idea of Pythagoras, not so much as a wispy dreamer imagining celestial music in his mind's ear, but as someone who had become significantly aware of the orderly design of the heavens and of the world around us as though it might be a magnificent piece of construction. That in itself is a remarkable thing – just as remarkable as the more poetic idea of celestial music, captivating though that may be.

Harmony is a compelling concept. It has connotations which are profoundly good. It is something we long for in our lives, in our environment, in our cities, in our politics, in our intimate relationships and among our friends and neighbours. It commands, or should command, our respect – universally. The central importance that Pythagoras attached to it is a measure of the positivity and optimism of his thinking. It contrasted markedly with the gloomier cast of the thinking of Heracleitus. Yet the age of Pythagoras was one whose mental world was, as we have seen, much more rooted in the physical and sensual than ours. For this reason it was natural that he should first express the satisfying connection which he was to observe between order and beauty in the universe around us in concrete terms, through a physical analogy from the realm of craftsmanship. The impetus for the subsequent change, in which the word moves slowly from the carpenter's joint towards something more like what we understand today as 'harmony', can reasonably be attributed to Pythagoras. We cannot be sure, yet it would be obtuse to insist, after all the evidence of later writing, that he did not focus primarily on this specific word and imbue it with this new and important significance. It is one of the hinges of his philosophy – and of much subsequent philosophy.

'Philosophy', φῐλο-σοφία, is itself another word which it seems probable that Pythagoras helped on its way towards meaning what we understand it to mean today, even if he did not invent the usage himself as some writers later claimed. Once again the word had an earthier origin than its meaning possesses today: *'sophía'* referred originally to a talent or craftsmanship (such as of a carpenter who is capable of a good *'harmonía'*), a kind of experienced 'know-how'; but from there, it soon expands out into a more generic idea of intelligence and that cumulative knowledge which we call wisdom. Once we put this together with *'phílos'*, which originally conveyed the idea of an intimacy with something or of an attitude of affectionate respect for another being or thing, we start to have the more subtle concept of an open-ness towards knowledge and intelligence. It is like *'philó-xenos'* which appears early in Homer and Pindar, implying a welcoming and hospitable nature, open to the unknown stranger, the *'xénos'*. In this way *'philo-sophía'* may well have implied a welcoming attitude towards knowledge, both that which is familiar and that which is unknown or new or strange. In other words, for Pythagoras, *'philo-sophía'* may have had more a sense of 'receptivity' than of 'acquisition'. Only later did the word come to have the more acquisitive feel of the 'pursuit of knowledge' which it possessed in the time of Plato and Aristotle.

Κόσμος – significant order and arrangement; ἁρμονία – congruent and functional relationship between entities; φῐλοσοφία – receptivity to knowledge and insight. What is interesting about these three words is that they are all profoundly good in what they imply. They have a moral force to them – not the straightforward morality of recommending doing good deeds towards others, even though that is what they may ultimately lead to – but rather they make us aware of a universe in which the aesthetic and the moral overlap and share at times the same domain. It is this that makes Pythagoras stand out from his contemporaries. There is in him an instinctive empathy for the human aspiration for betterment and for beauty.

These three newly evolving words do not exist in isolation in Pythagoras's thinking but rather they mutually reinforce and help to define one another like the three sides that constitute a triangle. *Kósmos* speaks of the state and nature of our world and how we can come to understand it; *harmonía* is the dynamic element which unites us in dialogue with *kósmos* and informs the living relation between phenomena; philosophía is the route by which we, as individuals, arrive at greater *harmonía* within the *kósmos*. *Kósmos* cannot come alive without *harmonía*, and it exists for the human mind as a result of an awareness of it arrising from the practice of *philosophía*.

Most systems of belief have been built around some kind of active participation of the individual through meditation, contemplation, ritual, spiritual exercise, prayer – whatever form it may take. *Philosophía* was for Pythagoras the equivalent of these – a kind of meditation or prayer: it was the route by which we could become more aware of the universe around us and come closer to understanding its beauty. It was not 'philosophy' in the sense of some complex argumentation, but rather a deep attentiveness to experience and awareness of the phenomena that surround us. The shepherd, in his momentary wonderment at the heavens above him, is engaged unwittingly in one of the first and most fundamental acts of *philosophía*.

This remarkable expansion in the meaning of these words is more than a mere philological curiosity, however: it is an expression of a change in human cognition. The mind is beginning to see in ways that it has not seen before, and in order to communicate this new experience to others is reaching for words from its familiar environment – carpentry, hospitality, adornment for the face – and applying them in quite different and novel situations. The literal is moving into the realm of the metaphorical. Like an aeroplane taking to the air, the word still possesses its earthbound nature, but it is now in space; it has taken off from the realm of physicality and is moving freely in a new domain.

When, in the thinking of Pythagoras, a word such as *harmonía* acquires a new and universal significance, it shows how he has lifted our habitual way of looking at something to a higher level, from which we can observe it as a concept rather than as a physical phenomenon. He has found us a hill on which to stand. Understanding this process of visualising the particular in a new and universal context, of heaving ourselves up to look at the familiar as if from a vantage point and to see the labyrinth as if from a low hill, helps us to understand why it came about that an elementary musical demonstration of harmonic sound, possessed such significance for Pythagoras. And it is to this that we should now turn our attention.

---

[1] *Odyssey*, Book XIII, l. 77

[2] *Iliad*, Book XIV, l. 187

[3] *Odyssey*, Book V, l. 248

[4] *Hippolytus*, l. 162

[5] *Prometheus Bound*, l. 551

[6] ἐξύφαινε, γλυκεῖα, καὶ τόδ' αὐτίκα, φόρμιγξ,
Λυδίᾳ σὺν ἁρμονίᾳ μέλος πεφιλημένον Οἰνώνᾳ ...
"Straight away, weave out, sweet lyre, the beloved strain with
Lydian harmony, for Oenone.. etc." Pindar, *Nemean* 4.45

Oak tree at the site of the Oracle of Zeus at Dodona

Sound

The ear of Antiquity was more finely attuned to pure sound than ours. The greater silence of its world shaped a different mind. At the ancient sanctuary of Zeus at Dodona in the mountains of Epirus, oracles were revealed by the sound of acorns dropping into bronze bowls from a sacred oak tree: these bowls were of varying sizes and would have given rise to different pitches of resonance and durations of sound before reverting again into silence. In the intervals of silence, the rustling of the tree's leaves would also be listened to attentively. Visitors and pilgrims would sit for long, waiting to hear these sacred sounds. They did this not out of foolishness or ignorance, but because, by listening, they put themselves into a receptive state of mind. Receptivity is fundamental for the relation to experience which Pythagoras advocates: wisdom and insight are things that we cannot go and get, but rather we receive them – like house-guests, asked or unasked, or like swallows that may or may not choose to nest beneath our eaves.

Our contemporary and more simplistic conception of an oracle is that you go to it, ask a worldly question and sit and wait for an answer from a divine source, transmitted through some strange and particular medium. This, at least, is the image of them that has been common since the time of the first written accounts. But the coming of literacy itself taught us to think in these more mechanistic and reductive ways: writing seeks, and lives by, explanation. Oracular sites are not explainable as mechanisms, which is why we do not wish to have them today. They were places for learning receptivity, where the simple act of waiting and listening – not listening *for* something, just plain listening – was often revelatory. This perhaps sheds light on one of the most revealing precepts of the Pythagorean School which the philosopher is said to have founded towards the end of his life in Croton in Southern Italy, that novices should pass their first five years in silence. This, at least, is what Iamblichus tells us [1]. Imagine: no words (in the context of the School at least) for five years.

In an age when background noise was almost non-existent and birdsong was vividly present, where distant horns communicated simple messages across the open landscape or announced the arrival of a military force, where the powerful resonance of gongs marked ritual moments or the thinner sound of the reed-pipe a funeral, and when the human voice in song was to be heard wherever there was humanity, pure and simple sound was a richer and more meaningful experience. This is the quality of sound to which a person of Pythagoras's era was accustomed, and it helps to explain how it was possible that his single most important philosophical idea arose from the consideration of sound. In his thinking, words do not come first: sense-experience comes first and words then follow. It is certainly important to look, as we have just done, at the significant words which Pythagoras bequeathed to our vocabulary with the meanings that they now possess for us: they are central to our understanding of what he is showing us, and in their time they expanded our awareness of the universe. But by starting from the words, we are putting the cart before the horse. Our question should rather be: what was the experience which led Pythagoras to reach for these revealing words in the first place? It was not merely by coincidence that he caused the meaning of the word *harmonía* to shift away from carpentry into music.

The experience in question was the realisation that harmony between acoustic tones was simply a kind of geometry made audible; and, furthermore, that both the harmonies and the geometry possessed a common purity and beauty. We take it perhaps for granted now that the harmonic musical intervals between tones are defined by simple arithmetical relationships that exist between the lengths of the two tensioned strings that produce them. Measurement of the proportional lengths show them to be defined (in modern terminology) as: 1:1 a unison; 2:1 (or half the length of the string/to its entire length) an octave; 3:2 (or two thirds of the length of the string/to its entire length) a perfect fifth; 4:3, a perfect fourth; 5:4, a major third; 6:5, a minor third; and so on. We also know today a considerable amount about the nature of sound waves and the way their frequencies interact when they come into sympathetic harmony with one another. But all this was virgin territory for Pythagoras. Sound had appeared up until then to be just a phenomenon without structure; yet here was evidence that it possessed an underlying rationale which was clear and simple.

There may have been several moments of epiphany in Pythagoras's life [2], but the moment in which he first came to this realisation must have been as great a revelation as any he would have wanted to have. It is difficult for us who belong to a world of predominantly scientific thinking even to imagine the surprise, novelty and vibrancy of this idea as it appeared to the mind of someone two thousand five hundred years ago – that, from out of the amorphous body of noise and sound, emerged a structure based on simple ratios of whole numbers. And if this was so, what other areas of experience in our world were likewise underpinned by these numbers and their ratios? It was a bridge which seemed to unite the senses with the abstract world of ideas. What we heard with our ears and gave us inexplicable pleasure was the incarnation of that order which Pythagoras felt was fundamental to the existence of the cosmos.

Pythagoras was most likely introduced to the idea of the mathematical structure underpinning sound through existing Babylonian musical knowledge. Giorgio de Santillana [3] suggested that this knowledge was already current in Babylon by the late 2nd millennium BC. But as far as we can tell, Babylonian thinking on the matter, although highly sophisticated in its grasp of the technical aspects of tuning, had stopped at the observation itself and had not gone on to explore its wider implications. In the mind of Pythagoras, however, which belonged to a later period and to another world, it acquired far greater resonance: for him it was the point of intersection at which the world of the physical senses could pick up a direct awareness of those abstract concepts of *kósmos* (order) and *harmonía* (congruence) which were the fundamental components of the universe as he conceived it.

A modern monochord with calibrations and movable bridge.

To demonstrate this materially, it is believed that Pythagoras used an elementary instrument such as a monochord or a di-chord – a sort of very basic zither. These intruments were calibrated to show length and they permitted the easy measurement of the lengths of strings when they sounded in consonant harmony, revealing indisputably the arithmetical ratios which related them. Teachers of musical theory still sometimes use monochords today, but as a scientific tool for measuring tonal intervals rather than as a musical instrument. There is no reason why Pythagoras should not have demonstrated what he needed to show on a seven stringed lyre, known as a *cithara*, a distant ancestor of our modern *chitarra* or guitar. He could well have used pipes of varying diameter or length also. But, whatever acoustic instrument he used, the result was the same. The same ratios between tones could be found in whatever produced a pure tonal sound because these ratios constituted a law of nature. And it was the idea that there could exist such things as universal 'laws of nature' that inspired Pythagoras's thinking. It is for this reason that his name is associated with the geometric theorem – not because he invented it, but because he saw the significance which lay in its universality.

The virtue of this simple demonstration was that it spoke to everyone and there was little room for argument. The difference between a note which is in perfect harmony with another note, and two notes which are not in harmony with one another is readily appreciable to anyone whether they believe themselves to be 'musical' or not. It is a given of physics and of psychology. A consonance of notes gives sensual pleasure and a feeling of inner expansion: a dissonance creates anxiety, a sense of unease and contraction. This is a simplification, of course: but it is the distinction between these two primary sensations that forms the basis of the emotional complexity of musical sound, which has been its singular fascination throughout time.

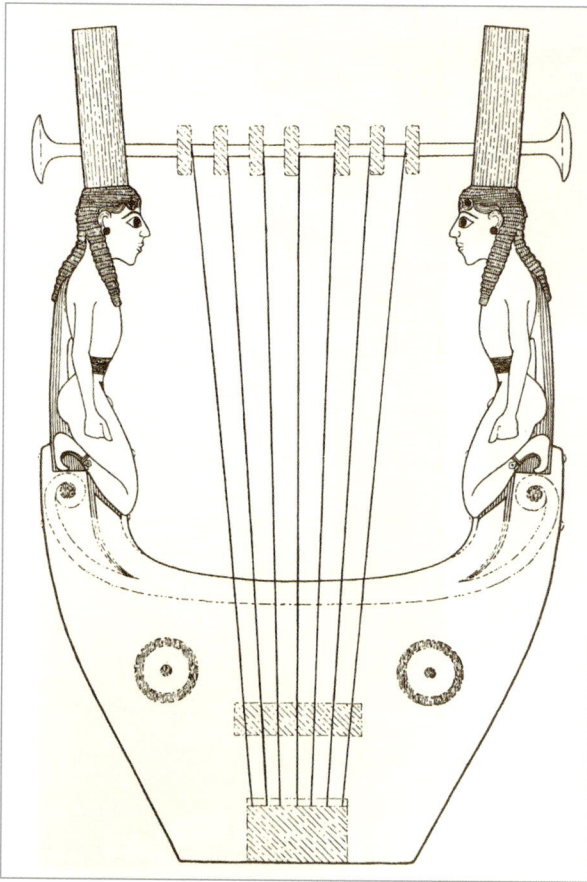

Samian cithara or lyre of the time of Pythagoras.
(Reconstruction from one of the ivory carved human figures - interpreted here as frame supports -
in the Archaeological Museum of Vathi, Samos.)

To any lesser mind the wider significance of this humble demonstration with the monochord would have passed unnoticed. The originality of Pythagoras, however, lay in the universality he attributed to it. Pythagoras placed harmony at the heart of his conception of the world. For him, order and harmony gave rise to beauty; and beauty and our reception of it, wherever we should find it, was what gave meaning to our existence. Without it our lives were just noise.

Nor did he stop there. He seems to have suggested that the lesson of acoustic harmony be the guiding principle for the conduct of our lives. To his mind, harmony possessed divinity and the force of a moral injunction.

How laborious the explanation of Pythagoras's insight becomes when it is written out in prose like this: how easily can ideas suffocate when they are wrapped up in words. But when we hear the sounds speak from themselves, or even see them in geometric form, it is clear and immediate. For Pythagoras the beauty of the demonstration was the way in which it perfectly circumvented the need for words. Nothing was being described: a fact was simply being made manifest to our senses. There were no words in the way, there was no explaining, no ingenious Socratic dialogue required. You could hear the harmonic sounds and see the proportionate lengths of the strings giving rise to them, and understand the inherent significance without a word being uttered – like a speechless revelation.

Why was this circumventing of words so significant? Words of course help us to think about things; but they also impede our true and complete understanding. They give us vision; but only partial vision. If we did not have words we would not feel that the world were impossible to comprehend; we would be content with just *being* it – as birds and animals are in the wild. When we encounter serious problems contemplating the world in which we live, more often than not we are experiencing problems with words. Take away the words and the problem goes; but whole areas of thinking also go with them. We created words ourselves, and yet they define the world we inhabit. Or rather we should say they define the world we *think* we inhabit.

The problem, in it simplest expression, is this: thought, experience and our world itself are multi-faceted, pluridimensional, perceived in many ways at many levels, through several senses and various modes of intuition, while language is a narrow tube of linear temporality down which ill-fitting and approximating words must be stuffed in strictly sequential order. In what possible way can the latter do justice to the former? While one part of our mind is occupied in the time-consuming task of articulating the verbal material to stuff down the tube, the instantaneous and non-sequential intuitions or connections which the other part of the mind is sensing are being lost. This is why descriptive or analytical writing is often the greatest of all human frustrations. We live lives and we experience a world which we can neither comprehend nor describe adequately because of the limitations inherent in the language itself which we have at our disposal. What chance do we have of making sense of our world through words? Great poetry alone is able to break this log-jam.

Music, on the other hand, arrives in our consciousness by another, quite different route. It is not 'making sense' of anything: it speaks without 'talking about' anything. We are jumping the gun a little in speaking of 'music' at this point, because Pythagoras's demonstration relates just to simple acoustic tones and intervals. There is a difference between agreeable (harmonic) sound – which he is speaking about – and composed music. And certainly when talking of ancient music we must remember that it was something so different, tonally and harmonically, from what we understand today as music, that it should almost be given another name. For this reason the demonstration of Pythagoras was nothing more than a beginning.   It aimed only to make a simple point about simple sounds, and that point was about relationships *between* sounds not about the single sounds themselves. It was the living relationships which interested Pythagoras because it was these that had universal application. And music, of any kind, is only a more complex structure of such intervals and relationships which still owe their meaning to the simple phenomenon illustrated by the monochord.

The ratios revealed by the demonstration are a way both of seeing the geometry of sound and of hearing the sound of geometry.   Neither the sound nor the form comes first in any kind of precedence; they are just different expressions, both appreciable to the senses, of the *kósmos* inherent in the universe.   Pythagoras would not have failed to see that proportions and ratios similar to those in sound harmony were at work also in spatial relationships and that there was therefore a similar science of number behind the pleasure we take in the purity and regularity of certain geometric forms and volumes. Such simple harmonic ratios could be, and were, applied to the proportions of a building or a particular element of architecture and would give rise to a comparable sense of pleasure which we would recognise as harmonious. He would have seen these proportions at work in many aspects of the enormous temple of Hera which his compatriots Rhoikos and Theodoros were building in Samos, on the edge of his city; and he would have seen them present in the canon of proportions used by the sculpture workshops in bringing to life the form of the great marble *Kouros* of Samos.

In the laborious transmission of Pythagoras's ideas through the subsequent centuries of intellectual history, his basic observations were built upon and re-worked into countless more complex theories of harmony, notation, musical temperament and tuning, architectural propriety, numerology, symbolic geometry and so on. These are a quite different matter, even though they may occasionally still bear his name. They are the fodder of that station 'Radio Pythagoreanism' which so often blocks out our reception of the intermitting signal coming from Pythagoras himself. The interest in Pythagoras lies not in any prowess he may have had as a technical theorist, but rather in the profound and clear connections he made between different areas of knowledge. Unfortunately, our perception of this has been dimmed by the volume of so much later commentary.

There are some exceptions, however, when his ideas re-emerge in a closely related form: the architectural theory of Andrea Palladio and his followers in the 16th century, for example, which favoured the use of simple harmonic ratios in the proportions of interiors and buildings, stands out as particularly relevant in its return to the essence of what the thinking of Pythagoras implies. But most of the body of so-called "Pythagorean philosophy" on these matters has neither more nor less relevance to Pythagoras himself than the abstruse theology and canon law of the Middle Ages had to do with the words actually spoken by Jesus of Nazareth in the first century and the challenges and precepts he may have wished to leave with us in this world.

The observations of Pythagoras were not of huge complexity. They did not aim to describe the totality of experience; they were merely the beginning. They showed the way. Anyone of Pythagoras's intelligence would have seen that the beauty we find in the human face and body or in the forms of the natural landscape and its flora and fauna is of a complexity that cannot be readily comprehended or analysed by the human mind, let alone reduced in its entirety to arithmetical ratios. So also with birdsong and musical composition. But he

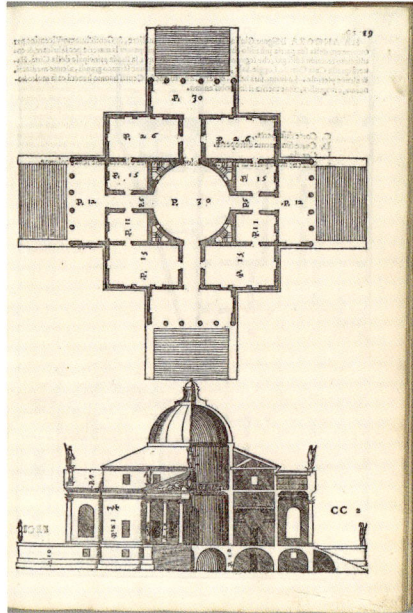

A page from Andrea Palladio's 'Quattro Libri dell'Archittetura' (Book II, page 19), showing a wood-cut made from a drawing for the Villa Rotonda near Vicenza.

sensed correctly, and for the first time in history, that their potential beauty was based at the most fundamental level on an order which *was* comprehensible to us. And it suggested most importantly that our reception of beauty was a valid path to philosophical understanding, and that music and sound themselves constituted one of the most direct of those paths.

If this seems an opaque or esoteric statement, we should recall the number of times that Einstein, in our own age, is said to have acknowledged the role of music, directly and indirectly, in the creative/intuitive process of scientific perception. "I often think in music. I live my daydreams in music. I see my life in terms of music" [4]. "The Theory of Relativity occurred to me by intuition, and music is the driving force behind that intuition…. My new discovery is the result of musical perception." [5]

These words, coming from one of the greatest of all scientific minds, are astonishing. What is musical perception? How do we "think in music"? A part of the answer lies in the fact that both music and mathematics release us from the burden of words. It is the capacity of music to free the mind that Einstein is referring to. It allowed him to perceive the order which lay behind the mass of material before him, and which ultimately he was able to distill into an equation of great simplicity and beauty.

There is a sense of a deep gratitude to music that lies behind Einstein's comments. Pythagoras must have felt something similar, many centuries earlier, when he became aware of the exactness of the numerical proportions that were manifest in pure harmonies of musical tone. Because it conjured clarity and order out of amorphous sound, the realization itself quelled anxiety; it brought a sense of relief, and for that he may, like Einstein, have felt a profound gratitude.

Einstein in 1941, playing the violin made for him by Oscar Steger in 1933

---

[1] Iamblichus, *De Vita Pitagorica*, Ch. 17

[2] The Platonic philosopher, Proclus, writing a thousand years later than Pythagoras claims somewhat fantastically that, upon his discovery of the geometric theorem which bears his name, Pythagoras sacrificed an ox in gratitude. The *'eureka'* like moment is unlikely to have occurred since the theorem was almost certainly something Pythagoras learnt from Babylonian thinking and his sacrificing of an animal furthermore remains a contentious question (see Chapter 14).

[3] *Hamlet's Mill*, 1977, Giorgio de Santillana and Hertha von Deschend

[4] Alice Calaprice (Ed.). *The Expanded Quotable Einstein* – p.155 (Princeton University Press, Princeton, NJ, 2000) Quoted from interviews with Einstein.

[5] Shin'ichi Suzuki, *Nurtured by Love - a New Approach to Education* – p.90 (Exposition, Press Smithtown NY, 1969, repr.1981.) Conversations with Einstein recollected.
For the many citations of Einstein speaking about music, see also:
Schilpp, Paul. (Ed.). (1979). *Albert Einstein: Autobiographical Notes*. La Salle, Ill: Open Court.
Wertheimer, Max. (1959). *Productive Thinking*. New York: Harper and Brothers.

'Le Silence', Antoine-Augustin Préault, 1843,
Plaster model, Museum of Fine Arts, Houston, Texas.

Silence

L et us pause for just a moment to take stock of what we have so far, and to see what exactly is implied by these three words that Pythagoras chose and the simple acoustic phenomenon which he laid before us.

Pythagoras is important to us not just for being a participant in the earliest scientific observations of human thinking, but for seeing and exploring the spiritual implications which they raised. This is his particular contribution. His idea of harmony does not finish at the physical phenomenon: for him it takes on a spiritual and universal dimension. Although a source of pleasure to the ear and to the mind, it acquires in his thinking a quality of divine significance. It does this because what it had shown about the nature of sound suggested to his mind that, within the single embracing concept of *harmonía*, there was the unexpected fusion of the ordered with the beautiful – the mathematical correctness of a just harmonic interval with the beauty of the sound produced.

Our language and thinking to this day still favour a clear distinction between the moral and the aesthetic, between what is good and what is beautiful. Yet to see these two qualities as effectively separate does not respect the truth. There is not an option or an alternative here: the moral and the aesthetic interpenetrate one another at every point, in many different ways, and to constantly varying degrees. They are hard to separate because by nature they should never be completely separated. A good life of supposed moral perfection lived in ignorance of beauty is every bit as valueless as a life dedicated only to the beautiful and lived in ignorance of the moral. The two are symbiotic – sustaining and modifying one another, and aspiring, between themselves, towards an intelligent equilibrium. The appropriation of the one without the other leads to disharmony. It seems unnecessary to have to say this; and yet through centuries of Western thinking, because of its prevailing religious beliefs, this perception has struggled to be given space. Much less, however, in Eastern thinking. For example, in both the historic tradition of Japan as well as in its contemporary culture, there is no inattention to, or *de*-emphasis of, the importance of the aesthetic in matters both of the inner and the outer life. In the West we have a greater apathy towards discordance and ugliness, and it has amounted in recent times to a conscious pursuit of disharmony in art and music, which speaks of a profound anxiety at heart.

Throughout later Antiquity Pythagoras was renowned more as the teacher of a way of life than for anything else, and it was the spiritual dimension to harmony that was the inspiration of that life. Its true teachings – even if the description of them that has come down to us from much later writers implies something more banal – must have centred on the different ways in which a growing awareness of harmony could be assimilated into our lives. The first step was our becoming aware of its presence and its nature (the part that Pythagoras himself had performed by giving it a name and demonstrating its universal nature). The next step involved our making it incarnate in our lives and our surroundings, and absorbing it into our whole way of being: this involved our relations to others, to other living things, and even to the inert things around us; it encompassed our way of eating, our manner of behaving, of speaking, of loving, of sex – everything. Finally, once it had taken root as the principle by which a person lived a life, it is natural that it should become an aspiration of the Pythagorean life also to die and to take leave of this life in harmony and without anxiety, as much as circumstance might permit.

In many ways this was an idea too simple and perhaps too abstract to survive. Pythagoras must have known that it would be a hard sell to a world that had very different expectations about what was divine. Abstract ideas of harmony, however beguiling they might be, are no substitute for a crowd of colourful and magical deities, sharing the forms and emotions of humans and animals, and wielding supernatural powers: humankind needed then, and still needs now, those vital companions on the playing-field of life. It is perhaps because of this realisation that the life he proposed would appeal to so few, that he is said to have said, 'μὴ εἶναι πρὸς πάντας πάντα ῥητά' [1], "all things are not to be said to all people". And in the end, it may well have been the charge of this kind of perceived 'elitism' that inspired the popular revolt, led by Cylon in the city of Croton, which saw the schools founded by Pythagoras destroyed and his followers hounded out of the city.

The philosopher Porphyry, in his life of Pythagoras written late in the third century of this era, laments that what Pythagoras "said to his followers no one can tell for certain, since they kept such exceptional silence" [2]. There were several reasons for that silence. One has just been mentioned – the diffidence Pythagoras may have felt in regard to the acceptance of his ideas. Another was that he may have foreseen the distortion that would inevitably occur – and did occur on a significant scale – as soon as his intuitions were wrestled into the written word and codified in an institutional doctrine over which he, after he was dead, would have no control.

But the greatest reason for the silence was the emphasis which Pythagoras wished to place on receptivity, on silencing the mind so as to listen and be open to the possibility of receiving intuition – to be as attentive, in other words, as the early visitors to the oak trees at Dodona had been. The emphasis was on openness of mind and observation as opposed to speaking and preaching. And, lest we should fall into the trap of thinking that such listening to things invisible might be a sign of passivity or of weakness, it is useful for us to remember that we are endowed with ears by nature to alert us to danger. Animals are perfect listeners: they have to be if they are to survive. So it is for us: being receptive, attentive and still, is not just a matter of tuning into the ether for the joy of it; it may also give us vital warning of disharmony and danger. It is a key to both spiritual and material survival. Although the gains in our empirical knowledge have been huge following the opening of the scientific mind in the

Banryutei garden, Kongobuji Temple, Koyasan, Japan.

119

6th century BC, by the very same process of awakening we have lost whole areas of intuitive interaction with our natural environment. We have become deaf to the communality of creation. The consequences of this long and continuing process can be seen all around us today. They threaten to overwhelm us together with our world if we do not soon start to pay attention and to listen once again.

The exhortation to listen and to be receptive still rings oddly in our ears today. When Shunmyo Masuno, one of the most celebrated living designers of gardens in Japan, mentions in his writings the importance of letting the rocks which are to be the backbone of a new garden tell us where and how they should be set in the ground – in his words, the importance "of hearing what they themselves have to say about how they wish to be laid out" – his words, to Western ears, seem oddly counter-intuitive. Rocks are inert blocks of limestone: how can we listen to them? Yet all that Masuno is saying is that we need to be receptive to the forms and the potential for harmony that may lie in *anything* that we see. Once we become receptive we see things that we were blind to before, and the problem – in this case the creation of a garden around a particular rock or rocks – dissolves.

Pythagoras would surely have concurred. Everything that is even distantly verifiable in his meagre oeuvre seems to suggest to us the fundamental importance he attached to receptivity. His musical demonstration was about listening intently. His precept to those who joined his school in Croton was about being silent and attending. And his creation of the word '*philosophía*' for us was an exhortation to be receptive and open to *sophía* – awareness and wisdom. It is for this reason that, although it is only recorded centuries later by the philosopher Iamblichus, I cannot help feeling that the idea that the new arrivals at his school should be silent for five years, reflects albeit distantly something that Pythagoras himself must have wished. That it became a 'rule', however, and was quantified at five years is almost certainly the work of later generations; but the initial idea of the silence and of the self-dicipline of just listening and receiving are surely original to Pythagoras himself.

A great deal depended therefore on the simple acoustic experiment of the monochord. In the hands of Pythagoras it became a narrow gateway into a whole realm of physical, moral and spiritual considerations. It was also the beginning of the technical study not just of sound, but of music. Often it is said that music is a window onto the human soul: perhaps we should say rather that it is a part of the human soul made momentarily incarnate. In fact, music presupposes the existence of a soul because its meaning is received not just by the mind and by the senses alone, but by something else which lies behind them both. What should we call this 'something else' if not the soul?

Let us look now at what Pythagoras may have had to say about the soul.

¹ Aristoxenus, *Rules of Pedagogy,* Book X, quoted by Diogenes Laertius, *Lives of the Eminent Philosophers, Book VIII*

² Porphyry, *Life of Pythagoras 19*

Ancient rhyton (a pouring cup for ceremonial drinking) in the shape of a dog's head,
with decoration attributed to the Brygos Painter, working in Athens c. 490 - 470 BC;
Museo Nazionale Etrusco di Villa Giulia, Rome.

Animals and Souls

Humans and animals: what a chequered history lies there. Some of it good; most of it terrible. We live in the midst of nature and yet we are often as orphans in its world. The collective memory of exploitation, disturbance and invasion of territory has meant that we terrify most of the rest of creation and we are unable to get close to it even when we want to. Yet when we do establish close relations with animals it can be a source of wondrous curiosity to us. The simplest thing done for an animal can bring an unexpected, almost disproportionate, sense of joy or gratification. Why ever should we not have meaningful relations with animals? The pity is that we don't have more.

Those few historically constructive relationships that we have formed with animals through history – with the horse in so many parts of the world, with the dog since time immemorial, with the elephant in South Asia, the camel and the falcon in Arabia – have come about through a strange concoction of fear, persistent inculcation, mutual benefit and mutual receptivity. Like children these creatures awaken in us a range of reflex feelings. Unlike children, however, these animals to which we are close can, if they wish, at any moment do us mortal harm; yet miraculously they don't, unless provoked, because the bonds between us are felt by them, at least, to be somehow inviolable. Much of our own purpose in desiring to be close to them is utilitarian. Yet, once such a relationship is established, a sense of our kinship with them starts to break upon our consciousness. At that point the uneasy question arises as to whether, behind their animal eyes, lies the repository of a soul.

This question held a fascination for Pythagoras, as we have seen. In that one surviving anecdote about him which dates from his own time, he gives us an insight into his thinking both about the soul and about animals. The anecdote is told by Xenophanes, a philosopher who often delighted in satire. Xenophanes originated from the city of Colophon on the mainland of Asia Minor across the water from Samos, and geographical and temporal proximity makes it perfectly possible that he and Pythagoras could even have known one another in person. Xenophanes's writings are lost to us, and so the anecdote only exists as a quotation from his work recorded by Diogenes Laertius [1], the biographer of Greek thinkers mentioned earlier who wrote in the 3rd Century, probably in Asia Minor: it is thanks to him that this glimpse of the person of Pythagoras has survived at all. In a manner characteristic of Xenophanes, the anecdote appears superficially to be making fun of Pythagoras's thinking. A literal translation of the verses would read:

> And when approaching one who was beating a puppy, they say, he
> [Pythagoras] had compassion and spoke out as follows: "do not beat it!
> It is the soul of a man, a friend of mine.
> I recognised the voice when I heard him cry."

καί ποτέ μιν στυφελιζομένου σκύλακος παριόντα
φασὶν ἐποικτῖραι καὶ τόδε φάσθαι ἔπος:
"παῦσαι μηδὲ ῥάπιζ᾽, ἐπεὶ ἦ φίλου ἀνέρος ἐστὶ ψυχή
τὴν ἔγνων φθεγξαμένης ἀΐων."

Using an interesting and not common word, Xenophanes says that Pythagoras 'felt compassion as he approached', παριόντα … ἐποικτῖραι. The root of the second word *'ep-oiktîrai'* is the more common verb *'oiktéiro'*, meaning 'I pity'; but the addition of the prefix *'ep-'* or *'epi-'* implies a more active involvement in which the compassion felt is both reinforced and specifically directed towards the unfortunate dog.

Quite plausibly this story could have been a sort of parable used by Pythagoras himself, which then came to be retold as an anecdote about its author. Or maybe it was merely a philosopher's gesture of humour and self-irony. But irrespective of who said it and with what words and in which context, irrespective even of whether the anecdote is pure fabrication or not, it still tells us something very clear about what people understood to be Pythagoras's beliefs. In the encounter he is seen to show an unusual compassion. He understands the cry of pain coming from the dog in this case because he senses it to be the cry of a dead friend whose spirit now inhabits the body of the puppy. This could have been seen as the sort of well-intentioned madness people had come to expect from philosophers: alternatively, we might be looking at one of the earliest rationalised expressions of a peculiarly dignified human trait – namely empathy, the feeling and understanding of the suffering of others, including in this case the suffering of those commonly perceived as lesser creatures. People may have found Pythagoras's behaviour laughable, but he could equally be admired for giving philosophical significance to the act of human empathy, by drawing our attention to it and seeking, in an apparently bizarre way, to explain its origin. Howsoever we wish to gloss the anecdote in the end, the fundamental message from Pythagoras is still quite clear nonetheless: stop beating the dog. As simple as that.

Why then so 'bizarre' an explanation? This is, after all, the object of Xenophanes's satire. Is he perhaps taking aim at what he sees as an old-fashioned and superstitious 'animism' in Pythagoras, against which he saw his own more pragmatic thinking in contra-distinction? Or is it something which possesses a wider significance?

The transmigration of the soul from incarnation to incarnation and the wheel of constant rebirth appears to have been an idea so widely permeating the beliefs of much of Asia at that time, that it comes as a surprise to realise that it could possibly have seemed unusual or funny to the Aegean Greeks of the 6th century BC. We are hampered by understanding little about the cultic practices and beliefs of the much earlier Aegean world in the Bronze Age, but no evidence so far discovered points to a cycle of reincarnation as necessarily being an element in its beliefs. Nor is there in Homer's gloomy view of death and the afterlife any sense of possible reincarnation. It appears that it is only with the arrival in the 6th century BC of the curious Thracian cult of Orphism, based on the story of the musician-saviour Orpheus, that the ideas of transmigration and reincarnation begin to have currency in Greek lands. Some commentators both ancient and modern have even seen Pythagoras as a co-creator of this new cult of Orphism, while others have suggested he may have been greatly influenced by it. Certainly the centrality given to music and its transformative power in the myth of Orpheus resonates closely with the thought of Pythagoras. The connection between the two figures is likely to remain deep, yet obscure.

The exact route by which Orphism came into Thrace and the Black Sea area in the first place is also unclear. The cult's particular focus on the redeeming power of the god Dionysos points to somewhere deep within Asia: Dionysos as a deity is said to have come back at some point into the Greek world from India (which is often 'myth-speak' for somewhere a long way to the

East), riding triumphantly on a leopard and bringing with him that vital Asian climber known to us as the grape-vine. Grapes and the spirit-liquor which is produced from their maceration and decay have kept their powerful association with the soul and its afterlife well beyond the extinction of the Pagan world, in the Christian use of a sacramental wine as the central symbol of its celebratory ritual.

Dionysos riding on a Leopard, Hellenistic mosaic from Pella, Greece

We can approach the idea of transmigration in a literal or a metaphorical way. To Western ways of thinking, the literal tends to predominate, meaning that we get caught up on the question of its mechanism. In the West we have come to view our individual selves as irreducible, our earthly lives as single and unique, and the consequences of our actions as ratified in a cosmic moment of judgement after death. We look at the idea of transmigration therefore with the same linear and consequential logic that was taught to us originally by Aristotle and Plato. We think immediately about *how* it might work; and in doing so our tendency is to oversimplify it. We see it reductively in terms almost of an absurd fable in which our possible rebirth as, say, a cockroach, subsequent on our death in this life would clearly be due to the misdemeanours of our life in this existence, whereas our birth as a person of compelling beauty and limitless means on the other hand would signify the opposite: best of all would be if, by concentrated spiritual evolution, we were able to pick up sufficient moral velocity to escape the gravitational pull of the cycle of rebirth altogether, as Buddhism teaches. All this is seen as a progression along an axis of time. Amusing as the image might be for us, being born again as a cockroach is not what transmigration is about. Because of its emphasis on identity, linear consequence and on mechanism, this simplistic way of reading metempsychosis – the transmigration of souls – amounts to little more than an unconvincing game of Snakes and Ladders without end.

The other way of looking at transmigration emphasises what it implies rather than how it works. If we can heave ourselves up a little above the board of Snakes and Ladders, we begin to see a different significance to it. First we need to suppress that desire to seek the explicable mechanism and to allow the wider implications inherent in it to come to the fore. In this way it no longer presents itself to us as a process which is purely reflexive, but rather as an expansion of our being into a greater dimension; not specifically as a sequential narrative about "past" or "future" lives, but rather as a metaphor of our growing consciousness.

In the anecdote recounted by Xenophanes, Pythagoras is asking us simply to acknowledge the inescapable communality that exists between our own being and the being of the dog. If, like the man who is beating the dog, we persist in seeing our lives and our selves as wholly distinct from that of other beings, we treat such beings or persons in any way we wish because they are, to us, merely objects. But as soon as we begin to comprehend how our actions affect them, hurt them, upset them or delight them, and we perceive how those actions reflect on ourselves to nourish or diminish us, we are no longer seeing our lives as separate from theirs. Something of the colour of our own being starts to infuse theirs. There is an intermingling such that we sense that our lives are not ultimately discrete or separate. A person who unthinkingly beats a dog has either never possessed or has momentarily suspended the faculty of empathy. Likewise, the oppressor is able to oppress only because the satisfaction to his own ego in so doing occludes any space for considering how his actions either affect the oppressed or, just as importantly, how they reflect on him.

Once we can escape from the perception of our lives as isolated and linear, and conceive that existence may have a cyclical character, even that the structure of time and space might possess a (to us unimaginable) geometry such that the oppressor is, was, or becomes the person oppressed, the torturer the tortured, the lover the beloved, the falcon the rabbit, the horse the rider, the daughter the mother, and so on – at that point we come closer to understanding what the idea of the transmigration of souls is telling us. It pushes us to see how our lives are related in a way similar to the individual leaves on a tree – superficially separate, yet at the same time indissolubly linked through their participation within the greater organism. All that Pythagoras is asking us to do is to be aware of both the individual leaves *and* the tree. His appeal in other words is to an understanding of the universal kinship of all living things – a kinship that does not exclude even stray dogs or cockroaches or Banyan trees. We do not need to ask, and must not ask, what the mechanism is by which a deceased person might so soon turn up as a dog in the marketplace, and let alone be recognised by his erstwhile friend, Pythagoras. That is not the point: the meaning here is not literal. The transmigration of souls is a metaphor to explain something which we are born, alas, to forget: that our millions of separate lives are also a unity; that what we do to others – bad, cruel, hateful, loving or kind – we are ultimately and inevitably doing to ourselves; and that the awareness in us of harmony and the cultivation of compassion through *philosophía*, as ways of deepening our understanding, are of such importance that they constitute the meaning – in one sense, the whole purpose – of our present existence.

Harmony; universal kinship; compassion; purpose. Who in the West had ever contemplated our earthly existence in such terms before Pythagoras? It is hard for us to comprehend the newness of this way of seeing things. Yes, a good part of it was imbibed through his contact, direct or indirect, with the East and with ancient Sanskrit literature; but he imparts to that wisdom a crucially new architecture of thought through his emphasis on the universal relevance of *harmonía*, which arose out of his observations of acoustic harmony. In the body of literature which precedes him in the Greek world – in the works of Homer, Hesiod or Sappho – there are moments of profound humanity: but there is no real aspiration towards an overarching philosophy of life. Nor do we find this in the reported thinking of either Thales or Anaximander, who precede him by a generation. With Pythagoras, all that changes. He raises questions for the first time about the meaning and purpose of our existence. And the appeal of later spiritual teachers – among them, Jesus of Nazareth – to these same questions, builds upon his legacy. Pythagoras prepares the way for these movements – not in the superficial sense that he 'influences' their teachings, but rather that he advanced and opened the philosophical awareness of the human mind towards the concepts of compassion and harmony. He had created a state of mind in humanity that could now be receptive to the teachings of one such as Jesus of Nazareth, who spoke both of compassion and of the meaning of our lives in a quite particular way.

The core teachings of Christianity and of the later spiritual movements and religions that have formed our mental culture, have so greatly habituated us to this cast of thinking that we no longer grasp how radical it was for the world of the West in Pythagoras's time. Two thousand five hundred years ago Pythagoras quite simply opened a door in our consciousness and ushered us through.

In our thinking about the anecdote which Xenophanes recounts there are two further over-simplifications which we must try to avoid. The first is seeing an incarnation as a dog in the market-place as necessarily a *bad* state of affairs or as some kind of 'punishment'. The cosmos is not in the business of punishing us: it is rather that the soul is in the business of learning. It as if our consciousness travels; and, as it journeys, it grows. In a way that remains mysterious, it appears to know its own route through the maze of existences. It seems to know its choices well, and to see its way. It understands what it needs: and in each new incarnation it is aware at a deep level of familiar situations and repeated fears, joys or problems. It recognises both what and whom it loves, and what and whom it must avoid. We sense the pull of these forces at many moments in our lives – even though we do not always heed them.

Avoiding the second oversimplification requires us to be open to the idea that reincarnation does not of necessity mean the reincarnation of the wholeness of our self as we know it in this existence, but that only what is unfulfilled and unevolved in us returns and returns until it eventually acquires what it needs for its fulfilment. In this way of seeing, only some part of Pythagoras's friend has become the dog in the market-place – the unfulfilled and incognisant part of him. The fulfilled parts, by contrast, neither seek nor need to return. In this sense, transmigration becomes a constant process of purification, of winnowing or of filtering out – even though the different parts never lose the connected sense of their identity as a whole. This is not a simple idea: we will return to it again in the final chapters of this book.

In the end, these two interdependent concepts – of the transmigration of the soul and of the unity of living beings which are intimated in the thought of Pythagoras – point to a conclusion that challenges more than comforts us. They suggest that we alone are responsible for our destiny and for who or what we momentarily may be in this life. No deity is choosing us, punishing us, testing us or rewarding us; we are never the passive recipients of a destiny, but rather the creators of it, not just in this life but in the general trajectory of our many different lives. We create what we are; and the decisions we take and the things we see as 'happening to us' are fed by our countless other existences in different places, times and states of being which, like tributaries, swell the stream of what we become.

The story, the joke, the fable – whatever it is – of the dog being beaten in the marketplace is used by Pythagoras as an image to make manifest the unity of all living beings. Its point is to lead us away from thinking of our lives just as single leaves or branches, and to turn our attention to the primary importance of the life-bearing tree to which those leaves belong – and to which, at the end of each season of life, our being willingly returns.

It is a curious coincidence that a number of finely observed images of dogs start to appear in Archaic and Classical Greek art around the time of Pythagoras's later years and shortly after his death. The sleek hunting dog (*image top right*), from the Acropolis of Athens, sculpted by the so-called 'Rampin Master' in Parian marble in the late 6th century BC comes first to mind because it is the best known. But there exist also many humbler objects, such as the ingenious ceramic pouring cup or *rhyton* produced and painted by the atelier of the 'Brygos Painter' in Athens, an image of which heads this chapter. And then (*image bottom right*) there is the succinct and elegant design by the artist known as the 'Euergides Painter' of a dog scratching its ear. Turned round upon itself in circular fashion, drawn within a circle and depicted on the circular floor of a wide drinking bowl, the image seems to intimate the cyclical recurrence of

Hunting Dog in Parian Marble by the 'Rampin Master' c. 520 BC;
The Acropolis Museum, Athens

The Euergides painter, Athenian red-figure cup, late 6th c. BC,
Ashmolean Museum, Oxford.

transmigration to which Pythagoras alludes. Yet, more than that – as is the case with all thoughtful art – its timeless beauty of design suggests something important: that works of art themselves, which are the vibrant products of our inextinguishable human urge to create new kinds of order and *kósmos*, are themselves entities to which we, by the act of creation, have imparted souls. The meaningful work of art is only meaningful in as much as it, too, possesses a kind of soul. Such creations have been a vital sustenance for humanity throughout its evolution. They accompany us in our lives, they nourish us, admonish us, counsel us and console us. Our own existence is the product of an impulse of creation, and we give meaning to our own lives through that same act of creating.

It is understandable that, from such a belief in the kinship of living beings, the abstention from eating meat and the killing of animals either for food or some other utility, may logically follow. For this reason it is highly likely that Pythagoras, as is widely maintained, was one of the first advocates of ethical vegetarianism in the West of whom we have any information. We have to say "in the West" because abstention from meat may have been for a much longer time a tenet of life for certain spiritual groups in India; and we need to say "highly likely" because we cannot be certain that Pythagoras advocated complete vegetarianism because there are so many conflicting reports about this in later centuries. Most of the later Pythagoreans appear to have followed vegetarian life-styles; some later writers (for example, Onesicritus quoted by Strabo, and Eudoxus – who goes so far as to say that Pythagoras would not even have anything to do with cooks and hunters – quoted by Porphyry) say that he was contrary to all killing of animals of any kind; others (for example, Porphyry himself, Iamblichus, and Aristotle cited by Diogenes Laertius) say he abstained from eating the meat of most, but not all animals; and then there is Aristoxenus, quoted by Aulus Gellius, who appears to deny that he was vegetarian at all. All these comments date, at the earliest, from long after the death of Pythagoras, and they contradict one another so freely that there is little hope of knowing the truth. This tends to be the norm with statements about Pythagoras. What Pythagoras himself did and believed, and what those in later centuries thought he did and believed, may rarely coincide. At best, we can say that the ambiguity that has arisen speaks for Pythagoras's lack of dogmatism. Dogmatism tends to be incompatible with wisdom and with *philosophía*. He may have firmly believed that the killing of animals for food was wrong in principle; but that if nonetheless it should be necessary for some particular reason, then it should be done in full cognisance of, and gratitude for, the life that was being sacrificed. In this way it was not just an empty rule to be obeyed, but rather the adoption of a standpoint of responsibility. As so often happens with Pythagoras's teaching, it may have been the nuanced and undogmatic way in which he thought and expressed himself that has left behind the legacy of confusion.

The questions both of vegetarianism and of the transmigration of souls lead us back once again to India, the only other intellectual culture which shared at this time a similar thinking on these matters [3]. However we choose to explain it, it is clear that Pythagoras is listening to and picking up on thought coming from the earliest of the Sanskrit compositions of wisdom – transmitted to him we do not know exactly how, but most probably through the geographical intermediary of Babylon and the Persian Empire. This transmission could have been direct, if we accept that Pythagoras did travel into Mesopotamia, or indirect if we wish to maintain he learnt such ideas from others – perhaps even from Pherecydes [4], the shadowy poet and philosopher of the island of Syros who was sometimes said to have been the teacher of Pythagoras. But that leaves unanswered the question of how Pherecydes himself might have received these ideas.

We noted earlier that the genius of Pythagoras lay in what he did with the ideas he picked up in his listenings, readings and journeys, rather than the formulation *ab nihilo* of the remarkable acoustic, mathematical and astronomical concepts that are central to his thinking. In the centuries following his life he was frequently referred to as the most learned of the Greeks of his age. This epithet riled the most celebrated Ionian philosopher of the next generation, Heracleitus, who appears to have felt that Pythagoras was somehow phoney and that his knowledge, gathered from other sources – many of them spurious in Heracleitus's view – did not amount to anything that could be dignified with the word 'wisdom'. Since these opinions of Heracleitus are the only other approximately contemporary comments we possess about Pythagoras's thinking, we should now give them a careful hearing since they may hold the key to a deeper understanding of the minds of both of these two remarkable individuals.

Goya's Dog

---

[1] Diogenes Laertius, *Lives of the Philosophers*, VIII, 1. 36

[2] See Diogenes Laertius, *Lives of the Philosophers*, VIII.1.8 where he cites Ion of Chios to this effect.

[3] Scylax of Caryanda speaks of people he encountered on his Indian periplus who ate nothing that had animal life.

[4] Pherecydes's principal work, the *Pentemychos* or *Heptamychos* (the 'Five' or 'Seven Recesses'), was about the origins of the cosmos, explained in allegorical fashion. It is only known through fragmentary citations in other writers and was considered to be one of the first works of Greek prose. His interest in the immortality and transmigration of the human soul, alluded to both by Cicero and Saint Augustine, has led to his close association with Pythagoras: Diogenes Laertius says that some considered him to have been the teacher of Pythagoras. Pherecydes is sometimes included as one of the 'Seven Wise Men' of Ancient Greece.

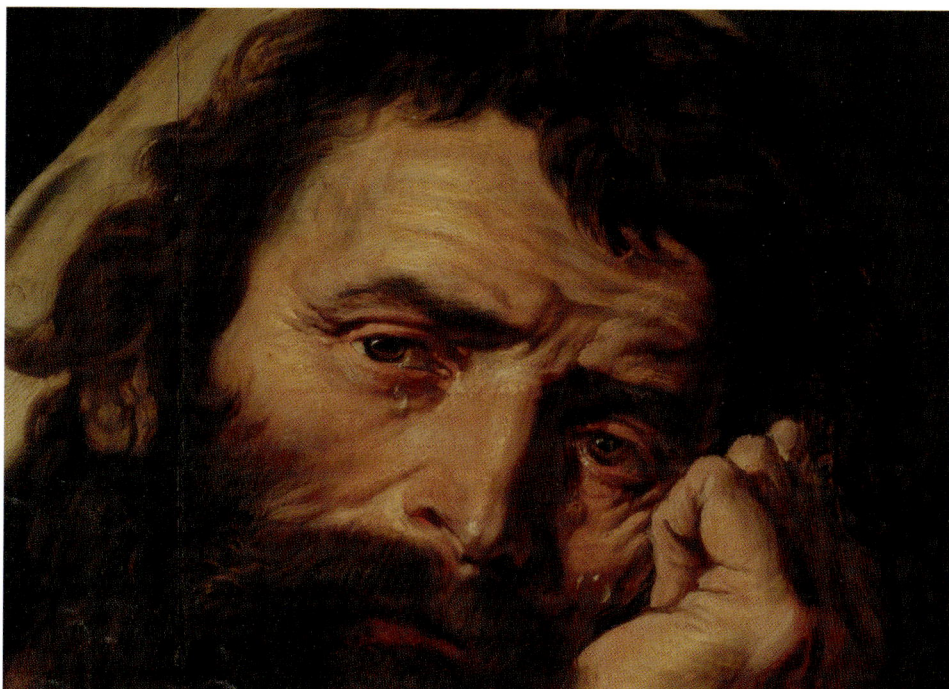

Abraham Janssens, the Elder – 'Heracleitus' c. 1602: oil on wood panel.
(Private Collection.)

Pythagoras
and Heracleitus

So far there has been a simplicity and coherence to the picture which is emerging of the thinking of Pythagoras. It is when we turn to the criticisms levelled at him by Heracleitus, however, that the situation changes: other than Xenophanes's anecdote of the encounter with the dog, these comments constitute the only glimpse we have of Pythagoras from approximately his own era. And with them our theme moves into a different key.

Heracleitus was a generation younger and is unlikely ever to have met Pythagoras, who had probably long since left the Aegean area and emigrated to

Southern Italy in the years in which their adult lives overlapped. The contrast between the two thinkers could not be more revealing, not just because it shows two great philosophical minds of starkly different cast, but also because it comes to the root of the short-comings of both of them.

Those whom we revere as great thinkers, great oral teachers or gurus, come into existence as such in the minds of those who hear them. They do not just occur in isolation. If either Jesus or Mohammed had not spoken to some deep and real need felt by the people of their own epoch, we would have no Christianity and no Islam. The expectations of an audience, furthermore, in any period of history determine significantly the manner in which such a figure will be recreated in the imaginations of those who receive and hear. A messiah can only come about, if there is a real cultural appetite for a messiah. If a person today from Bangalore or Bangor professed herself to be a messiah she would probably be received with scepticism. People might value her teachings, her great wisdom and her calling, but would struggle to see her in their minds as a messiah, however much she might profess herself to be one, because 'the messiah' is not part of the cultural grammar or vocabulary of our age. The minds that hear and receive are, in other words, as important in the creation of a cult as the one that speaks. People who wish to see wonders and miracles will see them; and those who crave a messiah will find one who answers to their needs. Jesus would present himself to, and would be received by, our minds quite differently if he were to be living in our world today. This does not diminish his teachings in any way; it is just a recognition of the historical fact that our minds function differently and have different expectations in the 21st century from those of two thousand years earlier. We see and hear Jesus through the eyes of those who came after him and wrote the story of his life from memory through the prism of their own emotions, desires, apprehensions and prejudices. Saint Paul, perhaps the single most influential interpreter of his teachings, never heard Jesus speak but rather drew his lessons and conclusions from received teachings in terms of his own mental and cultural world – that of an educated, Hellenised Jew with forceful and at times dogmatic opinions, as manifested in his prior persecution of the first Christians. For these reasons, we need to try to understand what we hear of a great thinker of the past by making allowance for the desires and expectations of those who received and then transmitted the information and the teachings to us.

What might those expectations have been in the case of Pythagoras? We must recall again the world from which Pythagoras emerged, and the dramatic changes which he and his contemporary thinkers wrought upon it. The seventh and sixth centuries BC were a period of crucial cognitive transition when a very ancient imaginative world, dense with animism, magic, ritual and shamanic power began slowly to give way to another, in which ideas and constructs little by little replaced spirit magic as the explainers of phenomena. This was a process which changed human conciousness for ever. It was not immediate but evolved imperceptibly over a long span of time, and like all processes it had to be far advanced before anyone realised even that there had been a process going on at all. Our growth from infancy into adulthood is a reflection of this, in so far as we can never say at exactly what point the milestones of our cognitive development occurred: we have to become an adult before we realise what it means to be a child. Pythagoras emerged from this forest of ancient lore replete with its multitude of divinities and invisible powers and shot through with magical and esoteric knowledge, proposing a vision of our universe as a simple and precisely wrought idea. A page was turned by him which portended great change. But many of those who either heard him or heard of him, still remained on the previous page. They knew of his travels in the East and Egypt, of his reputed knowledge in so many fields – geometry, music, astronomy – and they made of him what they particularly longed for: a home-grown magus in the mould of the renowned priests of Zoroaster in Persia.

The figure of the wise man with special powers, the magus or *mágos*, who had travelled to distant lands and learnt the lore of ancient peoples, was a deep-rooted archetype. Magi appear later even at the Nativity in Bethlehem. This persona of the magus haunted Pythagoras and he could never shake it off. He may even positively have encouraged it: we cannot know. The ancient magi imparted precepts, prohibitions, rituals and interpretations of the movements of the planets in the firmament, and they were expected to possess special powers of divination. For this reason it was natural that when Pythagoras spoke or reflected out loud on different and quite unconventional matters, in many of the minds of those who heard him his words and ideas were understood through the filter of those expectations: a metaphor became a precept, a reflection became a ritual, an observation a law, a curiosity a dogma. And because nothing was written down by him to suggest otherwise, such interpretations stuck.

Relief from Daskyleion showing Magi, with their faces partly masked, performing a ritual sacrifice. (Istanbul Archaeological Museum.)

This phenomenon was anathema to Heracleitus who instinctively abhorred cult of any kind. The Christian theologian, Clement of Alexandria, writing in the late 2nd century in his *Protrepticus* or 'Exhortation' (to the Pagan to turn to Christianity) cites Heracleitus many times, quoting the philosopher's withering comments about Mystery rites and pagan cults. And on the subject of Pythagoras himself, Heracleitus says: "Pythagoras, son of Mnésarchos, practised research more than any man, and making extracts from these treatises he gathered together a wisdom of his own [which was] an accumulation of learning, a harmful [deceptive] craft." [1] Those last two expressions in the Greek are: πολυμαθίην ('*polymathíeen*', literally, much learning or aggregated knowledge) and κακοτεχνίην ('*kakotechníeen*', literally, evil or misleading art). This corresponds largely with what we know already, namely that the inspiration for much of Pythagoras's thinking came from his exposure to existing Eastern sources of knowledge; but Heracleitus is implying something more by the word 'κακοτεχνίην', namely that Pythagoras's knowledge was a kind of empty and dishonest rhetoric rather than a true wisdom – which was something that Heracleitus believed he alone possessed, because only he realised that "what is wise is set apart from all things" [2].

Heracleitus was no easy friend to anyone. He defined himself by polemic: his nature was to be contentious and his character was famous for its perceived misanthropy. It appears that he eschewed the power and influence of the prominent position in Ephesian society into which he was born: he avoided human company and philosophical dialogue, and neither sought nor even desired to have students or followers, or to make himself or his pronouncements agreeable to others. His thinking has that rare capacity to move the ground on which we stand – and to do so in the space of a few words. He was paradoxical, vatic and oracular in his pronouncements, which often possess the quality of the greatest poetry in their terrifying simplicity and brevity of metaphor and the unforgettable visuality of the words on which he plays. In his famous apothegms – "the road up and the road down are one and the same" [3]; "war [strife] is the father of all and the ruler of all…" [4]; "it is not possible to step into the same river twice" [5]; "all thing flow [or are in flux]" [6] – our realisation that so much of significance can be said with so little means still troubles, excites and chastens us profoundly.

Pythagoras was in distinguished company as the object of Heracleitus's scorn. Homer, Hesiod and Archilochus (the three poets widely considered in Antiquity to be the greatest in all of early Greek Literature), as well as Xenophanes and the historian-geographer Hecataeus, were all cut down to size by him. Homer and Archilochus should, according to Heracleitus, be "eliminated from the [poetic] contests and flogged" ; Hesiod was ignorant for "not understanding that day and night are one". And as for his fellow citizens of Ephesus, Heracleitus wished them wealth only in order "that they might be convicted for their wickedness" [8]. Although his negativity may begin to pall after a while, his vision and his own poetic mode of expression never cease to enthrall.

The common thread of Heracleitus's comments about Pythagoras, is clear: great learning is one thing, and wisdom and insight are another. Nobody would disagree with that. But, according to himself, Heracleitus possessed the latter and Pythagoras only the former:

> Much learning does not teach understanding [νόον]; for it should have taught Hesiod and Pythagoras, and again, Xenophanes and Hecataeus.[9]

Given Pythagoras's extraordinary power of intuition which may have become evident from the preceding pages of this book, this is an odd criticism to level at him. Pythagoras did amass a lot of learning, for sure: respectable authorities – Herodotus in the 5th century BC, and Aristotle in the century after – are in agreement on this. What it appears Heracleitus does not give Pythagoras credit for, is the use to which he puts his immense learning, translating it at times into a genuine νόον ['nó-on'] – in other words, insight and understanding.

In the shortest and sharpest of his references to Pythagoras he speaks of him as "chief of charlatans" [10]. Heracleitus saw Pythagoras as someone who dealt in material which he considered to be hocus pocus. It galled Heracleitus that people might be duped by this learning which he had gathered on his journeys both physical and intellectual (i.e. the "treatises" he read), and that this might increase Pythagoras's fame at the same time, attracting to his person a devoted following of disciples and acolytes. It took, in fact, little time for the reputation of Pythagoras to attract followers and students: and just as quickly it began to spawn improbable stories and the circulation of a welter of sententious material related to his name.

Heracleitus, perhaps foreseeing this danger for himself, avoided with rigour all possibility of a following of potential intellectual heirs [11]. Unlike Pythagoras who left nothing written behind, Heracleitus left his own written testimony in a work entitled *On Nature* (Περὶ Φύσεως), which was well-known in Antiquity and of which fragments only have survived today through citations and discussions in other texts. He even took the trouble to deposit the text for safety in the Temple of Artemis at Ephesus. His thinking therefore stands more authoritatively on its own, with much less of the third-hand renditions and Chinese whispers that afflicted Pythagoras's legacy. Pythagoras left no written testimony and, maybe in order to substitute for that, he encouraged a following of pupils and adepts. The result was disastrous. History related his sayings and thoughts in as many ways as he had followers.

My sense is that Pythagoras responded deeply to what he experienced and learnt from the East, without perhaps even fully understanding why. It is an experience that the sensitive Western mind throughout history has had when it has come into contact with the otherness of the East. The encounter can be stimulating, and it can also be disturbing. It is not just a question of difference of language and custom: it is a difference of cognition. It is a platitude to say that travel into other cultures is good in that it opens the eyes to extraordinary scenes and introduces us to cultural habits quite different from our own. But the true gift of travel is that it makes us aware of a profound *cognitive* diversity in our world. It shows us that other peoples in other places can conceive of the same phenomena and of the same world as ours in a wholly different manner and on quite different premises. And this is a rather more significant – and liberating – matter. It was this that Pythagoras must have felt as he came into contact with the Eastern ideas which infuse his thinking. Heracleitus never gave himself the chance to see this. Since he did not travel, and saw no earthly reason to either, he could not understand that there were whole states of mind and different ways of being – ancient and in many ways alien to the hard-headed, pragmatic, mercantile cast of mind of the Aegean Greeks – which Pythagoras, by contrast, was concerned to comprehend and to transmit.

Pythagoras – instinctive listener and receiver that he was – accepted this otherness and understood its value. Encountering the highly advanced knowledge of Egypt, Babylon and India in the 6th century BC was like opening an encyclopaedia filled with technology, mythology, fantasy and natural observation, all mixed together and given equal status. The particular genius of Pythagoras was to have seen the importance and universal application of a number of the observations he found hidden within it: the observations on harmonic intervals, the ratios within triangles used in land surveying, methods of calculation for the relative movement of the planets. He picked these out and went on to transform Western thinking with them. But he may also have been unwilling just to ignore and throw away all the rest. There was much within this body of knowledge which regarded the soul, the divine, and the nature of our existence, all from a point of view to which he was not accustomed. To pass this on and to explain it to his own world, however, proved to be a struggle, and his attempt to talk about what he had picked up of this kind of knowledge was soon to go awry. Without writing anything down and instead entrusting his thoughts only to verbal transmission from person to person and generation to generation, the more time that passed, the further 'Pythagoreanism' strayed from Pythagoras himself. It was this process that left him open to exactly the kind of criticism which Heracleitus levels at him.

Although this interest in the Oriental and esoteric may have irritated Heracleitus, it was a deeper divergence of philosophical vision that fuelled his contention with Pythagoras. For Heracleitus the universe was an unending process of change and flux, in which the destructive, cleansing and regenerative power embodied in fire was its primordial principle: it is a vision reminiscent of the dance of Shiva in Hindu cosmology, which is a cycle of simultaneous creation and destruction. For Heracleitus things came into being through a tension of forces in constant opposition to one another, and it was for this reason that, for him, war or strife was the 'father of all'. Without this opposition things cease to exist: take night away from day and day too ceases to exist. Since this opposing of forces was the source of life and its phenomena, for Heracleitus the proposition that the universe might aspire to a *harmonía* which was the transcendent resolution of this war and which partook of a time-less and process-less beauty, as Pythagoras seemed to suggest, was nonsense. If the strife of oppositions was gone, then the phenomena were gone: it was simply nothingness and extinction.

Heracleitus's fulminating vision of the cosmos as a process is unimpeachable. But it is a description of the state of things, and it ends there. There are no suggestions in Heracleitus for the questioning human mind on *how* to be, how to live, how better to understand our human existence in the midst of these cosmic processes. Pythagoras, on the other hand, does give us this: he intimates a model of the universe and goes on to imply what it means to exist in this universe, to have a soul, and to elicit from our existence the harmony, beauty and fulfilment which is the most valuable gift we can take away from it. Pythagoras, unlike

Nataraja: Shiva as the divine dancer in a ring of fire, destroying while creating.
Bronze from Tamil Nadu, 11th Century. Art Institute of Chicago

Heracleitus, is an architect; he is one who constructs and composes.

The greatness of both thinkers lies in their intuitive intelligence, expressed through insights that occupy about as much *verbal* space as a lightning flash. The revelation of Pythagoras's harmonic demonstration in fact occupies no verbal space at all, nor does the theorem which bears his name. Heracleitus's apothegms, too, are almost as slim. But the trajectory of philosophical thinking in the following decades and centuries moved relentlessly towards occupying the realm of a more protracted verbal exegesis, a tendency which reaches an apogee with Plato and Aristotle. This is Plato writing on acoustics in the *Timaeus*:

Sound may be generally defined as an impulse given by the air through the ears to the brain and blood and passed on to the soul; and the consequent motion which starts from the head and terminates in the region of the liver is hearing. Rapid movement produces high pitched sound, and the slower the motion the lower the pitch....[12]

A different world, a quite different kind of mind – brilliant, of course, but far from the vision Pythagoras had turned our minds towards when thinking about sound. The long and laborious road of logical explanation and exegesis lies ahead. With Plato another profound change in human cognition will be under way.

Although he may be one of philosophy's first and greatest word-mongers, Plato nonetheless warns against the use of the fixed and written word in philosophy on more than one occasion. The conversation between Socrates and Phaedrus on the subject of writing [13] foresees clearly the problem intrinsic in putting speculation down in written form – the very thing for which he, Plato, is revered by history. Furthermore, in his *Seventh Epistle* – a piece of writing which, although often attributed to Plato seems to possess little of the feel of the mind and literary persona of the Plato we are familiar with from the writing of the *Dialogues* – he goes further, suggesting that true philosophy is somehow word-less and exists elusively in the spark of recognition or inspiration between teacher and pupil, philosopher and interlocutor [14]. At this point we are getting closer to the way in which Pythagoras conceived of it. In both instances, however, Plato confines his strictures mostly to the business of writing, and tackles only tangentially the deeper issue, which is language itself – not merely the written word, but rather the word itself.

Pythagoras could have written at length had he so desired: but he chose not to. Wherever possible he avoided the uneasy relationship between what is intuited and what can be expressed in words. He used other routes of communication – acoustics, mathematics, visual geometry. Let us turn aside, therefore, from the world of words and look finally at that word-less statement which is most associated with his name: the theorem regarding triangles.

All citations from Heracleitus are referenced to the standard collection of the texts of the Pre-Socratic philosophers by H. Diels and W. Kranz: Die Fragmente der Vorsokratiker. Zürich/Hildesheim 1964.

[1]   Fragment DK 129; & Diogenes Laertius, *Lives of the Philosophers* VIII 1.6

[2]   Fragment DK 108

[3]   Fragment DK 60

[4]   Fragment DK 53

[5]   Fragment DK 91; Aristotle, *Metaphysics*, IV.5.1010a, 10-14

[6]   Paraphrase of Heracleitus in Plato's *Cratylus*, related to Fragment DK 12

[7]   Fragment DK 42; Diogenes Laertius, *Lives of the Philosophers*, Book 9. 1

[8]   Fragment DK 125a

[9]   Fragment DK 40

[10] Fragment DK 81

[11] Even though Diogenes Laertius says that a group who called themselves 'Heracleiteans'
      sprang up after his death, it must have been a short-lived movement because we hear little more of them.

[12] *Timaeus* 67b (trans. Desmond Lee)

[13] *Phaedrus*, 274b, 275, 276

[14] *Seventh Epistle*, 341c, 341d

Albrecht Dürer, The Great Piece of Turf, 1503;
Albertina Collection, Vienna.

Alignment and
the Theorem

Is Dürer's extraordinary watercolour of a piece of turf, drawn in 1503, a work of scientific observation or a work of art? And are these two even exclusive of one another? No one before him had looked with such intensity and empathy at a microcosm of weeds, grasses and earth, and then chosen to immortalise them with such precision. Dürer happened to be sympathetic to millenarian beliefs: three years earlier, when he was only twenty-eight years old, he had contemplated the possibility that his world might end in the year 1500. Yet the world survived, and afterwards he began to look at it with the fascination of one who finds again an invaluable treasure that he thought he had lost. In the *Piece of Turf* he shows us – as William Blake also does with his grain of sand and wild flower [1] – how much closer we come to the divine through observation of the natural world around us than through any amount of theological exercise.

It is important for us to look at science in terms of its imaginative beauty, even if, at first glance, this may seem to be no more than a collateral aspect: in fact, if we see the beauty as at all insignificant we will not understand what the thought of Pythagoras is showing us. It is important for the simple reason that it prevents us becoming drawn into technicality to the point where we lose sight of the whole. The beauty keeps us focused on the intuitive truth and puts into proportion the exhaustive urge to define, pin down, describe and explain alone. That urge is a motivating function of the scientific process; but it is only a contributing part of something greater. Neither significant science nor important thinking is ever mere technicality; they both, at their best, aspire to the comprehension of the whole. Yet Dürer's pictorial study – combining seamlessly the vision of the whole with an intense attention to detail – shows us that there is another element as well: the empathy of the beholder. It may seem a strange thing to say, but great science is rarely void of human empathy because the contemplating human mind cannot be extracted from its process.

The solutions and models proposed by great scientific thinkers – Euclid, Copernicus, Galileo, Newton, Einstein – are all monuments of imaginative beauty. We do not diminish either science or mathematics when we emphasise their beauty: we understand them better and recognise a vital aspect of them which their greatest proponents also acknowledged. Towards the end of his life, Newton reflected: "I do not know what I may appear to the world, but to myself I seem to have been only like a boy playing on the sea-shore, and diverting myself in now and then finding a smoother pebble or a prettier shell than ordinary, whilst the great ocean of truth lay all undiscovered before me" [2]. There is a realisation here of the arbitrariness of the frontier of knowledge: all that we come to discover with great expense of insight and effort reconfirms our awareness of how little we ultimately know. Yet, even though his discoveries were for him no more than beginnings in the face of the greater ocean of undiscovered truth, Newton was not unaware of their beauty; the concept of gravitation, the process of infinitesimal calculus, the spectral composition of light and the laws of motion are all, in quite different ways, artistic creations of crystalline beauty and clarity.

And so it was also for Pythagoras. The geometric theorem, which happens to bear his name to this day, is important for us because of its many practical applications; but for Pythagoras its significance lay elsewhere – in the glimpse it afforded of a divine coherence to be found in the cosmos. In one sense it was like a poem: simple, perfect and clear, universally true and alive with a multitude of resonances – a poem, however, with no words.

The question which lies behind the theorem is as old as it is simple. A rectangle is a common and familiar shape; yet how can we know the length of its diagonal from that of its two sides? Like the demonstration with the monochord, the theorem or solution reveals a simple fact that is true, yet not self-evident: it shows that there is a universal proportion which relates the three components of the right-angle triangle, such that if we know the length of two of them we can always deduce the length of the third. That universal relationship between the two sides which form the right-angle (*a* and *b*) and the diagonal, or hypotenuse *(c)*, is expressed algebraically as $a^2 + b^2 = c^2$, and this equation is so familiar to us that we no longer look at it… Stop, therefore. It is never good not to look at things carefully just because they are familiar; so let us pause on it for a moment. Notice how when we seek to define the relationship between the simple lengths of three lines, the mathematics lead us immediately to relate them through *area*, through the squares on the lines, i.e. the theorem does not and can not talk about a direct and universally applicable relationship between *a, b*, and *c, except* through the spatial squares they each create, i.e. between a^2, b^2, and c^2. We need to keep this crucial observation in mind for later.

Read the other way, the theorem also shows that we can confidently create a perfect right-angle through the use of three measurements that conform to the principle of the theorem. That may seem trivial, yet the humble right-angle has been something of the greatest importance to human endeavour since earliest times: building, construction, wood-working and engineering all depend on it. The theorem also forms the basis for the trigonometry used in surveying and positioning, and it opens the way to many of the propositions of geometry later evolved by Euclid. But its simplicity, together with the thrill felt by the mind in being able to prove its universality, are what are brought to our attention by Pythagoras. That same thrill is described by Einstein, who at the age of twelve, proved the exact same theorem for himself: it was, he said, "the lucidity and certainty" of geometric proof that "made an indescribable impression upon me." Of the theorem in particular, he says:

> After much effort I succeeded in 'proving' this theorem on the basis of the similarity of triangles ... for anyone who experiences [these feelings] for the first time, it is marvellous enough that man is capable at all to reach such a degree of certainty and purity in pure thinking as the Greeks showed us for the first time to be possible in geometry. [3]

Einstein used for his proof the method of the similarity of triangles developed by Euclid two hundred years after Pythagoras, whereas Pythagoras himself would most likely have used the 'method of re-arrangement' instead as his demonstration (*see Appendix 3*). Whatever the method they used, however, that "indescribable impression" was common to them all. For Pythagoras, the equation above all else was confirmation of the perfect *harmonía* of the universe he had conceived, and it became the key-stone of his thoughts about *kósmos*.

Just as with the acoustic demonstration, the discovery of the relationship enshrined in the theorem was not original to Pythagoras. It is impossible to know how far back in time builders had been using the principle of the 3-4-5 triangle to create the necessary right-angle which guarantees that a rectangular floor plan can be laid out or a functional doorway can be constructed with confidence. Simple measurements in early Egypt were often made with ropes regularly knotted at exact, repeating intervals: it is probable that this method was practised just as early in India and Mesopotamia, too. It does not take long to discover that a rope, with twelve equally distanced knots in it, can be arranged in a closed triangle with sides of three, four and five knots respectively, and that a right-angle is by definition created between the two shorter sides thereby. This can be done equally well with pieces of wood of proportionate lengths of three, four and five units: the absolute length is irrelevant, only the ratio between them matters. This knowledge had been a convenience for centuries, long before anyone thought of extending it into a mathematical theorem of universal application.

Egypt, however, had other needs and one of them, particular to its own geography, was the rapid re-drawing of the boundaries defining parcels and allotments of cultivated land once the swollen waters of the Nile had receded after the annual flood. The previous year's divisions that had been eradicated by the flood waters needed fair and accurate re-apportioning – not least for state fiscal reasons. For surveying large areas of land, triangulation using the right-angle triangle provides a vital and transparent accuracy. The official surveyors entrusted with this task in Egypt were referred to in Greek as *harpedonaptai* [4], or 'cord-binders', because the tool of their trade was the knotted cord.

All of the early river civilisations – of Egypt, Mesopotamia and the Indus Valley – practised extraordinary skills of observation, measurement and calculation; and at some very early point the right-angle triangle was elevated from its simple origins as a knotted rope into a conceptual tool. Its evolution tells an interesting story. Otto Neugebauer, a pioneer of the history of ancient mathematics, points to the principle of the Pythagorean relationship being known in Babylon more than a thousand years before the time of Pythagoras [5]. A fragmentary clay-tablet from the Sumerian site of Larsa in the lower Euphrates area (catalogued as Plimpton 322,) dating from the early part of the second millennium BC [6], shows a list of fifteen 'Pythagorean triples' describing fifteen triangles of decreasing inclination: such triples are successions of three numbers that are integers and conform to the relationship of the theorem. Yet, at this point, there is no hint of a statement of a general theorem: it is possible that the triples may even have been developed through a systematic understanding of producing algebraic solutions to the equation $a^2 + b^2 = c^2$ rather than through the study of geometry. For a first recorded

Plimpton 322 (Columbia University, New York) –
a Babylonian mathematical text inscribed in cuneiform on clay;
c. 1800 BC from Larsa.

statement of the general principle, however, we must turn instead to early Indian science of the 8th century BC, Vedic period, where the theorem in its geometric form is expressed in the *Sulba Sutras*. The thinker and mathematician, Baudhayana, states that the square drawn on the diagonal of any rectangle will equal in area the sum of the squares drawn on the other two sides. And, as for a possible first proof of the theorem, we need to look even further East to a fundamental work of early Chinese mathematics known as the *Zhou Bi Suan Jing*

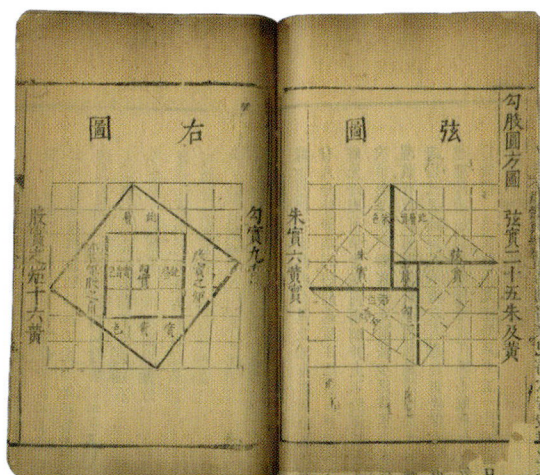

Pages from a 17th century printing of the Zhou Bi Suan Jing
showing a diagrammatic proof of the 3-4-5 Pythagorean triangle.

(or *Chou Pi Suan Ching*) which shows that this same knowledge was explored and finally given diagrammatic proof, possibly around the same time. As with many Chinese books of learning, however, the *Zhou Bi Suan Jing* is a compendium, and the exact date, therefore, of any individual element within it is hard to establish – the spread ranging from as early as the 11th to as late as the 3rd century BC at the two extremes. The knowledge of the particularities of the right-angle triangle was, in short, so old and so widespread that it is impossible to say where it first arose, if indeed it did not arise in different areas independently. There is no prize-giving here for the one who gets to the knowledge first, and certainly no prize therefore to Pythagoras for single-handedly discovering the relationship. But if it bears his name to this day, it was because he took its significance further and in a different direction from before. It also recognises the conjecture that he was the first person in Western thinking to prove its universality, using the method of geometrical re-arrangement [7]. In one sense, Pythagoras may have been merely the merchant who brought the study of this idea into the stream of Western thinking; but the reasons for his own fascination with the theorem are different from those of the Eastern tradition. Through its narrow window he saw a much greater significance – some of it reassuring, some of it, as we shall see, disquieting.

In a world without pencil and paper and fixed measurements and measuring aids and when everything had to be improvised, the elucidation of such ideas as these was substantially more difficult. We tend to take right angles for granted today: we have set-squares, protractors, T-squares, as well as more technologically advanced ways to determine a perfect 90° angle; but in ancient times it was not so simple. A right-angle could be obtained in two ways, either physically or geometrically: that is, either using natural tools or through mathematical concepts such as the 3-4-5 triangle. The physical method made use of a water level to define a horizontal line and a still plumb-line to define a vertical. Already at this point, as it would have appeared to an alert mind of the age of Pythagoras, there arose many interesting questions. How is it that undisturbed water appears to create a perfect level? and how can we assume that it will always do this in the same way in every place – especially if we are just beginning to have a growing suspicion that the surface of the earth might not be flat, but rather curved, in order for us to explain the perceived horizon and the fact that ships disappeared below it when journeying away from the viewer? And what reason do we have to assume that the plumb line will always give us the same angle of incidence against the water level? What makes it do that? And why was this particular angle of incidence the fundamental requirement for mathematical congruence in the theorem? These questions were to remain unresolved up until the time of Isaac Newton; but that does not mean to say that they did not pose themselves to earlier minds in one form or another. The plumb-line and the water level, in short, were marvellously useful in the construction of stable objects, doorways and buildings, but they raised as many questions as they solved: 99% of the time they were just put to good use; but if – in that 1% of time – some searching questions were asked about the reasons behind why these two curious and quite different indicators, one a receptacle containing water, the other a rope with a weight, invariably fell into such a particular and exact relationship with one another, all of a sudden matters of universal significance raised their heads. These tools were a great help, if you didn't think about them too much; but Pythagoras was not in the business of *not* thinking about things.

In looking at the matter in this way, all I am wanting to do is to arrive at some understanding of how these issues actually appeared, not to us today, but to the mind of Pythagoras two thousand five hundred years ago. Pythagoras shows none of the skills or interest of either his Babylonian predecessors or his Hellenistic successors of the 4th and 3rd centuries BC in ingenious and audacious calculation or even in complex geometry. His interest is not to *use* mathematics as a tool, but rather to think *about* what mathematics is – its meaning, its significance, its interaction with our own messy human world and experience. Our minds today are deeply numerate and literate; words and numbers are our everyday tools to a degree which we no longer are aware of. Even the person who claims to be 'un-mathematical' is more numerate than he or she might wish to admit, and has an ease with certain number-processes quite different from that of the age in which Pythagoras lived. For this reason, we need to put our own numeracy in abeyance for a moment, and try to see the way in which these various revelations which crossed Pythagoras's path must have appeared to his mind, and what rich suggestiveness they possessed for him.

First, they unexpectedly united quite disparate areas of experience. One of the interesting revelations for Pythagoras of his acoustic demonstration had been the functioning of what we might call the 'moment of alignment' – in other words the observation that the harmonic sympathy of sound, and all the feeling attendant on it, occurred only at a precise point and ratio, and that to deviate to either side of that ratio, by even a little, meant a relapse back into disharmony and stressful sound. Today, with our knowledge of sound as pressure waves of displacement in the density of the air, we understand both the mechanical and the mathematical reasons for this phenomenon. We can also make it visible graphically because of our understanding of the nature of wave motion. But to Pythagoras this quality would have appeared as something almost sacred or divine. Such a 'moment of alignment' was revealing to him because it appeared to relate the realm of the quantifiable, on the one side, to the realm of qualities on the other. The alignment was an exact geometric or numerical relationship; but its product was an unexpected quality of great beauty.

A similar moment of alignment occurs also with the triangle that is the subject of the theorem. An angle of 89° or 91° between the two short sides of the triangle will not give rise to the same equivalence implied in the theorem. It will not give rise to any equivalence at all which is meaningful or useful. The precision and the exactness were fundamental. In the acoustic demonstration it was governed by the fact that the ratio was between two whole numbers: in the theorem it was the right angle, which is also a perfect integral ratio in that it defines a quarter-turn or one fourth of the circular field of perception. This quality of the integral proportion may seem self-evident to the mathematician today; but to the mind of early philosophy it had profound significance.

True alignment is also a phenomenon which we sense physically, without the participation of either sight or hearing, through the position and configuration of the body in moments of profound, yet wakeful, relaxation when its weight is distributed perfectly along and around a vertical axis and our awareness of all the individual elements of the head and limbs and the relationships between them, though still apparent to our consciousness in a benign manner, appear nonetheless to be momentarily dissolved. A powerful passive energy accompanies these moments which is neither specifically physical nor mental but partakes of both and goes beyond, and which appears to arise out of the body's quasi-geometric alignment. I am not speaking of specifically yogic positions, but something much more common and accessible, arising without solicitation through a full awareness of our body and a willingness to answer its needs for internal harmony.

In many different ways, therefore, it would have appeared to Pythagoras that the fact of alignment itself was important. The other area of natural observation which repeatedly suggested significant alignments, of course, was that of the heavens, in the perceptibly regular movements of the bodies within them. When the sun and moon aligned the resulting phenomena were formidable and visible to all in the form of eclipses. But through the long traditions in Mesopotamia and Egypt of dedicated observation of the changes in the firmament it had become clear that there were occasions when the other heavenly bodies – the wandering planets – also came into particular alignments with one another, in conjunctions, oppositions and other triangulations; and, at the same time, into an alignment with the apparently fixed firmament behind them. We should recall here that the mapping of the firmament as the Zodiac with twelve characteristic segments – something which gave a crucial fixed frame of reference – had evolved relatively recently in time, perhaps no more than two hundred years before the lifetime of Pythagoras.

Before we say the word 'astrology', let us separate clearly in our minds the process of the vatic or psychological interpretation of the influence of these alignments, which is what we call astrology today, from the neutral astronomical fact that the alignments occur with varying regularity, and might – as far as Pythagoras could know – give rise to significant consequences in just the same way as the other kinds of geometrical and acoustic alignments which he had observed had done. Both to the Egyptians and the Babylonians, the observation and documentation of these celestial movements – to what appears to us as an astonishing level of detail and precision – was a matter of the greatest importance for the divining of auguries for the King or Pharaoh and the vital State matters over which he presided. To seek any signals that the gods might be giving through the movements and appearance of the stars was essential; but this study of the stars was not done by them for the pursuit of 'science' or with any explicit aspiration to understand why these movements should happen. That, on the other hand, was an aspiration that was peculiarly Greek in character, and it was to dominate Greek thinking from the time of Thales, Anaximander and Pythagoras forward. As far as Pythagoras was concerned the questions of divination were matters for the Babylonians and Egyptians themselves. His question would have been framed much more generally: if there were something intrinsically significant in alignments *per se*, was it not reasonable to hypothesise that a significance of some kind lay behind alignment in the heavenly bodies also? The question then was what exactly the nature of that significance might be. What we now understand as astrology was one possible line of pursuit; but it might well not be the only suitable one.

Second: underpinning these different kinds of alignment there was a more general encounter between the linear and the cyclical. The observation of this phenomenon had a particularly ancient history. Long before the exploration of sound or geometry, the observation of the solar solstices, for their importance to agriculture and the investment of hope in the returning cycle of the seasons, goes back into early human history and constitutes perhaps the first and oldest observation of science. At the solstices the cyclical encounters the linear: the progression of successive sunrises comes to a particular point on the local horizon at which, every year, it ceases to advance and begins its return in the opposite direction again. In similar fashion with sound, the linear progression of the intervals encounters the cyclical return of the octaves; and the wave motion of sound itself – as we now know, although Pythagoras did not – is in itself a resolution of cyclical and linear movement. Even the right-angle was intrinsically linked with the circle: it defined a quarter segment of a cycle and, as the theorem of Thales [8] had already shown, a triangle inscribed within a circle on its diameter will always give rise to a right-angle between its shorter sides. All of these phenomena arose from the incidence of the linear with the circular.

Then there was a third matter: the convergence of so many different phenomena on the same, simple, numerical relationships. The most accessible of the right-angle triangles, and the one known since time immemorial, was the 3-4-5 triangle used by the early engineers and land surveyors of civilisation. Three, four and five had a simplicity and an elegance to them as a group, and they were numbers that surrounded us everywhere. They defined the first three polygonal forms: the triangle, square and pentagon. They defined important sound harmonies through their ratios: the perfect fourth and the major third. They confirmed the perpendicular correctness in the elements of a building, an entrance-way or a table. And, in addition to all this, it happened that three multiplied by itself, plus four multiplied by itself, was equivalent to five multiplied by itself.

To Pythagoras – as it would to any curious mind of his time formed by the very different beliefs and suppositions of the world from which he emerged – this all must have seemed full of a fruitful interconnectivity between different areas of experience, which pointed to a broad coherence in the phenomena of our cosmos.

So far so good. But a disquieting aspect soon made its presence felt. Once we possess a conceptual tool such as the universal equivalence defined in the theorem of Pythagoras, we use it to deduce other values. It was at this point that the theorem revealed the existence of a species of troublesome and highly uncooperative numbers. There arose proportions which looked quite normal and harmless when drawn geometrically, but when expressed arithmetically they somehow defied definition. Starting from the simplest proposition of all – a right-angle triangle with two equal sides of one unit in length (in other words, the half of a 1x1 square cut along its diagonal) – and using $a^2 + b^2 = c^2$ we arrive at a value for the hypotenuse c of $\sqrt{2}$, the square root of two. The problem which now emerged was that the square root of two is not a definable number, since it cannot be expressed either as an integer or in terms of two other numbers as their fraction: it possesses an ungainly value which can only ever be expressed as an approximation, however minutely we may pursue it. Yet, in a two-dimensional drawing we can show it as a drawn line without the slightest difficulty. It exists geometrically, in other words, but not numerically.

This was no small problem. A fault-line had emerged in the fabric of our assumptions. There was the theorem itself: simple and universal. To one side it elucidated a coherence in geometric forms and gave rise to perfect solutions for building and surveying. To the other side it uncovered the existence of quantities that were numerically undefinable. Did this then represent the first crack in the structure of Pythagoras's cosmos? To his later followers, who had lost their teacher's intuitive grasp of the whole, it did indeed appear so; and, if we are to believe the chatter of subsequent centuries, they desired to keep the knowledge of irrational numbers secret for fear that it undermined their most basic propositions and their intellectual authority. Yet that in itself was a measure of the smallness of their vision. To Pythagoras, on the other hand, incommensurability must have seemed puzzling, but, all the more for that, a phenomenon of profound significance. It revealed a quite unexpected separation between arithmetical and geometrical perception; in other words, between the continuum of length on the one hand and the individual elements of number on the other, i.e. between what is continuous and what is discrete. This crucial philosophical distinction had not been given substance before; and it now came into the Western stream of thinking through Pythagoras.

The theorem had shown that the fundamental magnitude that we should be contemplating was not length but area. At the beginning of this chapter we paused to notice how, in the theorem, the mathematics led us immediately to the square on the sides of the lines whose relationship we wished to know, in the algebraic expression $a^2 + b^2 = c^2$, because it does not have a way to speak about the proportions between a, b and c as a group in their simple, linear form. The reason for this is that a triangle is not just the same thing as three lines: it has become a triangle and therefore possesses properties that can only be reconciled by reference to the spatial dimension. We may perceive with our eyes both the lines and the squares on the lines without any problem; but we can only *define* their relationship conceptually through the area of the squares and not through the lines alone. We must be satisfied merely to ascribe a symbol ($\sqrt{2}$) to the value of the line in the case of the triangle with two equal sides of one unit's length, because it cannot exactly be defined in any other numerical manner.

This curious situation perhaps explains the preference given to spatial geometry in early Greek thinking, mathematics and cosmology as opposed to the sophisticated computational arithmetic practised in early Babylonian and Egyptian science: and, as such, it is the reflection of a cognitive change. The awareness of the existence of certain irrational numbers and the attempt to approximate to an expression of their numerical value had – as we might expect by now – a long history pre-dating Pythagoras. A small cuneiform clay tablet (YBC 7289) from early in the 2nd millennium BC, approximately contemporary with Plimpton 322 mentioned above, shows the Babylonian mind meticulously grappling with this numerical monster – whose innocent conceptual appearance as just $\sqrt{2}$ belies a nightmare in quantification. The tablet shows a square with two diagonals, over-marked with a series of sexagesimal[9] numbers and measurements in cuneiform notation. These lead to a very refined approximation for the value for $\sqrt{2}$ expressed as the fraction 305,470 over 216,000 (or, in decimal notation, 1.41421296). What extraordinary skill of calculation this implies for the world of four thousand years ago! and yet what an expense of effort to arrive at

YBC 7289: Babylonian clay tablet from the early 2nd millennium BC,
showing a value for the square root of two.
(Yale Babylonian Collection, New Haven CT)

what is still only an approximation for the value of a line that is so exquisitely simple to draw.

The fact that the difficulty inherent in calculating the square root of two was known to students in Babylon a thousand years earlier, would suggest that Pythagoras was certainly not ignorant of the matter. Furthermore, one of his early followers, Hippasus of Metapontum, who may even have known Pythagoras before his death since he came from the city in which it is thought that the philosopher may have died, is said to have been punished by the brotherhood of Pythagoreans and, according to an improbable legend (arising from a conflation of comments made by Plutarch and Iamblichus [10]), pushed to his death from a ship because he had revealed the 'secret' of the incommensurability of the diagonal of a square with its sides. Whatever the credibility of this tendentious story, it does at least imply that not just the existence but the study of irrational numbers was known early on and was considered by the beadles of the Pythagorean brotherhood a skeleton strictly to be left in the cupboard. It is interesting furthermore that Hippasus is said to have been sympathetic to aspects of the anti-elitist sentiment of Cylon, the leader of the rebellion against the Pythagoreans in Croton which later culminated in the destruction of their schools. Once all the machinery of secrecy and the bogus sanctity surrounding the name of Pythagoras had begun to asphyxiate the spirit and the clarity of what Pythagoras himself had actually been saying, who would not have had some sympathy with Cylon?

Nothing is so revealing of this problem with the later '*so-called* Pythagoreans', as Aristotle liked to refer to them [11] – οἱ καλούμενοι Πυθαγόρειοι, 'kaloúmeni Pythagórei' – than this story of their apparently terrified reaction to the existence of incommensurables and irrational numbers. They were unable to see the wood for the trees. Because Pythagoras had proposed that the cosmos came into being through order, and that order was the result of proportions and clear relations between numbers, they had become snagged on the divine status of number alone rather than attending to the phenomena to which it gave rise. Number was the basis of the Pythagorean cosmos, for sure: but number was not *the thing itself* – even though this unfortunately became a mantra of later "Pythagoreanism", repeated to the point that it became dogma. And it was therefore for dogmatic rather than genuine philosophical reasons that they feared the existence of irrational numbers. What little we can gather regarding the nature of the mind of Pythagoras himself, suggests that he was not by nature dogmatic: like any intelligent mind, he appears to have warmed to dogs, but avoided dogma. His thinking and his life seem characterised more often by uncertainty. For him, as probably also for Hippasus, incommensurables and irrational numbers were a fertile and revealing lesson from the cosmos. They showed that there are situations in which we can only understand the world through its appearance (in this case, geometry) rather than through its arithmetical measurement.

The great sadness surrounding the fate of Pythagorean thought lay in precisely this inability of his followers to understand the spirit and the meaning of the thinking with which Pythagoras had entrusted them – not merely as regards mathematics and number, but in all the many aspects of his teaching. For Pythagoras – just as for Newton – his observations were the shells and pebbles which he had gathered from that same shore: they, too, were just beginnings. But his followers soon began to see them as ends in themselves, as doctrines and dogmas. And for this reason, in their unintended myopia, it was not so much Hippasus whom they were pushing overboard, but Pythagoras himself. Why, after all, did Aristotle insist on referring to them as 'so-called' Pythagoreans, if he did not have good reason to believe that there was a considerable element of pretence to them, and that they were not being true to the spirit of what Pythagoras himself had taught? Aristotle clearly gave a lot of thought to Pythagoras and it is a great loss for us that his essay *On the Pythagoreans* has not survived. It might have clarified many things about the disconnect which we sense between the philosopher himself and his followers, and which we are unable to understand for lack of information.

Albrecht Dürer, Melencolia I, 1514 (detail)

Eleven years after his study of weeds and grasses, came Dürer's famous etching of 'Melancholy'. How dejected poor Melencolia looks: despondency has descended on her and all the mathematical instruments and paraphernalia that surround her. She has magnificent wings that are ready to take flight; but she cannot stir. The crepuscular world of the bat, who unfurls the banner of the title, has darkened her mind; and in her self-absorption she seems not even to take notice of the celestial comet and the rainbow that illuminate the sky. Her thought is lost amidst the welter of tools, objects and symbols. She is the epitome of the fate of the Pythagorean cause as it lost its way and turned ever more inward with each successive generation of so-called Pythagoreans, who, as they grew more distant in time from Pythagoras himself, strayed further and yet further from the source of his thinking into a realm of sterile technicality. Plato, who was much indebted to the thinking of Pythagoras, played a role in this process that was not negligible. In the end, the vital beauty which Pythagoras himself had intuited was simply lost in translation and transmission.

Above Melencolia's head is a chequerboard of numbers, which bears the date (1514) of Dürer's etching in the central two figures of the bottom line. This is what is called a magic square. It takes the first 16 numbers, with 16 at the 'start' in the top left corner and with 1 at the 'end' in the bottom right corner. The intermediate numbers are then arranged in such a way that each row, each column, the four corners, each of the four quadrants and the central quadrant, the diagonals, and countless other regular and symmetrical permutations of four numbers within the square, all add up to the same sum of 34. In total there are more than eighty such geometric sequences which all make 34 within the square. In 1514 Dürer was 43. Whatever it signified for the artist, this magic square, too, stands as an epitaph for the soul of later Pythagoreanism: ingenious to a fault, yet ultimately a mesmerising and self-referential toy.

The thinking of Pythagoras was based on an insight that number could be seen as the primordial constituent in our earthly understanding of reality. In the hands of his later followers, and in their interminable studies of number symbolism, sacred geometry and numerology, number had become a mere obsession – no longer a key to understanding, but a game without end, void of meaning. Illumination and harmony had been eclipsed by a love for the abstruse. It is dismaying how rapidly what passed into history as 'Pythagorean thought' lost that life-giving alignment with its founder's original vision.

16	3	2	13
5	10	11	8
9	6	7	12
4	15	14	1

Dürer's Magic Square [12]

[1] William Blake, opening lines of *Auguries of Innocence*:

> To see a World in a Grain of Sand
> And a Heaven in a Wild Flower,
> Hold infinity in the palm of your hand
> And Eternity in an hour

[2] Sir David Brewster, *Memoirs of the Life, Writings and Discoveries of Sir Isaac Newton* (1855), Vol II Chapter 27 p. 407. Brewster was the inventor of the kaleidoscope, something that Pythagoras would have found fascinating for its ability constantly to create new, unthought-of patterns.
For Newton's simile see also W.B. Yeats's fine poem, *At Algeciras – A Meditation upon Death* (1928).

[3] *Albert Einstein: Philosopher-Scientist*, edited by Paul A. Schlipp, 1951; pp. 9-11

[4] Democritus, cited by Clement of Alexandria, *Stromata*, Book I. chap 15

[5] O. Neugebauer, *The Exact Sciences in Antiquity*, Lectures given at Cornell University, 1949.

[6] Plimpton 322, Columbia University, New York

[7] *See Appendix 3*

[8] Where the line AC is the diameter of a circle, any point (B) on the circumference of the circle with this diameter will give rise to a right-angle between the two lines joining it to A & C.

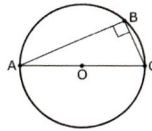

[9] This means with a base of sixty rather than the base of ten which we commonly use today. The sexagesimal system survives today in our division of time and of angles – sixty seconds in a minute, and sixty minutes in an hour; 360 degrees (60 x 6) in a circle, etc.

[10] *Plutarch, Life of Numa*, 22.3; and Iamblichus, *Life of Pythagoras*, 88 - (the conflation appears to derive from Pappus of Alexandria)

[11] Aristotle, *Metaphysics*, Book I, 985b

[12] Page 64, above, shows an image of Jain temples at Khajuraho, in India. In the temple of Parshvanatha (on the left in the picture) is engraved one of the oldest extant examples of a magic square, dating probably from the 10th or 11th century. Just like Dürer's version, it is a square of 4 x 4 numbers, whose many geometric permutations similarly add up to the total of 34: yet their arrangement is quite different.

7	12	1	14
2	13	8	11
16	3	10	5
9	6	15	4

Hellenistic mosaic of the 1st century AD, from the Sanctuary of Fortuna Primigenia at Palestrina, showing an imaginary African landscape.

The Shape of the World
and the Cosmos

Adventurous journeys lie at the heart of the Greek psyche: not just the historical journeys undertaken to found new colonies on alien shores or the distant travel of the merchants in search of new and exotic produce, but fantastical journeys also, such as that of Odysseus as he returned home from the long attrition of the Trojan War. Homer's great epic poem is, at a deep level, an allegory of that exploration of the surrounding world and of its phenomena in which the early Greek mind was so widely and profoundly engaged.

In the opening pages of this book, we looked at one particular maritime journey which was made famous by Herodotus who recorded it in his *Histories*, and yet, at the same time, cast a shadow of doubt over some of the unusual things which the mariners themselves had recounted. It was a long and arduous journey, lasting three years, which established for the first time the bounds of the continent of Africa. The possible cargo of gold, skins, feathers, ivory and rare woods, which the mariners brought back from it for the Pharaoh, could never truly have been such as to justify the years of challenging navigation in such difficult conditions. The greatest cargo that they brought home, however, was precisely that treasure-chest of extraordinary observations on navigation, meteorology and on the behaviour of the sun, the moon, the stars and the seas.

The expansion of human thought tends to go hand in hand with the exploration of the world. The circumnavigation of Africa was the just the first of many great expansions that the human concept of the world underwent over the next few centuries. A little later in the 6th century BC, Scylax of Caryander wrote of his exploration of the Indus river and the Indian Ocean, and of how he returned, around the Arabian peninsula, into the Red Sea after a period of thirty months [1]. The 5th century saw Hanno, the Carthaginian, explore the waters and river-mouths of West Africa. And the 4th century BC was to see the Greek mariner, Pytheas of Massalía (Marseille), make a journey far into the North Atlantic: he appears even to have circumnavigated the British Isles and penetrated possibly into the Baltic Sea. These are just the journeys which we know about. But with each new exploration – recorded or unrecorded – the shape of the world in the human mind came, little by little, into sharper focus.

The sheer extent of these explorations at so early a date surprises us today, perhaps because we underestimate how much travel and interconnection there was between different areas of the globe in early Antiquity – and, in fact, even earlier, in the Bronze and Iron Ages, as well. Such explorations altered irrevocably the shape of the world in the human mind. Once what appeared to us as merely our neighbourhood, began now to appear larger and larger – of almost unimaginable dimensions. The process has continued throughout the intervening centuries, constantly altering our conception of the planet on which we live. Today we know it to be no more than one insignificant body spinning through space in a universe so vast that it remains almost empty in spite of the millions of other stellar bodies to which it is home.

The first step into this greater loneliness was taken by the Pre-Socratic philosophers who began, in their speculation, to untether the Earth from its moorings. In our human perception, the world has always seemed to have solid foundations like a house or temple built on rock. But, one generation before Pythagoras, the philosopher Anaximander – by what was a huge force of imagination – suggested that the whole earth was somehow poised and floating and that the firmament spread not just above it, but around it and below it as well. For the first time the concept of Space had been created – an 'outer space', which totally surrounded our planet, so that the sun, the moon, the planets and stars which were observed to progress across the skies could continue their geometrical trajectories under and on all sides of the world on which we lived, even when we did not see them. It was one of the earliest feats of purely deductive speculation we know of. This wholly intuited awareness of Space – of the firmament as a vastness or depth, rather than as a solid lid above us on which the celestial bodies were fixed or engraved, as Homer had envisaged it, was Anaximander's greatest gift to posterity and to Pythagoras in particular. And he made it possible for Pythagoras to step back and to consider the universe in terms of his own ideas of *kósmos* and of *harmonía*.

Anaximander was from Miletus on the coast of Asia Minor, a city only thirty miles as the crow flies from Samos, and one of the most important and cosmopolitan trading ports of the Mediterranean at that time. He had a mind whose greatness deserves just as many pages as these on Pythagoras and, whatever the exact relation between these two men may have been, his influence on Pythagoras's thinking is profound. Anaximander himself had possibly studied with a fellow Milesian, Thales, who in his own brilliant way had grappled with these same cosmological questions.

Given how tenaciously the human mind will hold to the idea of the reassuring steadiness of the earth, it was no small matter for him to conceive that its whole mass somehow held to a fixed point at the centre of the universe, but yet was surrounded by space. Even now, in the 21st century we can find it disconcerting trying to imagine that penguins shuffling through the snow in Antarctica are not somehow hanging upside down, and that our planet rides through space at great speed, yet with no apparent support. Anaximander, with his extraordinary power of intuition, began the process of this awareness, however. Perhaps it is not merely incidental that his home, the Aegean area, is one of the most seismically active areas in the Western Hemisphere and that it shakes periodically – squeezed by the slow collision of the European, Asian and African tectonic plates. Earthquakes shake our faith in the permanence and fixity of things. Thales had tried to explain how earthquakes happen, suggesting the semi-mythical idea that the land floated ultimately on water below; but Anaximander took the matter to a more radical level, by cutting the earth lose completely.

In his conception of it, Anaximander did not see the earth yet as a free-floating sphere, but rather as something with the form of a drum, because he had somehow to reconcile two things: his intuited perception of its relation to the celestial bodies which cycled freely all around it, and the perceived reality of its having a flat surface. For this reason, he believed that what we saw with our eyes of the earth's extension was as the surface of a vast drum or column possessing the form of a cylinder.

Anaximander must have known the story of the circumnavigation of Africa. It would have been widely spoken about in the ports and trading centres of the Mediterranean where the Phoenicians were present. It had confirmed that Africa (or Libya together with Ethiopia, as it was then conceived) was in effect a vast island surrounded by ocean except for a small low-lying tract of land and salt-lakes at the top of the Red Sea which attached it to the rest of Asia – a single vast peninsula, but still, to all intents and purposes, circumscribed by water. The opposite side of the Mediterranean – the European land mass – he surmised must be approximately specular, because in nature things, including the human form, almost always had a symmetry to them; and therefore it, too, must be circumnavigable, like Africa. To the East, lay the rest of Asia which closed the circle, surrounded, he supposed, by its own body of water, the Indian Ocean. The total expanse of water that enclosed these three zones all around – the Oceanic River – formed the first, outer circumference of the world. In his imagination, the planet had ceased to have just a vaguely perceived mythical extension to it, but had suddenly acquired a distinct and circumscribed form.

Anaximander is said to have pulled these thoughts together with what information he had, and to have drawn the first map of the totality of the world. It must have come about through conversations with merchants and mariners who contributed this or that element. In a reconstruction of the map – based, here, on the version proposed by a scholar of Anaximander, Dirk Couprie – it would have looked something like this:

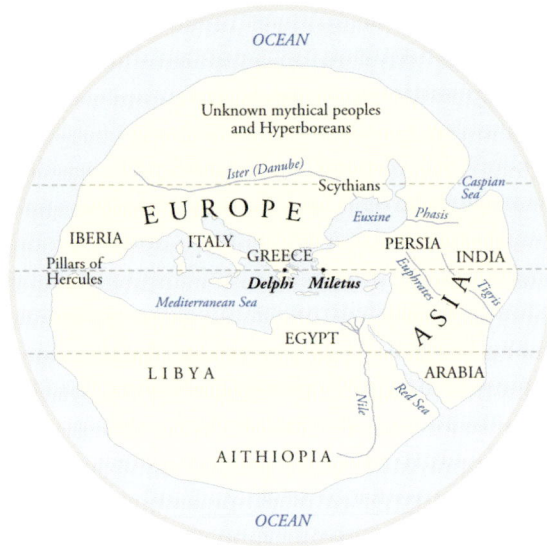

OCEAN

Unknown mythical peoples and Hyperboreans

Ister (Danube)
Scythians
Caspian Sea

E U R O P E
Euxine *Phasis*

IBERIA
ITALY
PERSIA
Pillars of Hercules
GREECE
INDIA
Delphi Miletus
Mediterranean Sea
Euphrates
Tigris

EGYPT
A S I A

LIBYA
ARABIA

Nile *Red Sea*

AITHIOPIA

OCEAN

In Prof. Couprie's rendering, the centre of the circle is marked by Delphi, which was for the Greeks the world's *omphalos* [2] and traditional centre, while Miletus, Anaximander's home, provides the reference for the band of seasonal variation of the rising and setting of the sun between the solstices, defined here by the broken lines that traverse the map horizontally.

For the benefit of legibility for the modern mind, all versions of the early Greek world-maps are oriented with a N/S vertical, so that it is arranged as would be the case with any world-map today. This makes it familiar and recognisable to us. Yet given the geographical situation of Miletus a N/S orientation is not the obvious default view, even though it may appear so to the modern mind, formed as we are since childhood by the use of post 16th century maps which have traditionally been oriented in this manner. Miletus looks out on the world to the West however; directly behind it, at the equinoxes, the sun rose over the heart of Anatolia and set over the sea in front. The more natural instinct therefore might have been to orient the map for reading on an axis rotated through 90° (*see opposite page*). It is for this same reason that Herodotus uses the words "to their right" (*see note note 2, on p.16*) rather than "in the North" when he speaks of the sun's appearance to the Phoenician mariners as they circumnavigated the most southerly point of Africa.

IBERIA
Pillars of Hercules
LIBYA
AITHIOPIA
OCEAN
EUROPE
ITALY
GREECE
Mediterranean Sea
Delphi Miletus
EGYPT
Nile
Red Sea
ARABIA
ASIA
Ister (Danube)
Scythians
Unknown mythical peoples and Hyperboreans
Euxine
Phasis
PERSIA
INDIA
Euphrates
Tigris
Caspian Sea
OCEAN

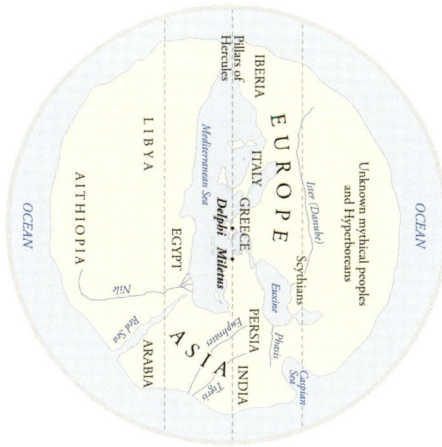

The resconstructed map, rotated through 90°

To map something is to visualise it conceptually. To conceive of a map involves a great effort of imagination in which the mind raises itself up from the level of our perseption on the surface, in order to imagine what the features that surround us look like from above, and how exactly they relate to one another. At surface level we have no clear idea how features relate to one another: the landscape around us, unless we are on the summit of a mountain, presents itself to us as a labyrinth. But as soon as the labyrinth is seen from above and is mapped, it ceases to be a mystery any more.

We live in a world so intensively mapped and our minds have thought so uninterruptedly in a 'cartographic' manner since the first great maps of the 16th and 17th centuries, that it is hard for us to un-learn this habit and to see the world as it was before the creation of the very first conceptual maps. When we read the word 'France', our mind sees immediately that unmistakable pentagonal form, or when we hear the name 'Korea', we see that rectangular peninsula protruding from the great curve of China. But before there existed proper maps, how did people visualise the form of their world? And, more practically, what might it have been like to fight a long military campaign with no birds-eye view of the lie of the land? What did it mean to set out 'to conquer the world' when you did not even have a map of where you were going? When Alexander the Great left Macedonia he would not necessarily have known that he was about to conquer a large part of the known world of his time: he had no

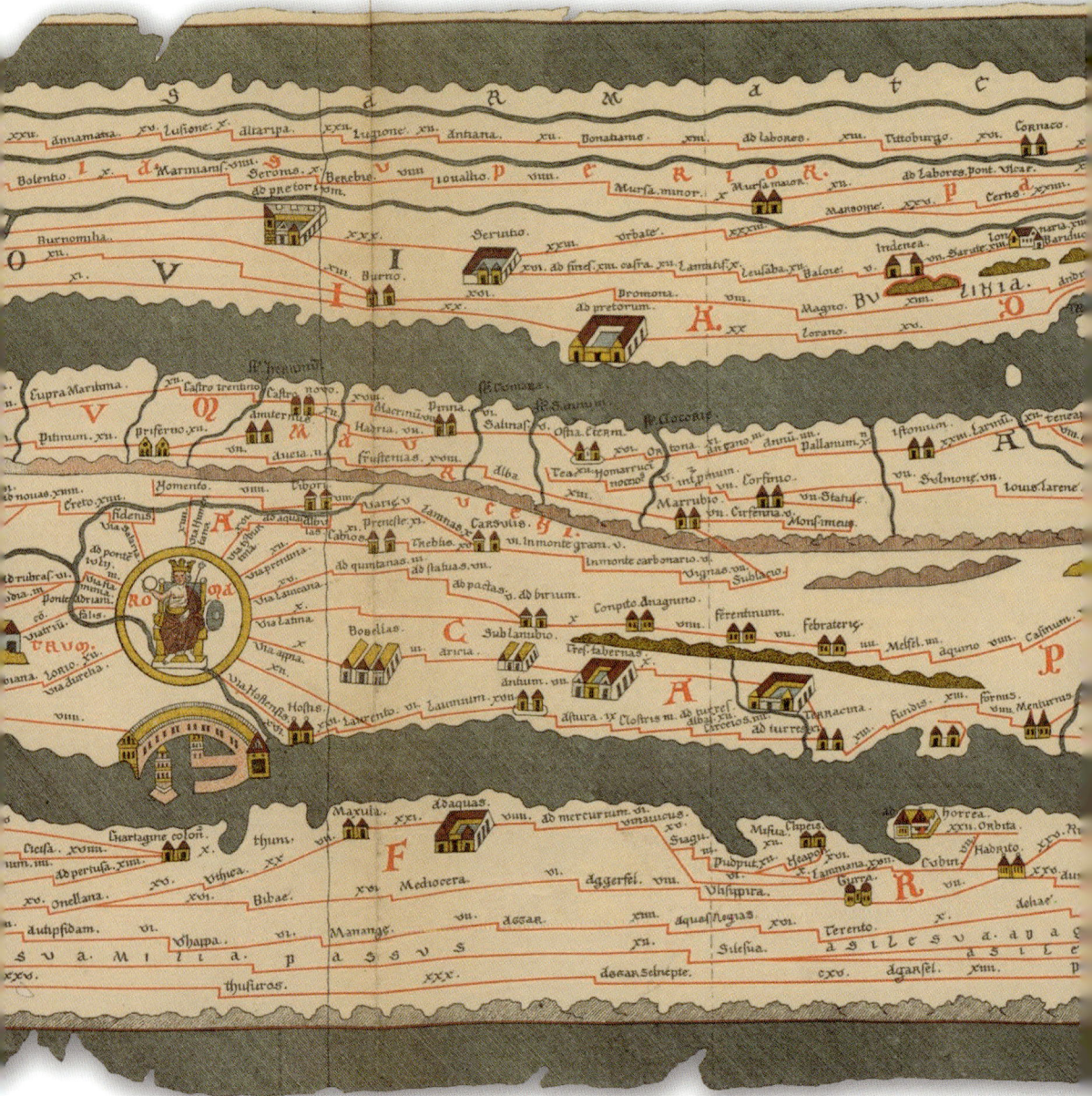

The central section of the Tabula Peutingeriana in the Austrian National Library, Vienna.
The north coast of Africa runs along the lower part of the map with the southern part of the Mediterranean Sea
directly above; in the middle level is the Italian peninsula with the mountain chain of the Apennines marked;
above that is the Adriatic Sea; and the west coast of the Balkans closes the top.

In the segment shown, Rome and its port, Ostia, are at the left side, and the Bay of Naples towards the right side. The fact that Pompeii, which was destroyed by the eruption of Vesuvius in 79 AD, is visibly marked (extreme right) suggests that the original map on which this was based dates from before its destruction.

effective idea of the shape and layout of the lands, seas and mountain ranges through which he would travel, any more than a beetle has of the pattern of a rug he is walking across. Alexander's scouts and local informants could tell him of the terrain for the next stage of his progress; but the overall shape of where he was going, what land he had taken, and what lay ahead of him, was hidden to his mind. The writing of Ancient History – not just the campaigns of Alexander the Great – can easily make assumptions about objectives and strategy oblivious of the utterly different nature of the knowledge that the Ancients had of the physical world which surrounded them. If Xerxes had had a good map of the Aegean, he would probably not have chosen to engage the Greeks in a naval battle in the straits of Salamis in September of 480 BC: and with a different outcome of the battle and a possible subjugation of Greece to Persia at that particular moment, the whole history of the West might therefore have followed a quite different course.

This helps to explain why the only comprehensive map from Antiquity actually to have survived in physical form down to our own times, the *Tabula Peutingeriana* (*see previous page*), is not a map as we understand it, but rather a linear itinerary giving the sequence of the towns, cities and features along the roads of the Roman Empire. The *Tabula* is a 13th century work on parchment, but it is believed to be a copy of a 4th or 5th century original which, in turn, was based on the map of the Roman world at the time of Augustus, which was commissioned by Marcus Agrippa around, or just after, the beginning of the 1st century AD. It is a long scroll of a map [3], twenty-two feet long and about one foot high, which begins with Ireland and Scotland at the northwestern extremity of the Roman world on the left and finishes with the southeastern extremity, India and Taprobane (Ceylon), at its right-hand end. Approximately half way along is Rome, *Caput mundi*, from which the Western world's roads then radiated. It is a fascinating work; but it in no way attempts to relate the forms and features of the world's geography spatially, but only in linear sequence. This is how the world appeared to the ancient traveller, merchant or general, but not as it appears to an astronaut today. The extraordinary thing about Anaximander's map on the other hand (although we should say, more precisely, Anaximander's attempt to map the whole world, because we do not possess any original image of it) was that it took a view of the world imagined as if seen by a person on the moon.

This way of conceiving planar space did not come about overnight. Two things prepared the way. In Babylon the use of pictographic maps for showing the form of a town and its surrounding plots of land had been in use for some time. A clay tablet (BM 92687), dating from around the same time as Anaximander's map, seems to show, again in pictographic form, the whole area of Mesopotamia: it is not impossible that it is based on a much earlier map, although that remains conjecture. But its scope is more limited and its thinking remains firmly in the realm of the symbolic. Anaximander's vision, on the other hand, of what the whole world might look like was something different. In its attempt to be descriptive and integrated, it was a quite extraordinary leap of imagination, and in every way more significant.

Imago mundi: Late Babylonian, 6th century BC, from Sippar;
British Museum, London, no. 92687.

The second thing that prepared the way for this manner of conceiving of space was the mapping of the celestial vault. The vision of a subdivided Zodiac with constellations emerged in Mesopotamia around the 10th or 9th century BC, it is thought. To map the night sky can be done directly from what the eye sees: but the eye of Antiquity could not see what the surface of the earth might look like from the sky, and it is this deductive vision that makes Anaximander's map – however approximate it is – such an extraordinary piece of intuitive deduction .

I don't doubt that Pythagoras would have been acquainted with the story of the circumnavigation of Africa, nor that the issues that arose from it exercised his mind considerably. He will also probably have known about and may even have seen the world-map of Anaximander, and have carried its image with him in a mental pocket of his mind on his journeys – not because it was any help with navigation or in choosing the best route, but because of its conception of the world as something circumscribed and with a distinct physiognomy. This fact is incredibly important. The human mind perceives the world from its local point of view as endlessly extensive; as we move, the horizon moves; as we come to the ridge of a mountain, more mountains or plains reveal themselves beyond; and the shore of an island or of a landmass itself appears only to be a change in type of extension in as much as the sea goes on stretching in front of us however much we move on its surface. But as soon as we conceive of the world as finite and circumscribed, its nature changes: it becomes knowable; it possesses a form, an individuality, an identity which is separate from the mind beholding it. The realisation that the vastness of Africa which seemed unending to the eyes of those that moved on its surface was in truth delimited and that it was virtually an island like Samos or Delos, only of unimaginably greater size; and that Europe and Asia might also be in the same way finite and might form together one continental landmass of the world that was itself only an island – all this meant a radical shift in perception that put the experienced and the conceptual into a new dialogue with one another. When we conceive of something as finite and bounded furthermore, we bring into being what lies beyond. In this way, in the minds of Anaximander, Pythagoras and their philosophically-minded contemporaries, the concept of Space (in the sense of 'outer space') was born.

We noted earlier how Pythagoras 'created' the cosmos for us, in a metaphorical sense, by stepping back from it, giving a name to it and showing that it existed all around us and was characterised by an order expressed as number. He created it as a distinct and coherent entity. Anaximander, building on what was revealed by the circumnavigation of Africa, had done something similar with the Earth: it was no longer just our experienced environment but existed as an object with a distinct form.

The early Greek mind was at its happiest thinking in terms of spatial geometry. It did so instinctively. In arithmetic and calculation, the Greeks of

Pythagoras's generation were newcomers: the Babylonian, Egyptian, Indian and Chinese observers and measurers had for long led the way in these fields. But with their integrated spatial conception, the Greeks introduced, quite literally, a new dimension of thinking. It was natural therefore that, with Pythagoras in particular, the question now centred on the specific geometric nature of the form that could be given to the Earth which was best suited to resolve these varying perceptions – those of his brilliant teacher Anaximander, his own thoughts and observations, the phenomena related by the Phoenician mariners, and those of our everyday, earthly experience of the world around us. Once again it was to be the aesthetic impulse of his thinking that may have suggested to his mind the possibility of a spherical Earth. The sphere was the purest of geometrical forms and, in its perfection, it reconciled boundlessness with a distinct, circumscribed form. You could travel for ever over its surface and you would never come to an end or a boundary: in this sense it answered to the experience of the terrestrial traveller and mariner. But it was also a discrete body with limits, size and circumscribed form, and could therefore exist as a physical identity within the spatial cosmos that he and Anaximander envisaged. The sphere presented itself like the perfect harmonic cadence which concludes a complex musical passage: its form fitted the problem neatly and brought resolution to all these disparate elements.

Did Pythagoras propose a spherical Earth? Diogenes Laertius [4] writes in the chapter on Pythagoras in his *Lives of Eminent Philosophers*: "we are told that he was the first to call the heaven, the universe and the Earth spherical [5] – though Theophrastus says it was Parmenides, and Zeno that it was Hesiod". Elsewhere [6], he attributes the same belief in sphericity to Anaximander. These comments are generally considered unreliable. Diogenes was not able to record with real authority what these philosophers actually thought, but only to relay what people after their time thought they had thought. All we can say for sure is that by the time of Plato and Aristotle, six generations later, the idea of a spherical earth had a more general currency in Greek thinking. An act of parturition had occurred: up until the age of Thales, Anaximander and Pythagoras, humankind had lived as if within the womb of nature, sensing it as its all-encompassing environment. Now, we were all of a sudden outside our mother's comforting womb and had a planet as our home. As with all births it was not an easy, but a necessary, passage.

The steps in this process of conception and birth follow one from the other:

1. The circumnavigation of Africa around 600 BC comes first.
2. Anaximander's map of the world, half a century later, is predicated on that journey.
3. Anaximander's most important thinking, however, regards the existence of a space all around the Earth, above and below, so as to permit the partially perceived cycle of the firmament's rotation to become a complete cycle.
4. His image of the Earth as a drum or cylinder poised at the centre of the universe, on the surface of which was our perceived terrestrial environment, was his method of integrating these two propositions, in other words placing his world map within his wider general cosmology.
5. Pythagoras knew of Anaximander's work and may even have been his student at one point: yet Pythagoras's whole cast of thinking gave ultimate precedence to aesthetic and geometric perfection. In his way of seeing it, therefore, everything that Anaximander had suggested both about the world and about the Space around it, could equally, but far more beautifully, be envisioned with an Earth which was spherical – the sphere being for him the most perfect of geometric forms. Whether or not he arrived at this conclusion we cannot know for sure, even though later commentators say he did.
6. The story comes full circle in as much as it can only be a spherical Earth that is able to resolve the conundrum presented by the statement of the Phoenician mariners after their circumnavigation of Africa, that in the middle of their journey the sun stood apparently to the north of them at midday.

This was a construct of great beauty. But had the world itself, so rich in colour and depth and life, been reduced to a drawing, a mere object, an intellectual concept, by this new way of standing back and looking at it from a distance? What did this mean for that sense of living reassuringly within the womb of nature? And where was the abode of the gods to be in this new and abstract construct? For sure, it was a very different aesthetic – a wholly new idea of what was beautiful. It was a concept in which the high-living Olympian deities, their banquets and their amorous escapades had no obvious place any more. Its divinity was of a quite other kind.

---

[1] *Histories*, Book IV. 44

[2] *Omphalos* is literally the 'navel'. This takes us back to the sculptors of the Samos *Kouros* and the other Archaic *Kouroi* who defined every part and contour of the body they were cutting in relation to one point selected as the navel.

[3] The full map can be viewed at: *https://upload.wikimedia.org/wikipedia/commons/5/50/TabulaPeutingeriana.jpg*

[4] Diogenes Laertius, *Vitae Philosophorum* VIII 1. 48

[5] Ἀλλὰ μὴν καὶ τὸν οὐρανὸν πρῶτον ὀνομάσαι κόσμον καὶ τὴν γῆν στρογγύλην: the phrasing in Greek is ambiguous as to whether Diogenes intended us to understand that the Cosmos and the Earth were both, individually, round in form, or whether it was just that the two together formed a round structure, in which it was left open whether the Earth were flat, slightly curved or spherical.

[6] *Ibid* II 1.1.

Ceiling fresco of a diver (early 5th century BC),
from a tomb in the necropolis of Paestum (Poseidonia), Italy.

The Push of
the Cosmos

Each one of these fragments of Pythagoras which we have looked at represents a way of thinking different from each of the others; yet there is one quietly spoken assumption that underlies them all. It was perhaps Pythagoras's greatest achievement – namely, to de-anthropomorphise the Deity for the human imagination. He did this some time in the mid-500s BC, and he did it in a manner that was calm and without polemic. It does not mean that he dispensed with the concept of divinity. Quite the opposite: he wanted, if anything, to increase our receptivity to what was truly divine. But he perfected a process that was already under way, to different degrees, in the thinking of the other philosophers of his time, and brought it to completion. He took human experience and suggested that the divine manifested itself to our perception in a multitude of ways, all of which belonged within the embracing concepts of *kósmos* and beauty. The world which we inhabit was, for him, not a passive receptacle into which a superior deity or deities poured down their will and judgement; it was a world in which all its living elements together built up awareness of the divine from their communality. Only by aligning ourselves with the constantly available potential for harmony within that living communality could we come close to understanding and being brought into a shared wholeness with the Divine. It was, at heart, a hopeful vision.

In this picture of the cosmos, harmony continuously creates and disharmony dissolves. Or rather it does not dissolve as if that were its 'will' or purpose; disharmony is simply the default state of things, a state which possesses no meaning. Harmony, on the other hand, was meaningfulness itself. All-enduring, yet never static, it existed between things and was constantly changing, disappearing here and appearing there, in an endless and infinite creativity, releasing many things in the process – beauty, hope, compassion. Wherever it was absent, the status quo of unordered disharmony reverted. The simple acoustic demonstration had furthermore shown Pythagoras that it was an innate quality of harmony to create always more than it receives from the constituents that give rise to it: two sounds become something much finer than themselves when they resonate as a harmonic interval. And it is not just that the resulting harmony is greater than the sum of the parts, but that it partakes of a higher nature, too. As our lives are played out in the midst of this, we need only to hold fast to the harmonious and the beautiful – to seek them out, to aspire towards them and to bring them into being wherever and however we are able to.

In such a picture, the divine could not continue to be seen in our minds as something separate, as a deity or deities with human or semi-human form who were above us, who judged and dispensed mercy or wrath; but rather as a presence encountered constantly at every turning, in every situation and in the other living beings that cross our path. To become involved with this divinity, we needed receptiveness; to further its harmony, we needed empathy. Sustaining these qualities through a lifetime was no easy thing; but like any habit it could be learnt with time and experience. The aim of the schools which Pythagoras is said to have founded in Italy must – at least at their outset – have been to further and foster this process of learning. The harmonious spirit built slowly; but once built, was never destroyed, neither in this nor in other existences.

The troubling distraction of anthropomorphic deities on the other hand was that they posed as many questions and conundrums as they solved. A god, either one or many, with a will or a mind or with judgements ultimately unravelled into contradictions or nonsense. In this way the mind became distracted from the divine and its questioning led down routes that were dead ends. The value of the idea of divine-order-as-harmony and harmony-as-divine-order which Pythagoras proposed on the other hand, was that it cleared the field: it created space for a more direct reception of, and a greater closeness to, the divine. The numerical ratios in geometry and music of which he spoke were no more than signposts: they stood as metaphors for the harmony that we should seek to foster inside ourselves, our thoughts, our feelings and intentions. It was not they themselves that mattered, but rather what that they pointed towards – namely that divine quality of *kósmos* which was immediately present to our senses in the life-giving forms of music and song; or in the proportions of a sculpture or a building or a doorway; or in the actions and faces of people whose being we valued; or in the beauty of the colours, forms, plants and creatures of the natural world. And because Pythagoras's mind was of a formation different from our own, emerging out of a past whose thinking was still deeply infused with an awareness of Spirit and spirits, it was easier for him than it is for us to see nature not as a mere play-thing for human convenience or as a domain donated to humanity to live within and to dominate, but rather as an environment alive with divinity that was continuously being brought into being by the order and harmony of which our own existence and consciousness was a creating participant.

Disassembling the anthropomorphic deity made this vision of things possible. That we owe to Pythagoras. It opened the way for speculation about our existence and its phenomena to be carried out untroubled by the fear of steering and revengeful deities, without taint of the 'will of God', or of one who insists we should belong to him and his tribe and not to others. It released us from a conception of 'good' that could sometimes be short-sighted and narrow, and made us free instead to understand the more complete and manifold goodness of all that is in harmony. Above all it allowed scientific thinking to happen – because science is not merely a technical game, even though that may be how it sometimes appears. Science involves also the discovery and revealing of beauty, and of the workings of harmony and of the divine. Science, at its best, is a study of the divine. Its evolving understanding of what lies in its purview – from the laws of motion to the genes which construct living beings, from the subatomic particles of matter to the processes of the cosmos beyond our planet – is not merely technical description: it can be spiritual truth of unimaginable beauty. True science and true beauty go hand in hand.

Human perception is partial – at least, in this existence. We have to content ourselves with that. In general, we glimpse and grasp harmony only fragmentarily and obliquely. Yet even so, in our lives there may occur moments when an aspect of divine *kósmos* appears to reveal itself to us through *harmonía* in what seems like completeness. We know immediately when this happens. For a moment which is passing but has no measurable length in time, fears and anxieties fall away from us without a sound, and we are like a child who is pushed out into deep water and swims instinctively for the first time, unsupported and out of depth, into the expanse of a benign sea. What was unacknowledged fear up until moments before, is now transformed into release and fulfilment. The water miraculously buoys us up and we are reassured and amazed to feel its support.

The sensation at such moments is of an unmistakable push. Nature launches us into her immensity – but does so with utter beneficence, and in a way that leaves us changed: we are now the independent swimmer, no longer the fearful shoreline paddler of before. We are master of a new element; we are a greater human soul as a result. These are the moments in which we are alive and for which we live. Anyone who has not felt this unmistakable 'push' of *harmonía* at some time or times in their life will find it more difficult to understand truly what Pythagoras is meaning.

PROBLEMS WITH PYTHAGORAS

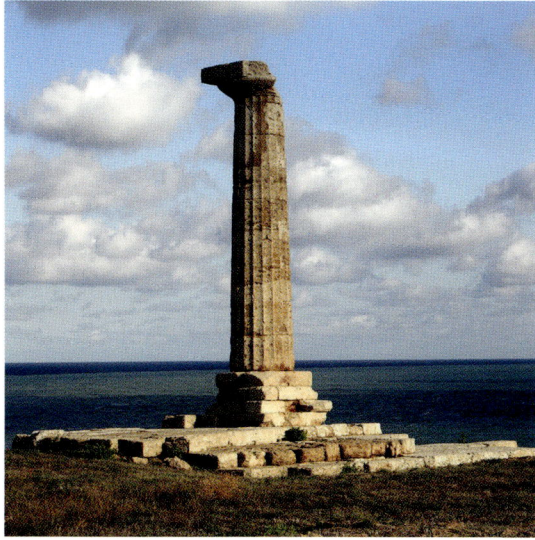

The single surviving Doric column from one of the grandest temples of Magna Graecia:
the Sanctuary of Hera Lacinia, at Cape Colonna,
near Croton in Calabria.

Pythagoras in Italy

L et us leave the splashing about in the cosmic sea for now, and turn to some rather more practical questions regarding what sort of person Pythagoras might actually have been and what was written about him in later centuries. Here we are brought up short by one great rock of a problem: the puzzling yet manifest difference between the depth and richness of implication in the thinking that we have been looking at up until now on the one side, and what is ultimately the scattered inconsequentiality and flatness of the sayings and doings which are recorded by later historians regarding the philosopher, on the other. They are aspects within the same mind which appear almost irreconcilable at times. The first belong to the early period of his life, about which he have almost no factual detail at all; the second, to the better documented period of his sojourn in Italy. The issue appears, in other words, to arise when Pythagoras leaves the Aegean world for Southern Italy, travelling westwards for the first time, in order to begin a new life among the area's already greatly prospering cities. What happened with him in Italy?

Since earliest times, Sicily and Southern Italy were to the Greek imagination what America was to Europe in the 18th and 19th centuries: vast, fertile, unconfined – a new land of hope and of economic potential and riches. The Greek cities founded there in the 8th and 7th centuries BC soon became conspicuously rich, enjoyed a lifestyle of great material ease and celebrated their success with the construction of buildings on a scale and quantity unmatched back in the Greek homeland. This was becoming true already by the time Pythagoras is said to have left Samos for Italy, and it may have constituted the appeal that the area and its mentality held for him. By the middle of the 2nd century BC, Southern Italy was already referred to by the historian Polybius as 'Great[er] Greece' [1], a usage taken on by the Romans who called it Magna Graecia.

Even to the eyes of the hero of Homer's *Odyssey* – the earliest literary glimpse we have of it – Sicily, in particular, appears as a land of seduction with lowing herds, fattened sheep, dense forests and flowing springs of water. Those who are familiar with Sicily today may be surprised at this description; but this is how the island appeared right up until the time of one of the first great human alterations of ecology in European history – the organised deforestation of the island by the Romans in order to satisfy their demand for timber to build navies and to fuel their thermal baths. In characteristically Roman fashion as well, this deforestation had its own logic in that they intended by the same process to transform areas of the island's interior into prairies for the cultivation of grain which was needed by the ever-hungry capital of their Empire. Only the later efforts of the Arabs who conquered the island in the ninth century – enlightened cultivators that they were – restored some ecological equilibrium to the island through intelligent irrigation and the wholesale introduction of a large variety of oriental plants which adapted well to their new home and soon became staples of Mediterranean cuisine – rice, sugar cane, citrus trees, almonds, pistachios, aubergines, durum wheat and, together with the latter, possibly even the making of pasta.

Migrations westwards, both in ancient and modern times, have traditionally been fuelled by the hope of starting over again, making good, becoming rich and, with luck, changing status in society; alternatively, it has been the need to seek refuge from persecution or from a lack of freedom back home. The reasons for which Pythagoras may have decided to leave the heart-land of Greece and emigrate to Magna Graecia were perhaps a mixture of the two – not, that is, that he sought riches and social advancement, but rather a new, fertile and open-minded intellectual climate in which to plant and cultivate his ideas. More than anything, though, he may have sought to avoid the political oppression which had built up in his native Samos under the autocratic rule of Polycrates and which would not have been sympathetic to him. This is the generally accepted thinking, although I sense, in addition, that Pythagoras was a person who did not relish debate, scrutiny and competition, and therefore to be free and distant from the intellectual hothouse of Ionia may also have had considerable appeal for him.

Shortly before he left Samos, Pythagoras would likely have met Democedes, who came to the island as the physician of Polycrates. Herodotus describes Democedes as the greatest physician of his day [2]; he later went on to become personal physician to Darius I, King of Persia – an example of one of the many talented Greeks who worked for a period deep within the Persian Empire. Democedes came from the prosperous Greek city of Croton in Southern Italy. That Pythagoras should have chosen apparently to settle in Croton, out of the many comparably attractive and interesting centres of Magna Graecia, suggests that the decision could well have arisen out of his acquaintance or friendship with Democedes while he was in Samos, or from the latter's recommendation to Pythagoras of contacts in his native city. However it happened, it appears that these two distinguished men, the physician and the philosopher, found themselves ultimately together in the same city. Herodotus relates how Democedes found a way to extricate himself with some semblance of official sanction from the court of Darius in Persia and to return home, using much the same kind of subterfuge that Marco Polo was to adopt centuries later in order finally to escape from the court of Kublai Khan [3]. Once back in Croton it seems Democedes would have found his old acquaintance Pythagoras already well established.

The city of Croton lies on the coastline of what is today Calabria, on the inside of the toe of the Italian peninsula, looking out to the East across the water towards Greece. It was one of a whole string of Greek settlements along the eastern coasts of Sicily and Southern Italy, and it is situated mid-way between the two most powerful economic centres of Magna Graecia – Syracuse in Sicily, and Taras (modern-day Taranto) at the top of the Gulf of Tarentum which forms the arch of the 'boot' of Italy. It was not coincidental that these two great cities occupied the two finest natural harbours in the whole of Southern Italy.

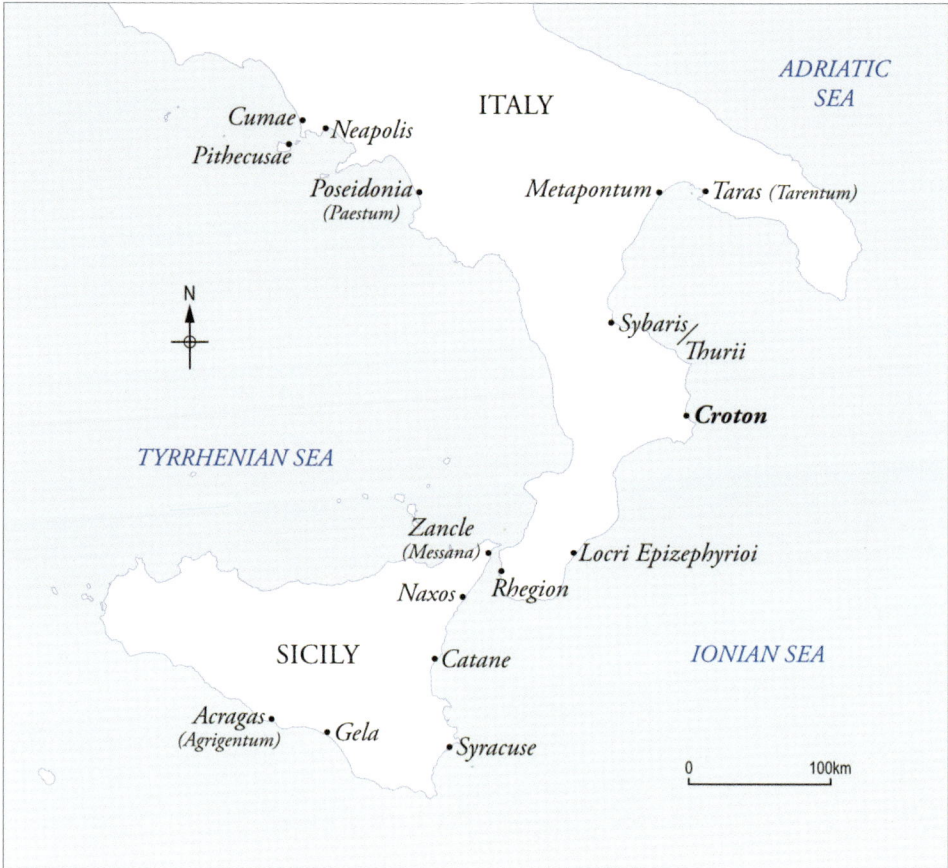

The Greek settlements of Magna Graecia.

This was an area very different in appearance from the lean, mountainous, indented coastline of Asia Minor with its scattered islands riding offshore. It was a landscape of long, unpopulated sandy shorelines, relatively calm waters and flat coastal plains which were irrigated by rivers descending from the mountains and hills of the interior – all features that were not that common in Aegean and mainland Greece. Above all there was openness and space. There was the possibility for expansion in every kind of dimension, including even the spiritual.

Croton was well-known in Antiquity for its doctors – not only Democedes who has just been mentioned, but also Alcmaeon, one of the first medical theorists, a pioneer of scientific dissection and a philosopher of physiology, writing half a century earlier than Hippocrates. Another, Calliphon, became possibly a close associate of Pythagoras and is said by Herodotus to have been the father of Democedes . The other field in which Croton excelled was athletics. Eusebius of Caesaria's list of the Olympic victors cites fourteen occasions on which athletes who hailed from Croton won an Olympic crown, and a further nine are mentioned in other sources. This means the city celebrated the greatest athletic accolade of the Greek world twenty three times in the two hundred years between the early seventh and early fifth centuries BC. On some of these occasions it was the same athlete who was repeatedly acclaimed as victor: most notable among these was Milon of Croton who won the Olympic crown in wrestling no less than six times, first as boy in 540 BC and then as an adult in 532, 528, 524, 520 and 516 BC. In addition, Milon won victories in the Pythian, Isthmian and Nemean Games which took place in the intervening years of the four year cycle of the Olympic gatherings. He was one of the most successful athletes of all time. Milon is also said to have given his daughter in marriage to Democedes on the return of the latter from the Persian court, thereby uniting the two fields of medicine and athletics in which the city excelled. All these achievements had already brought and continued to bring the city considerable renown in the time that Pythagoras is believed to have lived there.

Milon was a larger-than-life figure, about whom many colourful stories circulated. He was of such strength that he could snap a fillet tied securely around his forehead simply by clenching his temporal and maxillary muscles and expanding the blood flow to his temples. He was also a commanding soldier when required, and took to the field with the attributes of Hercules – the club and the lion pelt. This he did in the year 510 BC when the destinies of Croton and its most powerful neighbour, the city of Sybaris, came into direct conflict. The confrontation, which resulted in the destruction of Sybaris, one of the richest cities of all Magna Graecia, coincides with the period of Pythagoras's residence.

The fertile alluvial plain of the Sybaris & Crathis rivers, as seen in the 1940s
– site of Ancient Sybaris, north of Ancient Croton.

Croton and Sybaris, two large and prosperous centres separated by little more than sixty miles or a hundred kilometres of gentle coastline, assumed – in the minds of later historians at least – an allegorical significance as contrasting poles of morality: Croton, with its tradition of enviable athletic and medical prowess, and its association with the name of Pythagoras, was, to them, a paragon of the virtuous; Sybaris, with its inordinate wealth and worldly luxury, became on the other hand a symbol of immoderation, luxury and material excess, on which the gods looked down with some disapproval. The city's size, if we are to believe a probably exaggerated claim of Strabo, filled out a circuit of walls fifty *stadia* (or eight kilometres) in length; and the descriptions of its shaded and watered streets, its famous chefs and its leisured life in which – according to Athenaeus of Naucratis [7], who clearly enjoyed telling tales of the city's luxuries – not even cockerels were allowed to disturb the perfumed sleep of its citizens, make it sound like a place where one might with justification have taken considerable pride in the sybaritic life. But pride comes before a fall and, in spite of a warning from the Delphic Oracle [8], a forgetting of the proper respect and attention to the gods brought about the inevitable nemesis of the city's destruction.

There may well have been running disputes between Sybaris and Croton over territorial claims, but the confrontation of the two cities that occurred in 510 BC came about when Telys, the tyrant of Sybaris, expelled five hundred of the richest citizens of the city with whom he apparently did not agree, and seized their land and possessions. When these exiles took refuge in Croton the situation between the two cities became tense. Telys requested their immediate repatriation. It is at this juncture that Pythagoras makes a brief, perhaps token, appearance: it is claimed by Diodorus and Iamblichus that it was his intervention on behalf of the refugee aristocrats from Sybaris that decided the issue and convinced the fearful citizens of Croton, officially and on principle, to refuse the request of Telys. When, according to Athenaeus, a group of thirty envoys were then sent from Croton to Sybaris with this decision and were promptly butchered by Telys and their bodies thrown from the walls of the city and left unburied, Croton had no longer any choice but to act. Milon headed an expeditionary force against Sybaris, besieged the city and defeated it. Athenaeus adds the characteristic detail that the impressive cavalry of the city of Sybaris, which had been trained to manoeuvre to the sound of flutes, were deliberately disarmed by flautists in the Crotonian contingent who sowed chaos in their ranks with countermanding musical instructions [9].

Sybaris was destroyed – but the way in which it was destroyed was debated even in Antiquity and is still awaiting a clear archaeological verdict today. Strabo (and Strabo alone) claims that the confluence of two rivers, the Crathis and the Sybaris, which flowed close by, was diverted by the victors into the city which was then simply washed away to destruction [10]. A reference, however, in Diodorus to another siege of Sybaris thirty five years later suggests that the city continued to function and needed once again to be purged by Croton. In the end, a new Athenian colony, called Thurii, was created from 444 BC on the site of Sybaris in order to obliterate, through a change of name, the perpetuation of its memory. Sybaris and the Sybarites suffered a *damnatio memoriae*. It was in Thurii that Herodotus latterly lived and ended his days – curiously without making any reference in his writings to the memory of Pythagoras in the area. Pythagoras would still have been revered as one of the most celebrated figures of Magna Graecia at that time if we are to believe the generally received version, and he had died there a mere sixty years previously it is thought.

The elusiveness and invisibility of Pythagoras has been a theme since the opening pages of this book. He slips from our vision in a curious fashion all the way through his life, from birth to death. Nothing which is of a factual or historical nature remains clear. Diogenes Laertius, who does not speak about Pythagoras in relation to the conflict with Sybaris, glimpses him instead, in one of his sources, on the battlefield itself (or rather on the 'bean field') in a quite different dispute in Sicily:

> Hermippus relates that, when the men of Agrigentum and Syracuse were at war, Pythagoras and his disciples went out and fought in the van of the army of the Agrigentines, and, their line being turned, he [Pythagoras] was killed by the Syracusans as he was trying to avoid the bean field [11].

Another unsubstantiable – and, honestly, improbable – sighting; and another version of the philosopher's demise. Pythagoras's reported moral aversion to fava beans is something every bit as intriguing as it is famous: in the next chapter, we will look at this fact or legend – whichever it is – in a little more detail. But the reference to it here, by the philosopher-biographer Hermippus of Smyrna, as the inadvertent cause of his death, seems to push the bounds of credibility in the interests of giving his story an ironic and rhetorical twist at the expense of Pythagoras himself.

In the account of Pythagoras, and in particular in this period of his sojourn in Italy, on which the greatest part of all the material relating to him is concentrated, we are presented with a picture of unique opacity. About many of the early philosophers we know virtually nothing at all; about others we have a limited, but at least clear picture; only with Pythagoras is there such a quantity of material, and yet a picture which is so systemically ambiguous and contradictory. Diogenes's account of Pythagoras in Book VIII of his *Lives of Eminent Philosophers* is of importance to us because it is the very first dedicated study and biography we have of Pythagoras that has survived. It is by nature a compendium from many sources: hence he cites three quite different versions of Pythagoras's birth and origins, just as he cites also three quite different versions of his death. But, at the same time, it is a highly contentious work, claiming that Pythagoras wrote three separate books – 'On Nature', 'On

Statesmanship' and 'On Education'. Not only that: he mentions also that one of his sources, Heracleides of Pontus, says Pythagoras wrote another six works, including a treatise on the Universe and one on Croton, while another of his sources, Ion of Chios, says Pythagoras wrote poetry which he then ascribed to the authorship of Orpheus. All of these claims and conjectures leave us at a loss. Could they possibly be true? They sit there and look us in the face – uncorroborated and unsupported by any surviving evidence – like a row of dissembling schoolchildren.

It is curious, furthermore, that almost nothing in Diogenes's account of Pythagoras is seen – except in passing on a couple of occasions – as necessarily arising from what we have understood to be Pythagoras's overarching idea of *harmonía*. The word itself only occurs four times in his account. And it is this strange and inexplicable disconnect between the moral and spiritual qualities which Diogenes mentions on the one hand, and any wider philosophy which unites them on the other, that leads to the suspicion that there could be two different but not unconnected minds at work between Samos and Croton. Diogenes admits that the interests of Pythagoras included medicine, and celestial observation – and, for what it is worth, goes on to ascribe to Pythagoras, in his chapter on the philosopher, the observations that the "Evening and Morning Stars are the same" (para. 14), that "the moon is illuminated by the sun" (para. 27), and that the universe is "animate, intelligent, spherical, with the earth at its centre; the earth itself too being spherical and inhabited round about" (para. 25). But these amount to almost all that we receive of any sense of a greater cosmology. And the attribution of them all to Pythagoras is, in any case, highly questionable.

Notwithstanding the absence of information that we can rely on with confidence about the true nature and events of this final, Italian chapter of Pythagoras's life, a small number of themes -- largely relating to conduct in life – do emerge with a little more clarity from Diogenes's account. They are consistent within themselves and are confirmed by other writers. They include, for example: a striking emphasis on Pythagoras's own power of memory, and of the importance he ascribed to training the memory and mental recall (something he impressed also upon his students, according to Iamblichus); an emphasis on moderation in eating and drinking; on the avoidance of anger, vulgar joking, and of punishment or retribution given in anger; on the signal sacredness of friends and friendship, and of the communality of life and possessions between friends – which meant, for him, seeking even to convert our enemies into friends. There is a repeated emphasis also on Pythagoras's own personal gift for friendship. Other aspirations or 'teachings' which emerge clearly from Diogenes's account include: a constant, mental self-examination day by day regarding personal decency and morality of behaviour; an appropriate respect for elders and ancestors; a showing of gratitude to the Divine as well as towards good people; a commitment never to injure or to kill trees and animals that do us no harm; and, above all, to turn the soul always towards goodness.

All these things, which are touched on in passing in the anthology of information Diogenes Laertius gives us, create a picture of undoubted decency and rightness. Many remind us of Christian teachings which would come half a millennium later: making friends of enemies, moderation and temperance, and the avoidance of anger and retribution. Others lie outside Christian teaching: the avoidance of harm to trees and animals, the emphasis on memory training and the particular sacredness of friendship. But if they should seem unsurprising or unexceptional to us today, this is because we are ourselves the heirs to centuries of a Judaeo-Christian-Islamic acculturation which has overlaid these precepts with its own versions of them. But if we try to imagine a time before the coming of those faiths and influences in the West, an age which followed close on the heels of Homer's very different world, we can see how these qualities of pacifism, love and goodness were genuinely ground-breaking two thousand five hundred years ago. In this sense, Pythagoras was an extraordinarily powerful innovator.

Vicia faba – innocent subject of much controversy

[1] "Μεγάλη Ἑλλάδα": Polybius, *Histories*, II. 39

[2] Herodotus, Histories, III. 131

[3] Democedes found a way to guide a military reconnaissance trip into Greek waters on behalf of Darius, and then jumped ship at Taras (Tarentum) so as to return home to Croton (Herodotus, *Histories*, III. 134-7). Marco, Maffeo and Niccolò Polo offered to accompany Kököchin, a Royal Princess of the court of Kublai Khan to be wedded in Persia to Kublai's great nephew, Arghun Khan. Having delivered her to Arghun's successor (Arghun Khan himself having died in the interim), the Polos quitted their mission and continued home to Venice rather than return to the Mongol court.

[4] Herodotus, *Histories*, II. 125

[5] Herodotus, *Histories*, III 137/8

[6] Strabo, *Geographica*, VI, i, 13

[7] Athenaeus, *Deipnosophists*, 12. 518

[8] Aelian, *Vera Historia*, 3. 43

[9] Athenaeus, *Deipnosophists*, 12. 19

[10] Strabo, *Geographica*, VI 1.13

[11] Diogenes Laertius, *Vitae Philosophorum*, VIII, 1. 40

*Bronze head of a 'Philosopher', from an ancient shipwreck in the Straits of Messina;
5th century BC. (National Museum of Magna Graecia, Reggio Calabria)*

Who was Pythagoras
& what was he like?

W ho was Pythagoras, then? He was a man: that much we do know. A man – yet one with an important filament of the female in his make-up. That is not to say that he was effeminate; but rather that his being also comprised something of the innate receptivity which we associate with the female principle and with womanhood. He was a man; yet there was something about him that convinced people that he possessed divinity. Some spoke of his closeness to Apollo; others said he was actually the offspring of Apollo; and a few believed that he was an incarnation of Hyperborean Apollo himself [1]. He was a man, yet he seems to have maintained to the end that unease in respect of authority and confrontation which is often the hallmark of a certain kind of ceaseless, youthful dreamer. He was a hermit by instinct, who seems to have liked solitude and solitary travel; but a hermit who perhaps had a fatal weakness for the attention and admiration of others. He was a serious thinker, and yet he appears never to have written a word. He was fascinated by mathematics and by music, and yet those who came after him in Antiquity never spoke of him as a mathematician (as they did, for example, of Thales) or as a musician (as they did of Terpander). He sought to base his observations about acoustics and geometry on provable, logical consistency, and yet those who came after him seem to have been fixated with him more as a magician than as a logician. He was no ordinary man in the eyes of his followers: he apparently possessed a golden thigh [2] (whatever exactly that meant) and was seen to manifest himself in more than one place at the same time. He gave humanity a profoundly new way of looking at the cosmos; and yet the thing which his followers seem to have recalled most vividly was his supposed prohibition on the eating of fava beans. We can be sure of one only thing: he was highly irresponsible as regards his own legacy to posterity. He has left it to a poor individual in the twenty-first century to try to unpick the mess he has left behind.

Was Pythagoras a joker, then, at heart? Someone who took pleasure in teasing the credulousness of those who crowded around him? Even that is not impossible. There is, for sure, a sense of solemn seriousness and even of animus in Heracleitus: there is no mistaking that. Yet in Pythagoras, there is an elusiveness which amounts almost to a wilful desire to make fools of us all and of the seriousness with which human beings follow the lore and the laws of beliefs and rituals. His later followers and even modern, academic philosophers have performed somersaults in their efforts to explain Pythagoras's unexpected and famous prohibition on the eating of fava beans. Some said it was because the slippery interior of the pod was seen as a road for dead souls to the Underworld; others because of the visual similarity of the bean within the pod to the foetus in the womb; others noticed in them a similarity to testicles; while yet others say Pythagoras avoided them because dried beans were used as voting counters (though those were more likely black-eyed beans). The one thing we all know about eating a lot of fava beans, however, is that they can produce an excess of gastric wind. In the end we have to decide freely for ourselves whether many

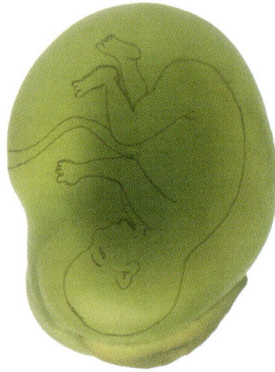

Fava bean.

of Pythagoras's reported precepts were themselves just so much gastric wind, or whether in them lay some profound insight: the fava bean issue is like an encapsulation of that very dilemma. When Pythagoras was speaking about beans, he may have been ironising about them; he may have been speaking metaphorically; he may have been telling a story; he may simply have had a personal problem with wind; or he may even have suffered from Favism, a rare genetic disease which makes the eating of fava beans potentially poisonous to the subject's blood.

If we wished, we could perform an experiment – not to consume an inordinate quantity of fava beans in order to see exactly what happens, but rather to talk about them informally and to see what happened to our discussion through time. I would tell you something harmless in an ironic tone, but I wouldn't write it down: I would only speak it in a classroom or a lecture hall, and we could ask those present to pass on to others, by word of mouth, what I had said. Then, we could reconvene after several centuries and see what had become of the original comment. There would be nothing left, of course: but that is because I am not Pythagoras. In the actual case of Pythagoras, however, the very fact that the prohibition on eating beans should still be the topic of animated discussion after more than two and a half thousand years can only be due to the compelling renown he must have had for wisdom, and the conviction among his followers that *whatever* he said was a truth of great import. We may not know what he actually had to say on most subjects; but many of his contemporaries, who were not ignorant people, apparently considered it all to be Law of the greatest seriousness.

Great learning; great insight; esoteric riddles; unconventionality; jokery. It is a powerful and enduring combination. These qualities, perhaps in varying mixture, bring to mind other figures in history – not just those of Pythagoras's time, such as Empedocles of Acragas, but much later thinkers, too: Leonardo da Vinci, William Blake, Voltaire.

By even asking the question whether Pythagoras might have been a joker – still a great thinker, but by disposition one who liked also to play games – I am merely trying to break the mould of our age-old manner of thinking of the Greek Philosopher as a sort of rabbinical sage, with long beard and humourless demeanour. Pythagoras has a right to be conceived in our imaginations also as a young person, as someone with humour and humanity, rather than with the aura of a bogus demi-god that his successors seemed intent to wish upon him.

Youthfulness is important. The mind is tempered during our lives. The intensity, imagination and intuition of youthful perception, the sheer leaps into the unknown that it is able to make, give way to a more earth-bound, critical and reflective kind of thinking in later life. To some, who have lived for intuition and intensity, ageing represents a loss of vision: the Romantic poets come to mind – especially Wordsworth who was acutely aware of this transformation in his own mind. To others, maturity can bring a welcome clarity. In Pythagoras the

Portrait in encaustic of a young man from Faiyum, 2nd Century.
(Antikensammlung, Berlin.)

change appears to demarcate two quite distinct aspects of his philosophy. To his youthful years – when he was still an anonymous figure, when he travelled on his own to Egypt and the East, when he observed and listened and assimilated other cultures and learning – belong those primordial insights which constitute the theme of the first part of this study. To his later years, after he left behind him the source of his inspiration in the Aegean and settled in Croton in Southern Italy, where he was surrounded by followers and admirers and was apparently much flattered by attention, are supposed to belong the establishment of the Pythagorean School and the (perhaps reluctant) experiments with the social and political application of his philosophical principles in his adopted city of Croton. The first period was a fulminating success; the second ultimately amounted to a failure. And the failure was further compounded by Pythagoras's refusal to write or to leave any authoritative record of his thinking for posterity. Pherecydes of Syros and Anaximander of Miletus – both thinkers cited in Antiquity as significant influences on, and maybe even teachers of, Pythagoras – are both known to have left important written works behind, even if they do not survive integrally today: Xenophanes and Heracleitus, too. Instead we are left by Pythagoras to rely on a sort of centuries-long twitter-feed initiated by those who were actually outside the room when he spoke.

This apparent change in the very nature of Pythagoras's thinking between these two periods in his life is a problem. How do we reconcile the clarity and lucidity of the concepts of his general ideas regarding *harmonía, kósmos* and mathematics early in his life, with the dispersive inconsequentiality of so much of the random mental pursuits, cryptic injunctions, practices and precepts – or *akoúsmata* ('things heard') as they were called – which have been transmitted from the period of the Pythagorean schools in Southern Italy? It is a struggle. They seem to be on quite separate mental flight-paths. If it were not for a relatively solid tradition that all of this material comes from the same Pythagoras, it would be easier to believe that there had been some confusion between two separate individuals – a Samian Pythagoras who travelled East, and an Italian Pythagoras who was settled in the West. This may seem a fairly improbable thesis; but, as we shall see in the following chapter, it is not an impossible one.

In the end, the best way we can reconcile this problem is by acknowledging that what was taught in the Pythagorean schools was, we are told, deliberately to be kept secret, and that our metaphorical 'tweeters' outside, upon whom we unfortunately depend, had little idea in truth what was going on and invented their own version of it all which has held fast throughout history. But even this explanation still leaves the problem of the secrecy itself: what was the necessity for that? Secrecy runs counter to the whole spirit of early Greek speculation which throve on open debate and competition among peers in the staring light of the public arena. Pythagoras by contrast, seems, deliberately or otherwise, to have hidden everything behind a smoke-screen. His instincts seem to belong more to the incense-laden world of Byzantine Greek thought whose heyday was to come a thousand years later.

Clearly the creation of a way of life through moral and philosophical teachings is a different matter from the passing on of insights regarding cosmology, and it involves a wholly different part of the psyche. Experience tells us, too, that an ethical way of life is imparted not so much by teaching, in any case, but by living example. The stories of countless saints, gurus, Zen masters and ascetics tell us this: it is not so much what these people said, but how they lived and were. They led by their physical presence and their very way of being. And communicating in words to posterity the reality of a great person's way of being is something well-nigh impossible.

If we imagine trying to reconstruct the life and teachings of Jesus of Nazareth, in the absence of the Gospels, from just a few remaining fragments, no more than a couple of parables and a reported miracle or two – the parable of the Wise Virgins or of the Prodigal Son, and perhaps the miracle of wine into water at the Marriage at Cana – we begin to comprehend the nature of the problem. Without the gospel books, we would be lost: they provide essential narrative context to the spoken words and to the teachings. They evoke a picture of the man, the audience, the background and the mission. But with Pythagoras we have none of this. The recorded sayings are fragmentary and dislocated. They feel like anonymous proverbs or folk-sayings. Some of them are clear, others impenetrable. One such saying, or *'akoúsma'*, which has come down to us, for example, enjoins us "not to stir the fire with a knife". When we stir embers in a fire we reawaken the coals, they become red and re-ignite. Metaphorically speaking we are resuscitating old grievances and former pains, things best left to die down naturally. The knife is the embodiment of cutting and division in the domestic context, and of aggression and the inflicting of pain in human interaction. Pythagoras's biographer, Iamblichus, enlarging on the interpretation of Diogenes Laertius, explains this for us: but it does not take a doctorate in philosophy to understand what Pythagoras might have been saying, even without his explanation. "Never pick up what has fallen from the table", is another *'akoúsma'*: it is a little less obvious and needs more contextual support, but we can suggest several ways to interpret it as a serious and valuable moral injunction, so long as we think of it metaphorically and not literally. Others, however, are even more bereft of context: "Touch the earth when it thunders" – a marvellously suggestive poetic image, but, without its context, even harder for us to place. And, in the end, without the invaluable guiding hand of a Pythagorean Saint Mark, recording the details and filling in the integrating narrative, the corpus of *akoúsmata* adds up to little or nothing.

Without any sense of the man's living way of being, his manner and presence, his human actions and interactions, this second part of Pythagoras's life – the years in Italy, in Croton – is, in spite of all the information we are given, virtually a closed book to us. It seems to be based on wholly different premises from the first act of his life, when he travelled and formulated the ideas which have so far been the subject of this book. The early thinking of Pythagoras stood out from that of his contemporaries, even the greatest of them, because Pythagoras sought demonstrable, measurable evidence for what he was saying through the monochord demonstration, or the universal equation of the theorem, or his mathematical and geometrical analysis. That he should have gone on, furthermore, to attempt to integrate those ideas with the spiritual revelations he had learnt and adapted from the East regarding the soul and the cycles of incarnation, is a project potentially of the greatest significance. This is the measure of the greatness of his mind and person, set against his contemporaries. And the importance of this thinking clearly resonated through subsequent centuries. But the secrecy injunction – *if* this were in fact something that Pythagoras himself, and not his followers, wished for – simply pulled the carpet from under his feet. If Jesus or Mohammed or Confucius or the Buddha had favoured a similar secrecy, what would we understand of their teachings and their lives today?

But there is another less obvious reason which explains why we have so little reliable information about the human nature of Pythagoras as a person. The Greek male mind, raised on values of military valour, athletic prowess and mental rigour, did not know quite what to make of humility, receptivity and courtesy. Greeks respected the role and the knowledge of priests and priestesses, especially the magical and prophetic skills of those of ancient or oriental origin; they saw clearly the value of intellectual skills in debate and in the public arena; but it was not to be until the arrival of Christianity many centuries later that humility came into its own as a positive personal quality. The image we have received of Pythagoras from his biographers and his followers is the result of a hard-won battle to squeeze his unconventional nature into the mould of the patriarchal philosopher-magos-guru – something that this author, at least, believes he never wished to be. It is revealing that we hear nothing specific about the nature of his opposition to the autocratic power of Polycrates in his native city of Samos, nor of his confronting the critical uprising of Cylon which ended in Pythagoras fleeing Croton for ever. His instinct appears to have been to side-step confrontation; and side-stepping was not yet part of the Greek cultural lexicon.

Courtesy: this may seem a strange quality to have mentioned a moment ago, but courtesy may well have been for Pythagoras one of the primary virtues, for the reason that it was a vital expression of *harmonía* between individuals. It is the embodiment of respect – universal respect. A flawed sense of what we think of as important in the West has meant that courtesy has been traditionally considered a question of surface or appearance, dispensable and of little more significance than the clothes we choose to wear. At times it has even been considered a sign of weakness. If our priorities were more evenly balanced, however, it would be at the heart of the way we relate towards one another, towards the world around us, and towards the divine. 'Courtesy' is a far from perfect word, but it is the best we have available and it comes without the undesired overtones of hierarchical deference which are implicit in the way we conceive 'respect'. Courtesy partakes of respect nonetheless: it is a preparatory disposition for the much greater concept of love.

We are not speaking here about the learnt code of courtesy, the dutiful following of acquired rules, but the natural and spontaneous courtesy which arises from within, from the simple and important fact of having respect for the inherent value of things, plants, animals and people, other than ourselves – as well as for the feelings and opinions of others. This is something we can draw from Xenophanes's anecdote of the man beating the dog: Pythagoras's point is not only about the reincarnation of souls, but also about showing respect for other living beings, even stray dogs. Genuine respect and courtesy spring from a standing outside of ourselves and a putting of our own life and feelings and needs honestly in relation to those of other beings, and for that reason they both partake of the nature of *harmonía*. Courtesy nourishes *harmonía*, magnifies its power and spreads its effects within us and between us. If, for Pythagoras, it was the first of virtues, this was because the other virtues flowed from it. To be respectful toward the food we eat and in the way we eat was a part of courtesy; to be respectful towards the autonomy of the natural world around us, likewise; to be mindful of the way we moved and related physically towards others was courtesy; to deal, trade and dialogue with others in honesty and moderation was courtesy; the right way of sex was a part of courtesy. Greed, rape, coercion and hurt, on the other hand, were what happened in its absence. It was above all a spiritual quality of primary importance, to be manifested in our attitude towards all – inferiors, superiors, animals, plants, lovers and enemies, and even towards our own destiny and lot in life. To be respectful towards divinity was to accept with dignity whatever fate might put in our path.

If Pythagoras then was renowned to later generations, as Plato suggests, for his creation of something particular and special in the 'Pythagorean life', it was not through a decalogue of precepts, but through the example of his own way of being which was a living inspiration in great and small to those around him. The problem inherent in this, however, was that, once he was gone, the memory of his example faded and the only way to perpetuate the aura which he seemed to possess, was through repeating vainly what he had said, telling stories about him and continuing the philosophical pursuits that he had touched upon. Yet without the central illuminating inspiration, such mechanical processes were not the same thing at all as they were in his living presence. If the *Mona Lisa* were destroyed along with all the representations and photographs of the painting, an effusive verbal description of the details and of the subtle beauty of the painting – such as the one written by Giorgio Vasari from recollection of the painting many years later – could never ever hope to be a valid substitute for the painting itself.

The reconstructions of Pythagoras's life written centuries later are every bit as well-intentioned as Vasari's marvelling description in words of the *Mona Lisa*, but they fall short just as much in giving no sense of the vital, living presence of the real thing. Memory is a remarkable human endowment; but it is not always a reliable one. For this reason, we should look for a moment at the many difficulties that were inherent in the transmission of history and biography in the Ancient World.

---

[1] Fragments 191&192, Valentin Rose, *Aristotelis…Fragmenta*; and Porphyry, *De Vita Pythagorae* 28; *Iamblichus, De Vita Pythagorica* 91–3, 135–6, 140–1 (Apollo was believed to be absent from his haunts in Greece for a substantial period of each year, during which he wintered in the land of the Hyperboreans, who were praticular favourites of the god and who lived in an ill-defined but paradisiacal land of perpetual, temperate sunshine, in the far North of the world.)

[2] Diogenes Laertius, *Vitae Philosophorum*, VIII.1.11: "Indeed, his bearing is said to have been most dignified, and his disciples held the opinion about him that he was Apollo come down from the far north. There is a story that once, when he was disrobed, his thigh was seen to be of gold" (*trans. Robert Drew Hicks.*)

[3] Giorgio Vasari, *Lives of the Most Eminent Painters, Sculptors and Artists and Architects,* 1550, Part IV: *Leonardo da Vinci*

The Historians
& their Pythagorases

A philosophy is never something fixed like a butterfly specimen in a drawer of history. It evolves and it has the liberty to have different emphases and to mean different things in different epochs. The reading of Pythagoras offered in these pages is one that inevitably reflects the particular interests and concerns both of the author and of the age in which it is written, and the reader is free to accept or reject these premises of interpretation. But there is a quite separate problem in the case of Pythagoras: it is that, within the body of material presented as the thinking and teachings of Pythagoras, the irreconcilability of some parts with others can make it appear as if it were an anthology of thought from different people and even from different periods, rather than the philosophy of a single person. In order to explore what may have happened we need to look now, not at Pythagoras himself, but at those who wrote about him and to try to understand some of the problems they faced in writing about him.

"The writing of history". The writing of history, *as we understand history,* that is. A kind of history that can be substantiated and is based on a disinterested accuracy of fact. The Ancients wrote what history meant for them; but we seek what history means for us, and the two are different. Benedetto Croce put it succinctly: *"ogni vera storia è storia contemporanea"* [1] – all true history is contemporary history. In other words, we cannot help writing and reading history through the lens of our own times, seeking what we in our particular period desire to learn from it and wish it to reveal for us. Every epoch writes history in its own way.

Benedetto Croce (1866-1952):
"All history is contemporary history"

So, when in the 21st century we are reading the (miraculously survived) words of an ancient writer of the 3rd/4th century, seventeen hundred years before our time, writing about someone who had lived a further eight hundred years before him, it is important for us, before we draw any conclusions about Pythagoras, to think about what exactly we are getting.

I am thinking, in this case, about the figure of Iamblichus who has left us the longest history of Pythagoras to survive from Antiquity as a complete text – his study on the 'Pythagorean Life', *De Vita Pythagorica*. He was the last person in ancient times, whose work still survives, to have written in detail about Pythagoras. He is therefore the closest to our own time; but by that same fact he was also the furthest away from his subject. In the eight centuries that had elapsed since the age of Pythagoras the world and its priorities and its ways of thinking had changed radically. What Iamblichus sought was not necessarily what Pythagoras gave. Nor is his version of things necessarily going to conform much to our own ideas of history either.

Iamblichus was a writer and philosopher from the eastern periphery of the Hellenic world. He was from rural Syria – either from the town called Chalcis ad Belum in the rolling steppe-lands between the Orontes and Euphrates Valleys or from Chalcis sub Libano in the Beqaa Valley, below the mountains of the Anti-Lebanon. Croton and Samos, the places most associated with his subject, Pythagoras, were many hundreds of miles away to the West. And the books that he needed to consult were scattered all over the known world. He might or might not find the texts he wanted in Antioch, or in Alexandria, or in Ephesus, Pergamon or Rome: he would need to travel there first to find out. There was no way to consult a catalogue before setting off; no articles on line; no books orderable through Amazon; no easy way to check and cross-check and gather the material which he needed; no laptop; perhaps no portable notebook and pencil even. His greatest tool was his memory – something which leaves us hoping that writers then had far better memories than we have today.

Ruins of the entrance to the Library building of Ancient Nysa on the Meander (Asia Minor), dating from the 2nd century AD.

Writing history in the fourth century was therefore no easy matter; but in spite of such difficulties he succeeded in his task and has left us with a valuable and generous portrait. Yet, for us, it is like a minestrone of re-cooked bits from other writers, combining impossibilities, improbabilities, inventions and contradictory comments about Pythagoras all within the same two covers, and attempting all the while to re-shape his subject and to squeeze it into the mould generally used for a saint, miracle-worker, mystic or charismatic preacher. In the rapidly changing world of the Roman Empire as it was transformed into a Christian state, this was the sort of figure that his readers were familiar with and wanted to hear about. His writing follows the form of the increasingly popular works of hagiography. But if this mould was not appropriate or relevant to the person of Pythagoras, how much use can it really be to us as an account of his life and thought? It tells us a lot about the preoccupations of Iamblichus and the world in which he lived, but rather less about Pythagoras. We find that once again Pythagoras has slipped away from under the lens.

Apart from the countless allusions to him in later litearure, we possess three dedicated lives of Pythagoras, written respectively by Diogenes Laertius in around 230 AD, by Porphyry in around 280 AD, and lastly by Iamblichus in around 300 AD. These three works build sequentially on one another, and are all trawling through more or less the same body of written and oral legends about Pythagoras. They are important because they are almost all we have: they may also contain some transmitted grains of truth embedded in their uneven texture. But because we have our own preconceptions of how history should be written and have our own ideas about what we want to know of Pythagoras, their tendentiousness can at times be simply confusing for us.

In the first place, the writers of this Late Antique period differ dramatically in their way of conceiving of written history not just from us, but also from the earlier Greek historians. For the reader familiar with Herodotus's disarming but thoughtful story-telling style, or with the intellectual clarity, authority and meticulousness of Thucydides and Polybius, or even with the less perceptive but nonetheless humane and well-intentioned thoroughness of Diodorus of Sicily, these later works of Diogenes, Porphyry and Iamblichus, though full of enthusiasm and a generosity of spirit, will seem facile, uncritical and highly disorganised by comparison.

Our way of thinking and of conceiving of history is very different from that of the age of Iamblichus; but his own mental co-ordinates were, in turn, quite different from those of the age of Pythagoras. Two major revolutions in cognitive habit had occurred in the interim: the first happened with Plato and Aristotle; the second with the arrival of Christianity.

Pythagoras was powerfully intuitive in his thinking and was learning to interpret and process that intuition through logic. The early, Ionian, pre-Socratic world is one of fulminating and transformative insights – his own, and those of Thales, Anaximander and Heracleitus. But that mental world changed rapidly and for ever with the methodology introduced by Plato and Aristotle, through their preferential emphasis on definition, verbal exegesis, the particular process of cross-questioning in the Socratic dialogue, and above all the passion for creating and perceiving categories and systems. Speculation became powerfully verbal and embodied in the written word. Their methods proved of great usefulness with time and have held good ever since; and it is for this reason that Alfred North Whitehead mischievously commented that the whole subsequent European philosophical tradition can be defined as "a series of footnotes to Plato" [2]. Yet the mental world of Aristotle in particular was at an odd angle to that of the earlier Pre-Socratic thinkers, whose intuitive insight now found its emphasis altered by the new urge to explain verbally, to systematise and to categorise. Aristotle and Plato were reasonableness itself, for sure; but the likes of Pythagoras and Heracleitus were not primarily interested in reasonableness. When we come to those writing in and after the age of Plato and Aristotle, what we hear about Pythagoras is interpreted strictly through the lens of their kind of thinking: a preference for critical analysis; for compendia of precepts (often removed from, and without relation to, their original context); for divisions and categories of the ages, physiology, humours or mental processes of human beings; for a laying out of rule-books for what is right to do and what is wrong, for diet, for behaviour. All in all, Pre-Socratic thinking had to submit to a greater concentration on technicality and on mechanical process. Thought became codified, and 'Pythagorean*ism*' was born out of what could be remembered of Pythagoras. It was already something quite different in quality however.

And then there came a second turn of the screw, another revolution in thought which followed as we move more than five centuries forward to the time of Iamblichus. As the new cult of the divinely-inspired holy person begins to permeate the Graeco-Roman world from the East with the arrival of the oriental cults of Isis and Syrian Sun-worship, and those centred on miracle-working Saviours such as Mithras and, most importantly, Jesus Christ, the method of writing about great figures from the past is changed to fit these new stereotypes, and to portray its subjects in similar light. Pythagoras, now long dead, is swept along in this current and, in the re-creations of his life by Porphyry and Iamblichus, he is seen through this lens. He becomes a sort of 'Saint Pythagoras'. He is even, at one level, put forward as a figure to be set up in comparison to Jesus – for Iamblichus even, as a sort of 'proto-Jesus' figure.

Iamblichus almost certainly assumed he was doing a great service both to Pythagoras and to history by re-casting Pythagoras as a holy man or saviour in this way. Hence the enthusiasm with which he recounts miraculous happenings, the swooning adoration with which Pythagoras was received wherever he went, the saintly and ascetic life he led and promoted, and the devotion with which his disciples laid down their bodies on the floor of a burning house to create a pathway so that the Master could escape unharmed. This was stirring stuff for the early Christian period, but how does it help us in the 21st century to get closer to the original Pythagoras? It is leading us, in fact, in the opposite direction. Some of the ingredients in Iamblichus's narrative will be based on a degree of truth, but since they have been mixed, blended and cooked into a minestrone, we find it almost impossible to distinguish them or separate them out any more.

The official story is that around 530 BC Pythagoras de-camped from Samos and moved to Croton in Southern Italy. The great majority of the material with which all the three biographers mentioned above are concerned relates to this second period of Pythagoras's life. It is the world of the beginnings of Pythagoreanism that really interests them, more than Pythagoras himself. It is difficult for us to recognise the same Pythagoras we have been speaking about so far in these pages, in the Pythagoras who emerges from the later histories which describe his activities as a cult leader, obscurely present in the cities of Magna Graecia in Italy. On the one hand we have the half-dozen resonating perceptions of Pythagoras that formed the first part of this book: on the other, we have the opaque accounts of religious secrecy, ritualism and quasi-miraculous happenings, devotedly recounted by our later historians regarding the Pythagorean academies of Southern Italy. We are left struggling with a square peg and a round hole. Either we have to explain this in the manner already implied – that it is simply the very different mentality of Porphyry and Iamblichus that leads them to compose their own Pythagorean agenda and to embellish, perhaps sometimes even invent, the material; or else we have to assume that something more radical has happened.

One possible way to resolve this question is to suppose that there has been a specific confusion in the transmission of the history regarding two different individuals. Because the essential biographical detail which our historians were using regarding Pythagoras is so intrinsically vague and contradictory, and often rhetorically back-written from later times, there is no conclusive reason to say that this is not possible. I understand and share the desire for a simple, logical, unified narrative – that Pythagoras left Samos for Italy where he lived out his final years and died: to say, in this way, that there was only one Pythagoras is by far the easiest and most reasonable assumption. But nothing leads us to say this with certainty or to contradict with equal certainty that there may in fact have been two Pythagorases confused here – our Samian Pythagoras, and another early and very charismatic Pythagorean follower.

If we possessed just one credible reference from someone contemporary with Pythagoras, from Anaximander or Xenophanes, or a barb from Heracleitus to the effect that, "Pythagoras, thank the gods, has finally pushed off to Italy…" – just one comment about him going there, then at least we could be relatively sure that our Pythagoras-of-the-early-insights was the same as the one who is said to have set up the academies in Croton and in other cities in Italy. What we have instead is a singularly unhelpful statement from Diogenes Laertius, to the effect that, "There were four men of the name of Pythagoras living about the same time and at no great distance from one another" [3]; after which he adds yet another five to the list, also of the same name. Among these nine Pythagorases were two sculptors, two athletes and/or athletics trainers, a man of Croton "with tyrannical leanings", a "bad orator", and a doctor "who wrote about hernia". One, already mentioned, was from Croton, and three of the others from Samos, including our Pythagoras, the philosopher. Diogenes had no earthly reason to make such information up: it is far too trivial a detail. But the potential for creative confusion here was immense. The reference in both Porphyry and Iamblichus to Pythagoras appearing in two different cities at the same time [4], suggests that something strange may be going on in any case.

The influence of a kind of teaching called "Pythagorean" was undoubtedly quite widespread across the area of Southern Italy by the end of the 6th century BC. The question is whether that was built around the same person of Pythagoras that we have been talking about so far, or around someone else who transmitted Pythagorean teaching to Italy, in the way that Saint Paul, rather than Jesus himself, transmitted the idea of Christianity to the Greek world and ultimately to Roman Italy. Paul's teaching is very different from that of Jesus; and he contributed perhaps more than any to the establishment of a Christian 'Church', theology and brotherhood – in just the same way as a Pythagorean theology and brotherhood was being created in Magna Graecia half a millennium earlier.

Saint Paul and Jesus had quite different names and cannot be confused. Pythagoras has the same name throughout his life: so is it merely perverse to suggest that there may be more than one Pythagoras involved in his story?

Let us suppose – for the sake of the thought-experiment itself and for what it might show us – that knowledge of the heard teachings of the charismatic figure of Orpheus had spread to the shores of Italy and had begun to acquire a considerable following; and supposing there were a citizen in one of the cities there who also, by chance, possessed the not uncommon Greek name 'Orpheus' and was therefore, quite naturally, attracted to the cult for that reason. Perhaps he even felt that because of his name the cult was in some way destined for his guidance or that he had a prior claim through his name to further it and to be its evangelist. He might set himself thoroughly to study the tenets of the cult, yet being of a quite different cast of mind, he would understand them in a different manner. He was clever, but did not have the spiritual insight and revelation of Orpheus himself; yet, in spite of that, he was successful at using his name as a sort of talisman which brought him fame and ultimately political influence. Throughout all this, however, he preferred to keep many aspects of the cult and its teaching secret so that not too many difficult questions were asked of him. He preferred even to hide his person and to speak to people from behind a veil.

This may all seem far-fetched: but the secrecy issue in respect of Pythagoras raised some questions for us already in the previous chapter. And Iamblichus, in his description of the process of Pythagorean initiation [5], relates that, during the long period of five years of silence to which he says initiates were bound, they could hear Pythagoras speak only from behind a veil or a screen and were

The Wizard of Oz, discovered behind his screen, declaring "Exactly so! I am a humbug".
Illustration by William Wallace Denslow for the children's novel,
"The Wonderful Wizard of Oz" by L. Frank Baum, 1900.

not allowed to see his face – something that recalls the ploys used by the Wizard of Oz. Is this really consonant with the picture of Pythagoras we have built up so far through the study of his early, inspirational thought?

And what if the person deliberately hidden behind this veil might not be either who or what he purported to be? And, in any case, could Iamblichus not be telling us inadvertently more about the nature of those early religious societies or secret brotherhoods which required initiation – Christian, Mithraic, Isaic and other – which existed in his own times, than he was telling us about the reality of Magna Graecia eight hundred years before the time he wrote?

Iamblichus inhabited a culture of a prevalent 'religiosity': Pythagoras did not. Spirituality and religion are not just different aspects of the same thing, they are different worlds. There may be some areas in which they intersect – at times even beneficially; but they stem from quite different human impulses. Spirituality is a quality of being; religion is an extension of social collectivity. They have little of necessity to do with one another. Religion involves a tribalisation of belief. It sets parameters of identity, faith, inclusion, exclusion, initiation, and authority both social and intellectual – many of the things which Iamblichus describes in his account of the Pythagorean Life. Religion is something that, by its nature, polarises as much as it unites. The spectacle of the often acrimonious arguments and fights between the inheritors of many kinds of sublime teaching recur throughout history and are no more edifying or infrequent than are family disagreements over the will of a much loved relation: Saint Paul, who never met Jesus of Nazareth, took issue against both Saint James, the brother of Jesus, and Saint Peter, the disciple whom Jesus apparently wished to be his inheritor; Ali ibn Abi Talib, the Prophet's son-in-law, took issue in a question of precedence against Abu Bakr, the Prophet's father-in law. There were fierce dissensions between the inheritors of the teachings of Confucius, the Buddha and Saint Francis; of Karl Marx and Chairman Mao. And we still live in our own times with the violent heredity of factional conflicts within Christianity and Islam. Pythagoreanism was also to have its fair share of distracting dissension. But this was a function of Pythagoreanism becoming a religion, not of Pythagoras himself or of his interest in the spiritual life.

In conclusion, all that we can say for sure is that, in the late sixth century BC, Pythagoras either in physical person or in reputation alone, arrived on the shores of Italy. That much is clear. Our alternatives at this point are three: the status quo; a very far shot; or a compromise. The status quo means holding with the official narrative and trying to make significant allowances for those very different, very tinted lenses through which the later historians were viewing their subject. The far shot, on the other hand, means supposing the existence of a second Pythagoras, a 'Pythagorean St Paul', who gave the philosopher's ideas the structure, ritual and theology it later acquired; and that this person adopted the persona of Pythagoras, and was perhaps even of the same name. But since this choice depends upon our instincts regarding a difference in manner of thinking, and since there is no positive evidence for it but only an absence of negative evidence, it should perhaps be our last resort. The compromise remains, however: it suggests that Pythagoras did come to Croton in person but was not destined to live there for very long; he came, he spoke, he laid out some ground rules, and that soon after his own demise not many years later, the cult took off in the hands of others and adopted a much more rigid and dogmatic and technical character; it began to assume the characteristics of the religion which Iamblichus describes, while, at the same time, the legends about the deceased founder took to the air. It is curious that the death of Pythagoras is as vague as everything else in his life and the versions are as contradictory as ever. No one can say for certain that he died here or there, in this year or that, in this or that manner, or whether he died of old age, was lynched, starved, or apotheosised and assumed into heaven. It is strange that no one at the time recorded the fact or the manner of his dying authoritatively. It would not have been a difficult thing to do for a person who was apparently so particularly significant to his contemporaries. It leads to the suspicion that he may well have died long before.

I have raised these spectres simply in order to say what has been obvious all along: that unfortunately very little of what was later written about Pythagoras can be taken at face value, and therefore we should not recoil from treating as quite separate things what we can deduce about Pythagoras's revelatory thinking from the few contemporary references to him on the one side, and what we are told much later about the things that transpired in his name in Croton, on the other. The first is a matter of great philosophical and spiritual importance to us and relates to the man himself; the second is a matter of fascination for the anthropologist and the historian of religion, and relates to the cult of Pythagoreanism rather than to Pythagoras. It therefore belongs to a different kind of study from this one.

---

[1] Benedetto Croce, *Teoria e Storia della Storiografia*, 1916.

[2] Alfred North Whitehead, *Process and Reality* (Gifford Lectures, University of Edinburgh 1927-8).

[3] Diogenes Laertius, *Vitae Philosophorum*, VIII.1.46 & 47

[4] Porphyry, *De Vita Pythagorae*, 27

[5] Iamblichus, *Life of Pythagoras*, 17

The endeavour of archaeology: piecing together a Bronze Age wall-painting from a myriad fragments.
Theran art of the 17th Century BC, from Xeste 3 at the site of Akrotiri on Santorini,
now in the Museum of Prehistoric Thera, in Firá.

Known generally as the 'Saffron Gatherer', this remarkably beautiful mural appears to depict a young woman (left) in a flounced skirt emptying a basket of saffron crocus onto a low offering-table. To the right of the picture, a goddess, wearing fine necklaces, sits on a winged throne; and, in the centre, a monkey, painted blue, acts as intermediary by offering a crocus flower to the goddess from the foot of the steps below her throne.

Depictions of crocus flowers dot the background of the picture.

The curse of Fragmentariness

The last and most obvious obstacle we encounter in trying to grasp the identity and the thought of a figure such as Pythagoras is one that is generic to the study of Antiquity – its philosophy, its art, its architecture, its poetry, its science, its everything: the lamentable fragmentariness of what has survived. The few words that remain from all that Pythagoras said and taught in his life would not even line the bottom of a small bucket; while the *Critique of Pure Reason* by Immanuel Kant has, alone, about two hundred thousand words. Why do we still trouble ourselves with what has been almost entirely reduced to dust?

To understand the magnitude of the problem, let us imagine a scenario. A cataclysm destroys the heritage of European art; all that remains are some salvaged household items from which future generations may reconstruct our art and material culture. What could they ever hope to understand of the real and immediate effect of a great painting by Botticelli or of the complexity of the Sistine Chapel from a few ceramic plates and some tableware decorated with famous images taken from these same masterpieces of Renaissance art, fragments of which happened, by chance, to have survived destruction? Not much. Yet this is, in effect, what we have left of the art of Antiquity: some decorated pottery, damaged copies made in another medium and in another age, fragments of sculpture – little more. When today we try to imagine the impact that the statue of the *Aphrodite* of Cnidos by Praxiteles may have had on the viewer, we are facing a similar situation. "Unforeseen amazement at the goddess's beauty seized us …" recalls the speaker, Lycinus, in the *Erotes* dialogue of Lucian of Samosata [1], after making a visit to Cnidos especially to see the *Aprhrodite*. The sculpture was, like Botticelli's *Birth of Venus*, one of the most celebrated works of art of its age: it became one of the earliest, artistic 'tourist attractions' of Hellenic Antiquity, drawing visitors such as Lucian on the long journey to Cnidos in Asia Minor. The original work itself is long lost, however, and all that we possess are mutilated copies and copies-of-copies executed by artesans working

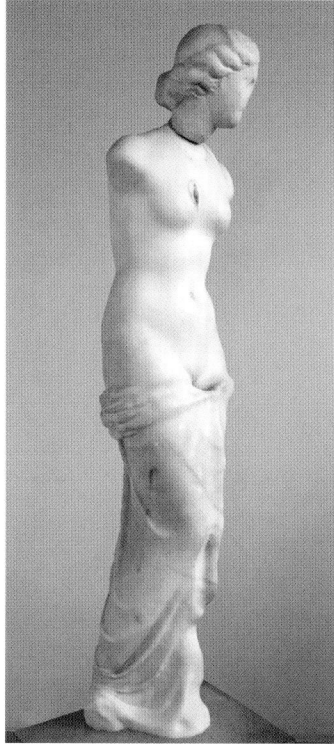

The so-called "Marine Venus", a mid-2nd c. BC memory of the Aphrodite of Cnidos of Praxiteles found on the sea bed near Rhodes. (Archaeological Museum, Rhodes.)

often centuries later – one of which happened ironically to be the inspiration for Botticelli's *Venus* [2], eighteen centuries later. Furthermore, we see these copies today in contexts (museums, galleries, books and magazines etc.) which are quite different from that of the original setting where the sculpture rose from a reflecting pool of still water inside a small temple with two entrances, set in the midst of a garden of flowering plants and trees, as Lucian describes it for us. How can we understand what effect it would have had, when all that remain are these poor and often amputated copies set up in lifeless museum galleries?

We have no shortage of verbal descriptions by ancient writers such as Athenaeus, Pausanias and Pliny the Elder, of the wonders of Ancient Greek painting and of the great works by the painters Polygnotus, Apelles, Protogenes and Zeuxis. Pliny recounts the famous anecdote of a bunch of grapes painted by Zeuxis which was so masterfully naturalistic that birds, believing the fruit to be real, would come to peck at the painting [3]. Yet, not a single portable painting has survived from Ancient Greece into modern times: not even one. In fact, with the exception of a few painted funerary chambers in Greece and Southern Italy we have no ancient Greek figurative, polychrome painting whatsoever dating from after the prehistoric period. By sheer good luck, a school of hybrid Greco-Egyptian painting of remarkable naturalism, first discovered almost two hundred years ago in excavations in the Oasis of Faiyum in Egypt, has survived

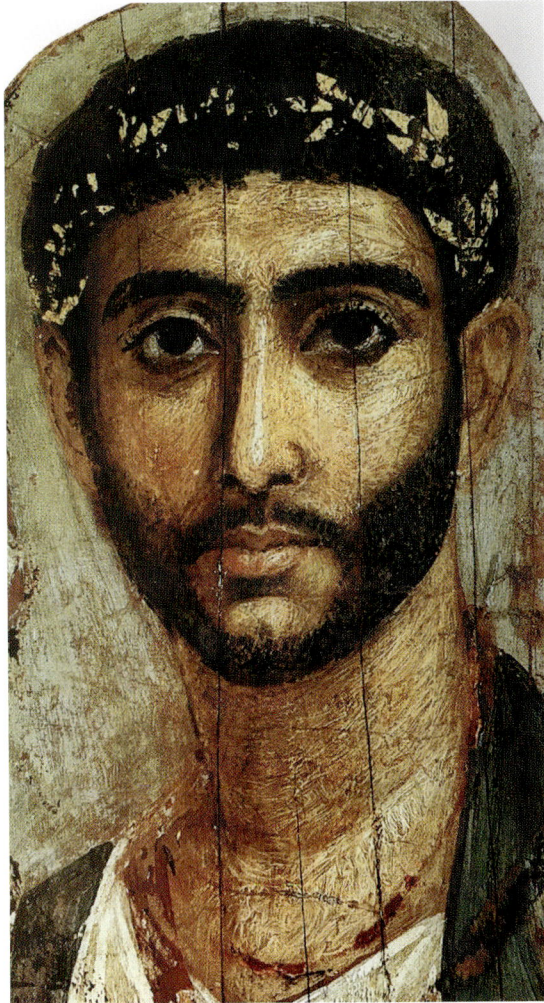

Greco-Egyptian portrait of a young soldier in encaustic technique
from the Rubayat Necropolis of Ancient Philadephia, Faiyum, Egypt.
Roman period, early 2nd century AD.
(Vorderasiatisches Museum, Berlin.)

to give us some intimation of the arresting quality of Ancient Greek portraiture. These were, in fact, no more than routine, funerary portraits painted by local artesans: but their striking beauty serves to underline the immensity of our loss in possessing no major Ancient Greek painting any more.

We do however have a considerable quantity of vase-painting, much of which survived because it was protected in burial chambers. But what can we really understand of the colour and magnificence of Antiquity's larger wall-paintings or set pieces from the mostly monochrome figurations on funerary or domestic pottery that may have been copied from them? Many ancient works of Greek painting were so famous that they were repeatedly copied in the murals of Pompeian houses in Italy centuries later. But the painters of those houses – who were not great artists but rather competent decorators paid by the square metre – had most likely never seen the originals which they were repeating, and they would possibly have been working from something like the Mediaeval artists' pattern-books of which some examples have survived. Given this, can we really expect these remote copies to tell us of the true quality of the original work any more than we would expect a decorator's version of the *Mona Lisa* found, somewhat damaged, in a suburban villa in a seaside resort to give us a sense of the genius of Leonardo da Vinci and of the living presence of his paintings? The celebrated mosaic of Alexander confronting Darius at the Battle of Issus, which covered the floor of a rich merchant's reception room in Pompeii, is a work of astonishing skill, psychological drama and aesthetic coherence: Pliny mentions a lost painting by Philoxenos of Eretria, of the 4th Century BC[4] on which it may have been based. What then might the original have been like? And can a mosaic copy ever tell us about the subtleties of effect which are inherent in great painting? Again, imagine for a moment Leonardo's *Mona Lisa* copied four hundred years later in a mosaic of tiny stone and ceramic *tesserae* … How can we even come close to an understanding of the painting of Antiquity from these fragments and approximations?

With sculpture and architecture the situation is no better. We are heirs only to the shattered ruins of buildings, bereft of their intricate decorative and chromatic surfaces and void of the light effects which they once possessed. And, out of the several thousand (according to Pliny's estimate) life-size, bronze figures which adorned the sanctuaries and cities of Greece, less than forty (life-size or more than life-size) examples have survived into our own age: some are

*Detail of a masterfully fore-shortened fleeing horse, from a Roman mosaic floor
in Pompeii, depicting the Battle of Issus.
Copy of a lost Greek original by Philoxenos of Eretria, of the 4th c. BC
(National Archaeological Museum, Naples.)*

not complete, some damaged, and all lack the subtle finishings which, for the ancient eye, gave them their perfection. Stone sculpture may have fared better quantitatively, because it was a less valuable material and less convenient to pillage; but, more often than not, the marbles that have survived into posterity are not only amputated and damaged, but lack the colour which once enhanced them – not to mention the beautiful effect of *ganosis*, the polishing of the marble surface with warm, tinted wax which is referred to by both Vitruvius and Pliny, and which imparted a warmth and translucence to the marble. This kind of finishing, of which not a vestige remains, appears to have been considered an art in itself: Pliny tells us that Praxiteles – sculptor of the *Aphrodite* of Cnidos – trusted only one living painter, called Nikias, to apply the colour and *ganosis* to his works [5]. These clearly must have been effects of the greatest aesthetic refinement and importance.

Valiant attempts have been made to reproduce the chromatic effect of the colours with which much of early ancient Greek sculpture was decorated, but the results are mostly unhappy. Colour is a phenomenon of immense complexity and subtlety: hue, transparency, tonality, the depth that a medium of application, or the treatment after application, may impart to it, are considerations every bit as important with ancient sculpture as they are with a Flemish painting of the Early Renaissance. Just because there are archaeologically verifiable traces of pigment still surviving on some statuary does not mean that the pure unadulterated colour which has survived was all that there was; or that it was not treated and modified with subtler surfaces above. It may only be what remains of an under-painted tone. All that archaeology can tell us is that there was colour in places on statuary, and what that *base* colour was; but it cannot give us a picture of the ultimate surface appearance. It tells us no more about the actual physical appearance of a masterpiece than saying that the sky in the background of a lost altarpiece by Giovanni Bellini was apparently blue.

And yet, in spite of all this – in spite of our ignorance of the original appearance, the lack of crucial context and the terrifying fragmentariness of the ancient art and architecture we have inherited – we turn to it, and we still find it compelling and moving. It still enters into a powerful dialogue with us, and this very fact should be of importance to us when we are confronted with the comparable fragmentariness of Pre-Socratic philosophy. Our aesthetic response to objects is no simple matter, and many elements participate to give

Fragment of the face of a female divinity in painted terracotta, 8th century BC.
Paolo Orsi Archaeological Museum of Siracusa, Sicily.

us pleasure. We respond to the perfection of certain formal details or of a captured visual phrase which are seen perhaps more intensely because of the absence of context. Often, though, it is the hidden-ness, the fleeting glimpse of something perceived only partially, the pull of ambiguity and mystery, which draws our imagination into the empty spaces and lacunae of ancient art. The imagination and the creative instinct play – and have to play – a vital role in our response to what is left to us of Antiquity. Its appeal is of a quite different nature from that which we may derive from great Dutch portraiture or the landscapes of Impressionist painters, and it stimulates a whole other area of the geography of our psyche. Its revelatory beauty, however, remains unmistakeable.

If the Ancient painters and sculptors of the time of Pythagoras were to come to our twenty-first century and see what remains to us of the creations of their era, they would be saddened of course by its terrible paucity, damage, erosion and fragmentariness. They would be mystified by our rapturous response to the impoverished bits of it that remain. The very fact that we view these incomplete pieces as something we call 'art' would be puzzling to them. The Ancient eye, in any case, seems to have viewed them quite differently – as creations with a specific narrative, ritual or social function: technical skill of execution was of paramount importance. What fascinates *us* about them, on the other hand, might be considered of negligible interest by the eye of Antiquity. Both parties would have some sense of what was mediocre and what was great; but our opinions would be unlikely to overlap.

The meaning and value of art is in a state of constant flux throughout history. Those qualities which the Greeks themselves valued in their own art, and which the Romans later cherished in it, and which the destructive Goths and the unruly Heruli failed to see in it, and which the pious saints of the Middle Ages feared in it, and which Donatello, Winckelmann and Ruskin may variously have admired and despised in it, are just so many mirrors that reflect our changing perceptions of the receding world of Antiquity. So it is also with our 'reading' of Pythagoras. There is much in common between the way we look at the art and architecture of Antiquity and the way we look at its philosophy; there is nothing wrong in that. What is beautiful in Pythagoras – the half dozen intuitions, revelations and observations at the core of his thinking – is of primary importance, and our aesthetic response to them is not misplaced. However, the elements of his legacy that were pored over later in the Hellenistic and Roman periods are a reflection of the thinking of those times, and their particular concern for technicality or dialectic.

Roman art, which copies Greek styles relentlessly, may *look* like Greek art, but it is never the same thing: it is an anxious, mechanical reworking of Greek schemes which betrays too often a hollowness at heart. Something very similar is the case with the later 'so-called Pythagoreans' and their relationship to the person and the thinking of Pythagoras. They copy as best they can from memory and from descriptions handed down through generations; but the animating lymph of the original is absent. The all-important context of the things of which Pythagoras spoke; the inflections, indignation, quizzicality, humanity or humour of the way he spoke; the colours of his way of being; the implied relations he made between one thing and other – all of this is lost. We have fragments, torsos and occasional amputated feet remaining from his teaching, unrendered and without colour. Yet, like the broken vestiges of a sculpture, they still are able to cast a spell over us.

Remains of a Hellenistic carved marble frieze at the site of
Ancient Tyre in Lebanon.

---

[1] Lucian, *Erotes* 12-14, trans. J J Pollitt.

[2] Whether the original piece which caught Botticelli's eye might have been the Medici Venus, now in the Uffizi in Florence, or the *Capitoline Venus* in the Musei Capitolini seen perhaps when he was working in Rome, or yet another as yet unidentified version, cannot be established given the lack of early information regarding the whereabouts of these pieces in the 15th & 16th centuries. The use of a very similar pose by Masaccio in his *Expulsion of Adam and Eve* for the Brancacci Chapel (c. 1425-27) suggests that something of this design was readily visible in early Renaissance Florence.

[3] Pliny, *Naturalis Historia*, XXXV

[4] Pliny, ibid, XXXV, 110

[5] Pliny, ibid, XXXV, 133

PYTHAGORAS
TODAY

Standing Buddha, from Gandhara, 1st century.
(Musée Guimet, Paris)

The Soul as
Work of Art

This striking example of the style of sculpture which emerged in the Upper Indus Basin, in the area of Gandhara on the borderlands of modern-day Afghanistan and Pakistan, during the 1st century BC exemplifies perhaps the most felicitous and beautiful conjunction of Asian and European aesthetic in the history of world art. It speaks eloquently of the movement of artistic ideas and styles across great distances and spans of time. The Gandharan artists were of an unusual heredity – a mixed Greek and Asian descent: they lived in the communities which had been seeded by Alexander the Great, and in the cities that he had founded during his sweep through the Persian Empire into Asia two centuries earlier. This remarkable hybrid gave crucial form and style to the first figurative visual art of Buddhism which had, up until then, been strictly abstract and symbolic in nature: at the same time it endowed it with a poignant humanity. In Gandhara, the Buddha appears as a human person for the first time in the history of art; furthermore, he appears dressed as a Greek teacher or philosopher. Through the long history of their interaction both in the realm of ideas and of art, the East has given sustenance to the West, and the West at other times to the East. Such is the intricate fabric of the world's artistic and intellectual history.

The Buddha as Greek philosopher: the Greek philosopher as Spiritual Guru. Two ideas from different parts of the world that became superimposed in one resonant image. In the same way, when perceptions from quite different sources and arising from opposite areas of the field of human experience come together – from within us and without, arising from a spiritual awareness inside of us and meeting with an observation of the world around us – the synergy and harmony they create can take us by surprise. As the musical demonstration of Pythagoras had shown, when two or more tones sound in perfect harmony (either together or sequentially), their beauty and their effect upon us is greater, by far, than the simple sum of their individual elements. It is for this reason that *harmonía* is central to everything that Pythagoras said and believed. We know instinctively when an intuition within us overlaps and resonates with a reality we perceive outside. It transforms what we see and how we see it. We cannot say in words what that sensation is, but we know it when we encounter it. This is the reason for which Pythagoras laid words and explanations aside and allowed the simple acoustic experiment to speak for itself. Those who understood what it meant, understood. Those who didn't see any significance in it – well, in another life, they would have the opportunity to understand perhaps.

Pythagoras is a horizon. He was the first mind we know of in the West to think in a truly integral manner about our world, our place within *it*, and *its* place within the cosmos. He was the first person to talk about all this without resorting to myth, anthropomorphic deities or allegorical narrative. And he was the first person to show how it was beauty that gave meaning to this whole – the beauty of underlying harmony and of a universal mathematical order. Others such as Anaximander and Thales before him had spoken abstractly of the design of the cosmos, but they did not choose to explore the participation of the human soul within it; while others such as Hesiod and Pherecydes had spoken in an allegorical manner about humanity within the cosmos, but without relating it to a rational cosmic structure. The perceptions of Pythagoras, for sure, built upon those of his older contemporaries. Yet we like to consider him as one of the creators, in his time, of a quite new way of thinking; and, although the reality is more complex, for convenience we conceive of that way as characteristically 'Western' because of the primacy he gave to number and geometry in his conception of the ordered cosmos. This laid important ground for the prevalently scientific method we use to understand our world today. But unlike his predecessors, Pythagoras was unable to leave aside from his enquiry the participation of the human soul. In this way he shows how great a part of his instinct remained within the sphere of what we would consider to be 'Eastern' thinking whose roots went deep into Asia and Ancient India. He was, in short, a creation of both East and West.

For him the mathematical study of acoustics could never just stop there, but led inevitably to a consideration of the significance of those sensations – of beauty and of rightness – which the quality of sounds gave rise to within us, and thence to the greater concepts of harmony and alignment that they suggested: that, in turn, brought him back again to *kósmos* – the arrangement and the beauty-within-arrangement which gave both existence and meaning to the universe we inhabited. Nor was he able to ignore those ideas about the journeying human 'soul', its immortality and its transformations which he was hearing from the ancient thinking of Asia. His genius, however – or rather his particularity – was to aspire to bring these two worlds together and to understand their relationship: both the world as understood by the mind *and* the world as lived by the soul; outer nature and inner life; science and spirit. Much has been made in the history of ideas of the undeniable influence of Pythagoras on the thinking of Plato, even if Plato himself seems never to have wished openly to acknowledge this: that influence however consists primarily in this one thing – the exploration of the interconnectedness of the soul with the material world of our experience.

The much earlier world of Pythagoras, however, was, in an important respect, quite different from that of Plato. Pythagoras lived on the threshold of the revolution which writing and the written word were to bring to human thought. Even though some of his contemporaries did leave written works behind, most of the speculation of their age flourished instead in the realm of live speech, above all in teaching, and also in living poetry and even in song. 'Song' may surprise us; but song is older even than language itself and spoken language has grown out of song. Sound and music possess profound meaning, and Pythagoras realised this. He is the first human being we know of who based his understanding of the world around him on an observation about the nature of audible harmony; and this remains a measure of his originality. Words, written or spoken, were not the only, or even the best, vehicle for his thinking: sound and mathematics were more finely adapted to his ends.

Yet this was precisely where his problems began. After his death, as the recording and writing down of speculation in words rapidly became more widespread, thinking became by this same process less intuitive and more word-oriented. What is crucial here is the particular nature of the written language which was evolving in the human mind. Since its very beginnings writing had been used primarily for practical ends, such as compiling inventories, recording information, or the codification of regulations, laws and treaties. All kinds of speculation, material and spiritual, therefore, had to adapt to a kind of linguistic expression whose character and structure was preferentially, and in origin, legalistic. Slowly, a kind of logical argumentation similar to the legal 'court process', with voices speaking for and against, became the norm in philosophical discourse – although how strictly 'normal' it actually is, remains open to question.

This was a language and a method that was little suited to the insights – part musical, part aesthetic and part mathematical – which interested Pythagoras. In the powerful machinery of logical sequences and Socratic dialogues which Plato and his followers promoted, what could still be recalled of Pythagoras's thinking was masticated, regurgitated and slowly transformed into something that would become quite different from its original nature. Later on, commentators and the "so-called Pythagorean thinkers" – as Aristotle disdainfully calls them – set to work on it too, plucking it more like a chicken than a musical instrument. And finally under the pressure of Christian theology – the intellectual juggernaut of subsequent centuries in the West – it succumbed and was flattened. Only much later, and then only fragmentarily, would pieces of its skeleton be exhumed around the time of the European Renaissance.

The survival and the perishing of ideas has always been a complex and unpredictable phenomenon. Many of the perceptions that great thinkers of the past have had are so effortlessly profound and clear that they are soon lost or overlooked. Ideas are akin to delicate plants that grow in a garden: theirs, too, is a mortal struggle for the light and for attention. Sometimes they survive; sometimes they don't. Nothing guarantees that they will not wither or be overwhelmed by weeds. But the greatest danger of all for an idea is when it is zealously embraced and propagated by those who only partially understand it. It becomes for them a talisman of power. They wish to possess it, to make it their own, to embellish it, to use it to their own ends and to entice others under their dominion with it, and, in the process, the idea itself becomes exhausted or changed beyond recognition. Even those who have the best intentions can inadvertently bring death to a way of seeing or thinking if they do not truly understand it. The thought will have occurred to us all about what exactly the Buddha or Jesus of Nazareth or the Prophet Mohammed might now have to say if they returned to the world of today to witness what is widely perpetrated in their name by those who claim to be their greatest supporters and interpreters. Pythagoras would recognise this problem, too. Once ways of thinking become 'tribalised' or institutionalised, a necrosis soon sets in; and slowly the core truth begins to decompose. This is what happened to the thought of Pythagoras in later Antiquity; and the objective of this book has been to lay that corrupting 'religiosity' aside, and to seek out from the confused and fragmented legacy of his thought those few luminous and transformative observations which

Pythagoras left with us.

The other thing about which we know Pythagoras spoke, in a manner that was undogmatic and undemonstrative, was the journeying of the human soul from one existence to another. The idea that our lives may not be just one, but many, is something which emerges from Xenophanes's anecdote of the philosopher and the dog. But if they are many, why is this so?

The evolution of a soul – that 'cosmos' in itself of desires, habits, thoughts, memories and intentions which constitutes our identity – across many lives, is like the careful bringing into being of a work of art. The artist who creates something new does so by combining and giving an ordered relationship to many different elements. Those elements need to work together, both functionally and in harmony in order to give rise to something that will be meaningful as an artistic creation – a painting, a song, a design, a building, a dance, a film, a story, a poem or any other product of the imagination. All this involves a complex process of refinement, of trial and discarding, of combination and interweaving, of reflecting and modifying, throughout the alternating despondency and excitement which characterise the creative process. Its end – the moment at which the composition may be deemed to be a finished work – is always elusive and arbitrary. No work of art reaches perfection; but it does aim constantly towards it. It is like this also with our many existences. We need the cycles of reincarnation in order to create, enlarge, correct and modify that 'work of art' which our soul is becoming. We have to learn and to reflect on our selves over many existences. We have to bring disparate elements into harmony, and make incarnate the soul's evolving composition from within. The process is one of creation and perfection: it is slow and cannot come about in a single life alone.

The diverse origins and the different routes of transmission of the concept of reincarnation, before the time of Pythagoras, are obscure and will for long be the subject of scholarly debate. The particular form in which Pythagoras took the idea seems most likely to derive from the intellectual milieu of the seventh and sixth centuries BC in Northern India, where the Sanskrit *Upanishads* were written: but this is far from certain. The understanding which he had of acoustic harmony, on the other hand, seems clearly to have derived from Babylon. In the mind of Pythagoras these two very different ideas come together for the first time. They suggested that the cycle of our many lives serves us like the tuning of an instrument, bringing our soul ever closer towards a perfect harmonic clarity. Once that is achieved it will have no need to be reincarnated or worked upon any further. Both life and death are processes of 'tuning', tempering, and of purification. The world itself – full of conflicted evil as much as beauty – is a realm of purification. The process is slow. At moments it can appear to stall or to turn back: but even when it does, it is still a way of learning and of purification. In this sense, the idea of transmigration and reincarnation is not without ultimate hopefulness. It does not aim to give us a logical explanation, but rather to help us balance the understandable emphasis which we give to our own self and our identity in this particular life, with an equal awareness of the greater whole to which we belong; to impress upon us the inter-dependency of living things in this world as well as the inter-dependency of our own many existences; to make us aware of the tree itself to which we belong, and not just the blooms which we momentarily are.

A weeping cherry tree in Matsumoto, Japan, in flower.

But what if the tree to which we belong begins to sicken? What are the blooms to do and think, when the tree itself, the source of their life, is in danger?

Pythagoras and our Garden of Eden

Asked about the uncertainty of the future, and speaking of the weight of apprehensions and fears that he observed to be latent in the dreams of his patients in the years following the Second World War, Carl Jung said in a televised interview in 1959: "the real danger that exists is Man himself. *He* is the great danger. And we are pitifully unaware of it. We know nothing of Man… far too little. His psyche should be studied because we are the origin of all coming evil."

Carl Jung, in 1950.

The impassioned emphasis of this wise and distinguished man on those words "*He* is the great danger, and we are *pitifully* unaware of it" is somehow hard to forget. What should we do with a danger of which we are so pitifully unaware, and which originates within our selves?

We live today – as Jung would willingly have conceded were he still alive – with a new and troubled state of mind in which the termination of our existence as a human race has begun to take conceivable form. In the estimation of some ecologists, an imminent environmental collapse on our planet is not just possible, but probable. We have for too long suppressed that sense of communality with the surrounding world and with its other living beings, of which Pythagoras speaks. We have come to view the world as an object and its creatures as slaves. We have exploited the natural world so relentlessly and so ruthlessly for what we think of as our 'needs' that it seems that we are now set to realise the consequences of that aggression.

This is dismaying, for sure; but why should it surprise us? We knew this from the beginning. Ra, the greatest and oldest of the deities of Ancient Egypt, grew so disenchanted with the lack of respect shown by the human beings to whom he had given life that he asked his own daughter, Hathor, to destroy humanity on his behalf in her terrifying guise as the lion-headed Sekhmet. A number of humans did survive, but only because Ra was so sickened by the slaughter he had provoked that he relented and managed to trick his daughter – now crazed by the lust for blood – into stopping her massacre. A similar divine impulse to

An image of Sekhmet, from Ancient Thebes, early 14th C. BC –
with the face of a lioness and the body of a woman.

destroy humanity is found in the Ancient Mesopotamian legend of Atrahasis. In the *Book of Genesis* also, humans were first of all evicted from the paradise they had been given and then, not long after that, destroyed by the Flood from which Noah and his family alone survived. Much later, Plato writes in similar vein about the destruction of Atlantis. It seems we have known all along about our bad behaviour. Nor are any of these narratives divine revelations: they are stories created by us. They are our own human voice speaking about ourselves.

On the question of our earthly survival, the religious faiths of the West have little guidance to offer us: our natural environment is not something they contemplate as such – except, rather curiously, as a point of departure. The story of the expulsion from the Garden of Eden comes right at the very beginning of the Judaeo-Christian narrative: it is not the concluding calamity, but rather the episode that starts it all off. If we are facing a calamity today, it will involve devastating change for sure. It will be painful at first, just as it was for Adam and Eve: the prospect of expulsion viewed from within the Garden must have been hair-raising for them. But it is possible that our changed state could also become, just as it did for them, the beginning of a new way of being for humanity. Once again our relation to all that surrounds us will change from that which we have known up until now. It will be another turn of the wheel of transformation, as if the cosmos itself were unfurling and our place in it spilling out like seeds from a blown flower.

The story of Eden, which is perhaps the most radical of all the myths in our psyche, is an all-or-nothing transformation; there is nothing gradual about it. One minute we are in the Garden, the next minute we are shown the door. This suddenness of drastic transition is a characteristic of many of the stories of our ancestors about creation and extinction. One minute there is chaos, and the next there is the world with everything in it. One minute humanity is created and the next it is flooded out of existence. One minute we are in this world, the next minute we are awoken at a Day of Reckoning and are sent to heaven or hell for eternity. There is little space afforded for adaptation.

Nature, on the other hand, is full of processes which are more gradual. We may have reservations about the mechanics of what is described in Darwin's *Origin of Species*, but what we should take away from Darwin's thinking is not so much the technicalities of what he describes, but the overarching perception that nature is everywhere in a constant state of evolution and self-transformation,

Giovanni di Paolo, The Creation, and the Expulsion from Paradise, c. 1445 ;
Metropolitan Museum, New York.

often in ways that to us seem strange and hard to comprehend. In early human history our consciousness was enmeshed within the fabric of the natural environment to such a degree that our inter-connection with it was seamless. It was as if the natural phenomena which surrounded us dwelt as much within us as around us. But with time, the act of observing, of noticing the cycles of days and seasons and the distinction between the predictable and the unpredictable in nature's manifestations, as well as a need to understand the reasons behind the fear and respect which they inspired, slowly and imperceptibly fashioned a different consciousness within us that began to balance that primordial 'oneness' of before with a new sense of 'separateness' at the same time. It was a process that never stood still but evolved unobserved, at times substantially altering course as it did with the new realm of awareness opened up for us by the thinking of Pythagoras and his contemporaries. This delicate equilibrium of oneness and separateness was always altering but it held good until the arrival of the technological advances of the last two hundred years, at which point the balance began noticeably to go awry.

The curious irony at the heart of all this is that Pythagoras, at the same time as advancing the awakening of a greater consciousness in our minds, is also part of the problem. Great thinkers of all ages and places change the trajectory of our thinking with their perceptions. They show us a 'hill' from which we can see the labyrinth from a higher or different vantage point. The very early Greek thinkers whom we group together under the title of Pre-Socratic philosophers, in particular, began to open the way to what we now understand as scientific thinking. And Pythagoras, by conceiving of the cosmos as an all-surrounding construct of order and great beauty, taught our minds to stand back and to understand it as something in one sense separate from ourselves, rather than as the greater skin and flesh within which we live. In doing so he helped inadvertently to create a distinction which has troubled the thinking of every human generation since his time – the necessary, but illusory, appearance of separation in our minds between mankind and nature, humanity and environment, us and everything else. And it is this mode of vision which is the foundation of the deeply problematic way in which we treat the natural environment today.

Yet without his thinking on the other hand, and without that implied separation and standing back from experience which he encourages in us, we could have neither the understanding we possess of our existence nor the wonderment and enrichment which we feel at the beauty of our particular cosmos. What, after all, can a 'sense of beauty' really mean in the pre-Pythagorean world? The early human mind must have experienced its interaction with its environment through a kaleidoscope of powerful moods and sensations of all kinds. But the *idea* of beauty as we understand it, and its evocation of harmony and goodness, can only come about by standing back and contemplating what is around us and asking what it is and how it works upon us.

A dual process has been at work therefore: as we have acquired a new level of awareness, we have lost comparably our immersion in nature – that sense of being embedded and of belonging within an organic whole. It is something we intimate only fleetingly now, and we have to work hard to regain its reassuring sensation. Pythagoras, however, lived, felt and thought both of these realities. His philosophy embraces them both, and he gave preference to neither.

When he speaks of the kinship of all living things and the soul's participation in different lives and aspects of nature through the cycles of incarnation, he speaks of our inextricable belonging to, and participating within, an organic whole. On the other hand, when he shows the universality of an equation in geometry, or the mathematical nature of the harmony which order and *kósmos* bring about, he appeals to that incorporeal beauty arising from our detached awareness of things. For him they were complementary aspects of the same *harmonía*, even though their relationship was constantly recalibrating. For him they were perfectly balanced and connected; but for us that balance has been lost, and they have become disconnected.

Our natural environment is the incarnation of a cosmic beauty. We come out from it – in this particular existence, at least – and into it we return; and for that reason we live on its sustenance, physical and invisible. In destroying it, we like to blame science and technology; but they are no more than our tools. The tool cannot be at fault, nor even the hand that guides it. It is within the mind that directs it, as Jung observes, that the problem lies.

Contrary to what is revealed for us in looking at Pythagoras, Western religious teaching has encouraged us always to think in terms of an un-crossable divide that separates us from the rest of the living natural world. For the religious faiths, this divide marks humanity out as something excellent and chosen by the deity for his special purposes; and it gives humanity the right to use the natural world and its fathomless life for its own benefit. In the interview of 1959, Jung comments with scepticism on our presuming of that 'excellence'. If we have become a danger, as he says, then it is because we have forgotten one of the most important lessons that we learn from the thinking of Pythagoras – that we are fortunate in being the conscious and incarnate part of a *kósmos*. We are fortunate to have a body and senses through which to receive, and a mind with which to understand, its beauty. That fortune inevitably brings with it a responsibility to maintain and be attentive to the *harmonía* which gives life to the cosmos. In hurting and abusing the outer reality of nature, we only hurt the inner nature of ourselves: in our destruction of it, lies its destruction of us. They are different aspects of the same process. Our subconscious awareness needs no telling that, as soon as we stop thrashing the dog, we will cease also the self-infliction of pain.

The age of Pythagoras was a fleeting moment of freedom for the human mind. It helped us to shed some of the fears that are born of superstition, and it did not yet know of those new fears which would later be brought by the great monotheistic faiths. Pythagoras and his clear-sighted contemporaries across one half of the globe – notable among them Gautama Buddha, Lao Tzu and Confucius – stood as if in a moment of calm between these two tides. The thinking of all of them aimed in different ways to free the mind of darkness and of unnecessary suffering from guilt and fear.

Even if, two and a half thousand years after his death, we still possess only the vaguest outlines of the identity and the thought of Pythagoras we do at least know that the handful of perceptions which his thinking encapsulates, and the principles which he taught through his example, were held throughout much of later history to be important as guides for a way of life which possessed both intellectual and spiritual integrity. They are few, but even so they are clear:

- *Do no deliberate harm to any living being – human, animal or plant.* The ultimate kinship between all living things and the cycle of incarnations mean that what we do to others now, we are also receiving ourselves at another point in the cycle of existence and experience. It is simple spiritual self-protection to desist from harm.

- *Foster and hold to harmony as the greatest aspiration of our earthly life and seek to understand its meaning* – harmony in all things, trivial and great, personal and general, domestic and public, from birth through to, and including, death. Things in themselves are not important: our relation to them is.

- *Look for beauty in all aspects of our life: create it and cultivate it with care.* Beauty and harmony, not "virtue" alone, are what give meaning to life. Virtue is a concept invented in the mind; it is definable. Beauty may only be intuited because it partakes of the divine.

- *Respect silence and remain always receptive to intuition.* We can neither grasp nor seek out the meaning in our existence by force of will: but if we learn to be receptive, it will come to us of its own accord.

- *Train and free the mind to think and reflect,* because the habit of *philosophía* brings spiritual growth and enrichment: for this reason we should watch, listen, reflect and create.

- *Be open always to other ways of seeing and thinking* – to live the thoughts and ways of others also; to be open to diversity, and to travel in mind and in body with sensitivity to otherness.

There could be others: this is merely my selection of the most prominent ideas or principles that I see emerge from the study we have made of the fragments of Pythagoras's life and ideas in these pages.

But imagine for a moment that these deceptively simple injunctions had been the backbone of our education and of our spiritual life for the last two thousand five hundred years… We could have done much worse. In fact, in many ways we did do worse. After these two and a half millennia of human civilisation since the time of Pythagoras, we can fly to the moon, transplant organs of the body and speak to one another live over vast distances. We can do previously unimaginable things, and our minds and skills have changed out of all recognition. But can it be said that in the same long period of time we have evolved to a comparable degree as human beings? Are we spiritually or morally, or even physically, any more developed, any wiser, kinder or more humane than our ancestors in Antiquity? Even to small degree? Most of the evidence would suggest not: in fact, given the dire predicament in which we find ourselves today, it appears that we have lost, not gained, this ground.

Why has this happened? Why have the great faiths that have moulded our cultures, shaped our education, and which purport to make us better beings – why have they failed us so badly in this respect? Have two and half millennia of Judaic, two millennia of Christian, and fourteen hundred years of Islamic teachings in our Western hemisphere cumulatively made us better creatures, more sensitive to the others with whom we share this planet, whether they be our fellow humans, or animals or plants? Or made us wiser, or happier, or more fulfilled than those who lived at the same time as Pythagoras? It would not be an easy case to make. They have brought us – and still bring us – conflict, intolerance and many different kinds of social and mental subjugation. This is not a reflection on the teaching of the central figures of these several faiths, but upon the fruitless and destructive human manipulation of their words and ideas. So many centuries have passed and so few lessons have been learnt.

What has gone wrong?

If we run through the half-dozen Pythagorean touchstones listed above, we see that they have too often been repudiated by the very Faiths that have purported to educate us: 'be open to other ways of seeing and thinking'; 'free the mind to think and reflect' independently; 'respect intuition' and above all 'seek and cultivate beauty'... What happened to the respect for beauty which might have restrained us from the appalling despoiling of our planet and collective home? And as for harmony and the doing of no harm, here these same Faiths have a yet more pitiful record. This has been a tragedy not just for the thinking of Pythagoras, but for the world.

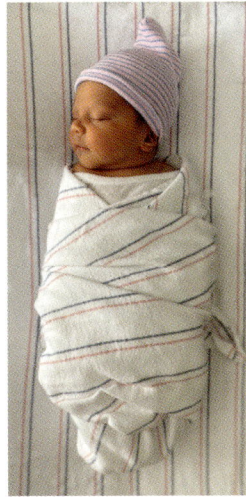

We are born with our eyes closed, and in each existence in a new way we have to learn again to see. Only by *seeing* the universe we inhabit do we ever become wiser and better beings. 'Seeing' the universe means understanding and being receptive to its beauty as Pythagoras shows us. Eye surgery and technological aids cannot help us to see in this way. Nor can the doctrinal teachings of institutional religions.

Pythagoras was not a saviour, nor did he ever pretend to be one. He simply gave us better eyes with which to see and understand. We can use them or not, as we wish.

And if we want to ask, 'Is Pythagoras, about whom we know so little and who lived so long ago, relevant for us today?', then this is the only answer I can offer.

EPILOGUE

Truth and Beauty

The vision that Pythagoras has given us of a cosmos sustained by the need for harmony, brought into being for us through *philosophía* in many existences – our own and those of others – stands and falls by its beauty as an idea. It, too, is neither more nor less than a work of art. That is not to diminish it, because all philosophies and all religions are ultimately works of art, not categorical or even possible repositories of ultimate truth. At their best they are magnificent creations of the human mind, just as extraordinary and as evocative as the imaginative impulse that brought into being the Taj Mahal, or the city of Venice, or the silent technology of our astronomical observatories. Until we begin to see a philosophical system or a religious system in this way we risk illuding ourselves about its scope. Even the Christian Church is one such vast and complex work of art, the collective endeavour of centuries with all its human pathos and beauty, and with all its contradictions, cruelties and blindnesses. Once we become convinced that it possesses an ultimate answer, we are severing our moorings: but if we look at it as a magnificent, multi-faceted work of art or as an epic of poetry and thought, then we can live at peace with it and understand it for what it truly, humanly can tell us – problems, warts and all. It can teach us an enormous amount, for sure, but it will neither save us nor damn us, nor tell us what happened to us before we were born or what will come about after we die; it will simply give us space to reflect if we allow it to, in the same way that any valid work of art does. At its best, it should aim to lift us out from the labyrinth and allow us to benefit from the wider view from the hill: but, at times, it may even do the opposite. This is just as true for Buddhism, Islam, Taoism, Pythagoreanism, and all other religious systems great or small that have ever existed. They are all remarkable testimonies to the vibrant artistic creativity of the human mind – and also to its defects and limitations.

What this book has tried to concentrate on is not the superstructure of subsequent reasoning but rather the power of the primordial insight – in this particular case, a number of transformative insights which emanate from the figure we know as Pythagoras. Although few, they were significant and revelatory. It is the structures, on the other hand, that have been built on top of those insights by his followers and by the commentators of later ages, that have led us further and further away from the insights themselves into fields of increasing irrelevance. This is a problem that lies deep in the nature of explicatory language itself, which, for the purposes of communication, tries to substitute itself for insight, but in the end never can. In just the same way, the insights of Siddhartha Gautama, of the Tao Te Ching, of Jesus of Nazareth, or of Newton, Marx and Einstein and a thousand other thinkers, teachers and scientists, are of vital importance to us, while the body of later elaboration upon their thought too often leads us, step by step, away from the power of the core insights into ever more unstable territory. Truth lives fleetingly in insight – in the elegant mathematical formula, in the parable which we never forget, in the aphorisms inscribed at the sanctuary-entrance to the oracle of Delphi or the maxims which Michel de Montaigne painted onto the rafters of his library. These insights have an independent existence of their own: they do not *belong*, as such, to the mind and voice that propounds them, which, in one sense, is only a conduit. They arise from somewhere deeper. Even Jesus is recorded as saying this. "The words that I speak unto you, I speak not of myself: but the Father that dwelleth in me, he doeth the works." [1] And the figure, known to us as John the Evangelist, who wrote those words and who was arguably the greatest artist and creator of the literary tradition of Christianity, must himself have felt the self-same thing. Heracleitus in the sixth century BC intimates the same in what is cited as the opening of his treatise *On Nature*; and Einstein in the twentieth century observes it about the manner in which philosophical and mathematical solutions came to him.

Although these pages concentrate only on certain aspects of the complex figure of Pythagoras, they have aspired to see his thought also in the wider geography, physical and cultural, of his world – its sounds, psychology, architecture and natural landscapes. No philosopher is an island, and no philosophy exists separate from the deep influence of the physical world out of which it emerges. Pythagoras's image of the cosmos – its wholeness, its internal coherence and the indivisibility of the life within it – imparted to us without any suggestion of human guilt, without pressure of faith, without fear or false hope, is a powerful expression of the clear-sighted and youthful mind of the early world of Aegean Greece, of its sea, its rugged earth and its unmistakeable brilliance of light.

A drawn tracing, made by Keats in 1819,
from an engraving of a Hellenistic Vase, signed by Sosibios,
1st c. BC (now in the Louvre, Paris)

Thinking about this remote world from his rooms in a grimy, nineteenth-century capital of Northern Europe, and viewing it through the tiny window of a drawing he had made of a decorated Hellenistic vase, which was about as close as he would ever get to the Greek world, John Keats, twenty-four years old and with tuberculosis already gnawing at his lungs, gave words to an insight which had been long waiting inside him to be born. The image which the vase offered him was of a world that was very distant, yet which to him felt strangely close. It would, he imagined, always "remain… a friend to man", teaching him that:

> *"Beauty is truth, truth beauty – that is all*
> *Ye know on earth, and all ye need to know."* [2]

Keats speaks here to the very essence of Pythagoras's thought. And the idea of being "a friend to man" would also have appealed deeply to Pythagoras who seems to have laid such emphasis on human friendship. In an age as frightening as our own, such friends are what we need and such ideas are what we must hold to.

It is curious that one of the greatest poets of the following century – perceptive and insightful as T. S. Eliot almost always is – found this couplet of Keats to be incomprehensible. "I fail to understand it… The statement of Keats seems to me meaningless." [3] I think that for much of my own life, I would have agreed with Eliot: I, too, never truly grasped what Keats meant by these words before. But now I do: and I am grateful to Pythagoras for having revealed their clear and profound significance.

John Keats,
shortly after his death, aged twenty-five, in Rome on 28 January 1821,
drawn by his friend Joseph Severn.

---

[1] John, 14, v.10

[2] Keats, *Ode on a Grecian Urn*, May 1819

[3] T.S Eliot, *Dante*, 1929

AFTER-THOUGHTS
& APPENDICES

APPENDIX 1

Celestial harmony &
Ancient music

....the isle is full of noises,
Sounds, and sweet airs, that give delight and hurt not.

(Shakespeare, *The Tempest*, Act III.ii.133/134)

Our pursuit of the arrangement of sounds into what we call melody and song is one of the strangest and most wonderful phenomena of our development as human beings. It has long been associated with magic, and we acknowledge this fact even today when we speak of a musician's performance as 'spell-binding'. Caliban, in his simple words which are the epigraph of this chapter, reminds us that the sounds and airs of music 'give delight and hurt not'. Music is not an idea or an argument or a point of view: it does not seek to explain or to convince, constrain or convert us. Even in its earliest and simplest forms, it manifests itself simply as an impulse of beauty.

Music brings together, where the tendency of language is to distance. The imperfection and approximation of language, its struggling incapacity to convey feelings or perceptions with exactitude, creates an invisible barrier. It makes us aware of the space between ourselves and others; and we rely on the support of physical and facial inflections, and modulations in the voice, to bridge the gap and to gloss what we are saying and the spirit in which we are saying it. At its greatest and best, language speaks obliquely in poetry; at its worst, it leads from differences of verbal interpretation into debate, discussion and disagreement – all things that reinforce our separateness.

Because music dissolves these distinctions rather than reinforcing them, it came more naturally to the mind of early Antiquity to share understanding through song and music rather than through the prose which increasingly dominates speculative thinking thereafter. The dramatic tragedies and comedies of Ancient Greece were intoned and always accompanied by the song and the deliberate movement of the chorus group who were located physically and metaphorically between the audience and the actors. Pythagoras preferred to avoid writing and to direct our attention towards music, for these reasons. Plato, a century later, in turning away from this very ancient manner of communication and reinforcing the primary value of word logic, transformed the nature of human cognition with his creation of the self-conscious and self-referential Socratic dialogue which has shaped the practice of philosophy and theology ever since his time. For Pythagoras, however, music and geometry always came before words.

Music has a transformative power on the human character: souls that are commonly melancholy, uncommunicative or taciturn can be transmogrified by the sound-creating instruments they play; and voices of exceptional quality emerge in song from women and men whom you could never have surmised had such music within them. The path which a skill in music cuts through humanity is rarely predictable. Children with a compelling musical genius have emerged throughout history quite unforeseen, often to the astonishment of their parents. For those who may have disabilities, in particular blindness, music can be a voice which releases the soul from within; it can help bring alive those with an emotional autism or a difficulty relating to others within society. Iamblichus tells us, among other things, that Pythagoras and his followers used music as therapy for the sick. Contrary to the rarefied world of philosophical disquisition, music illuminates mankind from the foundations up. Those who do not feel music and cannot at some moments in their life give themselves over freely to its power, are sorely disadvantaged in their worldly existence. Nietzsche famously observed that "without music, life would be a mistake" [1].

But the cosmos as music? Can such an idea have any sense? Pythagoras may have alluded only obliquely to this idea. His interest is primarily in acoustic tonal harmony; and what he may or may not have had to say about melodic music is unknown. The genesis of the poetically delightful idea of a 'harmony of the Spheres', which then became 'music of the Spheres', may have come later, acquiring its first unambiguous attribution to the person of Pythagoras only many centuries after his time, in a comment by Pliny in his *Naturalis Historia* [2]. Earlier than that, however, Aristotle, in his refutation of this idea of celestial harmony, does not mention Pythagoras by name, yet comments with characteristic pragmatism that "melodious and poetical as the theory is, it cannot be a true account of the facts" [3].

The apogee of the idea of Celestial Harmony comes with Johannes Kepler who pursued it with devotion and mathematical precision in his *Harmonices Mundi* of 1619, going so far as to explain (Book V) that our Solar System is composed as if of a choir of voices, in which the Earth and Venus were altos, Mercury a soprano, Mars a tenor, and Saturn and Jupiter were basses. Pythagoras, however, was not concerned with the mechanics of all this as it was later to be elaborated by his own followers and ultimately by Kepler; his point was that the heavens were a creation of beauty because they possessed order, and that the patterns of their movement and the apparent dance of the stars should ultimately be comprehensible to us. From Anaximander he had learnt to think in terms of the distanced separation of the planetary spheres and of how they lay one behind the other; and he may well have surmised that there was a correlation in those separations equivalent to the proportions of the harmonic intervals revealed by his monochord demonstration. In whatever way it may have been expressed, to yoke together acoustic harmony and the emerging science of the cosmos, or rather to explain one in terms of the other, was a courageous and remarkable intuition. The cosmos, and the way it might possibly work, is an idea, while the distinguishing quality of music is precisely that it is *not* an idea: rather it is something felt and understood deeply by the body and its senses.

'The body and its senses'… For the Greeks of Antiquity, μουσική – *mousikí*, was a fuller corporeal experience than 'music' as we understand it today. In its association with all of the Muses, it was rarely separable from movement and dance; and this indissoluble link is reinforced by the very arrangement of our human bodies. Nature has combined in our ears, in one and the same organ, both our response to sound and our sense of balance and awareness of movement. We referred earlier to the way in which music unites and dissolves invisible separations; with dance there is a yet deeper suspension of identity and communion between all who participate. The mind recedes; the body leads; and for a moment we sense what it is – and how benign it is – to be alive while released from ratiocination. In the unfolding of a dance; in the momentary dissolution of the individual into the sympathetic movement of a group or a couple; in the harmony of the music and song which inspires it and the rhythm that gives it structure; in the visual congruity of the movement; in the variety of physical contact between the participants; in the geometry of the figures and their changing patterns; in the display of colours; in the subliminal yet inherent charge of eros; in the transient uniformity; and in the forgetting of who we are – dance, any kind of dance – rudimentary and spontaneous, or complex and choreographed – is one of the surest and most accessible homes of human fulfilment we know of.   Happiness lies in a synergy of harmonies. So many kinds of harmony converge in dance that our physical being seems to become momentarily a harmony itself.

The Mark Morris Company in their 2015 (and frequently repeated) production of
Handel's 'L'allegro, il Penseroso ed il Moderato':
an inspirational example of the perfect integration of dance, music, words and visual spectacle.

Dance is not something marginal: it never has been. Among birds and mammals it is often the precursor to the most portentous of all moments, that of choosing a mate for procreation; among insects it is used for the communication of vital information. Between humans it exists for both. When we are in the presence of someone important to us – especially of a person we love or fear or for whom we care – our gestures become involuntarily choreographed. Dance is the ultimate extension of that body language which is innate to us all, just as music is the ultimate extension of the intonation and pausation of the human voice. The manner in which we speak to an infant or to an animal is strongly intoned, suggesting that musicality is a fundamental element in learning the skills of communication. In every-day conversation amongst ourselves we control the cadence and the pitch of our voice in order to communicate to our interlocutor all kinds of inflections and feelings that lie beyond the mere words we use. When these instinctive habits are further enhanced, and the intonation of the voice and the language of the body are shaped with order and harmony by the mind, they lead us to a different state of being. They return us, often effortlessly and without our soliciting, to the very core of our being.

From a number of papyri, inscriptions and fragments, we possess brief passages of ancient musical notation; and these have been carefully transcribed by scholars, studied and then reproduced using instruments which themselves are constructed rigorously following the design of those that have come down to us as archaeological finds, combined with a careful study of the visual and literary sources which describe them. It is tempting to think that, as a result, we can reconstruct the musical pieces that were played by the hands of ancient musicians. The result is scholarly; but it can sometimes have the astringent effect on our ears that a dish of Japanese pickles has on the palate. In part, this is because the notation defines only a skeleton and it has yet to be given that ephemeral flesh of rich improvisation. Of that we can now know nothing. We are used today to the concept of the comprehensive scoring of music, in which a piece, whether orchestral, vocal or solo-instrumental is defined, along the staves of the score, in the entirety of its notes, accents, inflections and phrasing. But a much greater proportion of the world's music throughout history is performed with improvisations – often working cumulatively out from a traditional melodic line or a familiar sequence of cadences, such as those that have survived on the ancient papyri, while building up its vital texture during the actual process of performance. This wealth of improvisation which wove around the melody line, the variety of its instrumentation, the speed and delivery, whether continuous or punctuated – all these very important elements are lost to us.

The brief stretches of notation which we have from Antiquity are almost certainly only guide-lines or mnemonics to the performers. We should never expect them to evoke the fullness of a piece of ancient music, yet there is every reason for us to suppose that ancient music would have been just as moving and beautiful and versatile for the people who listened to it then, as our own music is for us today. It may have been a thinner, purer, slower, perhaps more rarified sound, and its cadences and frequent intervals of silence might sound unfamiliar to our ears. But that does not mean it was less emotionally involving or less spiritually stimulating. For centuries a beautifully performed religious liturgy, or the recitation of an epic story, could move its listeners to tears – an effect, for the most part, lost on us today. In the far greater tranquillity of the ancient world even the sound of a distant reed-pipe well-played could elicit a shaft of joy or devotion, or a strongly elegiac sense of loss.

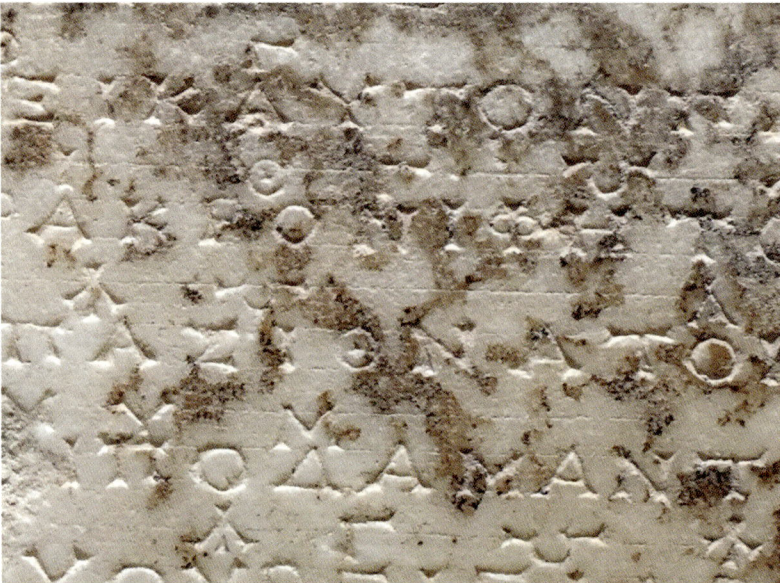

2nd century BC inscription from the Athenian Treasury at Delphi of a Hymn to Apollo, composed by Athenaios Athenaiou, with musical notation and punctuation marked above the lines of text.

---

[1] Friedrich Nietzsche, *Twilight of the Idols.* ("Ohne Musik währe das Leben ein Irrtum".)

[2] Pliny, *Naturalis Historia*, Book II, 20

[3] Aristotle, *On the Heavens*, Book II, ix.

The other end of Asia: Pythagoras, LaoTzu and Confucius

It is interesting that, at the opposite end of the Asian land mass from the world of Pythagoras, there was a comparable ferment of thinking during the same period, known in China as the Spring and Autumn Period of the Zhou Dynasty. China, in this early time, comprised many states and fiefdoms, and this gave rise to a plurality of beliefs and philosophies. Two of these in particular, however, had the critical momentum to survive and be transmitted through the subsequent generations and dynasties of Chinese history: the teachings of Confucius, and the philosophy of Taoism. There was no shortage of fruitful debate and opposition at times between these two currents of thought, but their deeply complementary nature ensured the survival of both. There is a solemnity and thoughtful traditionalism to Confucius: he directs his attention to matters of governance, family, and social responsibility in a philosophy which concerns itself with the worldly life of the human community. The unconventional appeal of Taoism, by contrast, is to the inner life and to the transcendental world of the spirit. Yet both these philosophies at heart concern themselves with the same profound question: how to bring humanity into fruitful harmony with *tian* (the celestial) and the principle of heavenly order.

Some of the same problems and ambiguities which beset us when talking about Pythagoras, also face the student of early Chinese philosophy. With Taoism there is a similar problem of biography. Popular tradition says that Lao Tzu, the spiritual figurehead of Taoism, was a historical person, and that he was the author of the *Tao Te Ching*, that he lived during the 6th century BC and worked as a court archivist. These details first take form approximately four hundred years after his supposed lifetime in a biography written in the *Shiji*, or

Lao Tzu Riding West, Mounted on an Ox. Zhang Lu, early 16th cent., ink on paper.
(National Palace Museum, Taipei, Taiwan)

Historical Records, by Sima Quian. In that account, Lao Tzu is said to have met Confucius who sought advice from him at one point, rather as a student might of a master. Notices of his life end with his travelling 'to the West' mounted on an ox, but only after leaving a written account of his thinking in the form of the *Tao Te Ching* allegedly at the insistence of a certain Yin Xi, a border guard who would not let him pass out from the western frontier of China until he had left this invaluable record behind for the guidance and enlightenment of posterity. It is a beautiful and ingenious scene. Where Lao Tzu subsequently went and where he died is not recorded: nor how far "to the West" he may have gone. Was it into the mountains of the province of Sichuan? Or was it West in the sense of the Himalayan world and India, home of the teachings of the Buddha who would probably have been his younger contemporary? Or was this journey to the West something simply metaphorical – a nod towards the inspiration for some of his thinking which lay in ancient India? And his riding on an ox, sacred animal of Hindu India – what was that really saying?

It is an abiding and comprehensible human impulse to desire an account such as this which sketches out a real human being with a real story, however unsure the truth may be, as well as a text which was authoritatively composed by a Master. But scholarship suggests something different, namely that the *Tao Te Ching* is an anthology of texts, sayings and parables from many sources and possibly from a considerable spread of periods, and that it is the product of several minds and traditions. The attentive reader may be able to sense this. The figure of a historical Lao Tzu as sole source of this wisdom is unlikely, even though he or his prototype may still have been one of the principal sources for some of the text. The name 'Lao Tzu' or 'Laozi' simply means 'old' or 'venerable man'; this already suggests that it may in fact refer to no one more specific than a symbolic sage. In the light of this, what then should we make of the meeting with Confucius that was supposed to have happened? Is this instead alluding metaphorically to a competition between rival currents of thought?

Just as with Pythagoras, whose biographical details are only marginally less ambiguous, the generations of followers and adepts and commentators of Taoism have cumulatively constructed a corpus of thinking and of biography around the persona of Lao Tzu, which has then been appropriated as a canon; and in this process they have shifted the emphasis. We now have a *story* of Lao Tzu, just as we have a *story* of Pythagoras, which occupies the foreground: but, behind them, we suspect there may lie a different reality.

There is a deeper level, however, at which Pythagoras and the *Tao Te Ching* share common ground. The *Tao Te Ching* comes immediately to the heart of something we have observed repeatedly in the case of Pythagoras, namely the sensed inadequacy of language to talk about the deepest perceptions of human experience. For this reason the *Tao Te Ching*, though written with words, begins straight off by stating how words are insufficient for the task in hand; and by extension, the acts of reasoning, discriminating and describing in words, as well.

> The way that can be spoken of
> Is not the constant way;
> The name that can be named
> Is not the constant name.
> The nameless was the beginning of heaven and earth;
> The named was the mother of the myriad creatures.
> Hence always rid yourself of desires in order to observe its secrets;
> But always allow yourself to have desires in order to observe its
> manifestations.[1]

The crucial thing which Taoism implies is *being* – being in a particular way in relation to our human and natural surroundings. In fact, in the supposed encounter between Lao Tzu and Confucius, Lao Tzu is at pains to show Confucius how his urge to impart precepts and to make discriminations between what is good and what is bad will lead him nowhere, and that he must seek instead the freedom of a spiritual listening. He must be led by the *tao*, meaning 'way' or 'path' – a word that has a few important affinities with Pythagoras's '*harmonía*'. He wishes to warn Confucius against the binary and dialectical cast of thinking. In early Western thought, no one stresses such listening and receptivity more than Pythagoras; he never sees *harmonía* as locked in opposition with disharmony in the way that good is with evil, because for him disharmony is not a definable or active force, it is merely the default state of things, a chaos. *Harnonía* for Pythagoras is the gift of meaning in the universe: like the *tao*, it is just there to be followed and it exists above distinctions. It leads us out of the labyrinth of choices and discriminations.

Pythagoras's insistence on teaching through music, geometry and mathematics is, in this sense, close to the spirit of Lao Tzu. It represents the way in which he chooses to circumvent so much of the distracting paraphernalia of verbalisation. Through them he reveals and helps us to observe things with the minimum verbal distortion. In such ways, there is common ground between the thinking of Pythagoras's early years and that of the sage or sages of Taoism.

In the story of Pythagoras's later emigration to the Western Greek world of Southern Italy and of his increasing involvement there in the social application of philosophical thinking, however, his philosophical persona moves much closer to that of Confucius. The abstract philosophy of his youth now gives way to a concern for the more mature consideration of the application of his thought to society, as well as to the preparation of the soul for death. Pythagoras, according to Diogenes Laertius, guided the governance of the city of Croton to what could be called "a true aristocracy, and government by the best" [2] . The politics of a small city of the Greek world in this early period was very different from the often degraded phenomenon which we understand today as the politics of a state. Good or bad, its functioning was never remote, but rather at very close contact with the whole of the citizenry. It was able quite credibly to embrace the desire for a genuine moral regeneration, as would seem to be the case with Pythagoras's participation in Croton. And in these concerns he reminds us of a sort of Western Confucius…

…and yet how different. To Confucius is traditionally attributed the compilation and editing of a large body of literature that he made into the primary canon of texts from Chinese Antiquity – the *Five Classics* – and which he is said to have seen as the basis of an ancestral knowledge which should inform the thinking and judgements of his own and later generations. Even if the attribution of all this work to him overstates his role, it seems clear that through his teaching he significantly contributed to the later canonic formation of these texts. The *Analects*, too, are a clear and vital source of knowledge about the thinking of Confucius and, even though they may not have been composed by him, they give the impression that he instigated and even guided, at least in part, their compilation by his followers. There is a seriousness of purpose in all of this which is the foundation of Confucius's greatness. And it is in stark contrast to the tissue of hearsay we have regarding Pythagoras. Nor could their lives have been more different. Pythagoras was a merchant wanderer from the decentralised world of Greece; Confucius belonged to the scholarly and scriptorial world of a densely sedimented society. He saw that harmony in society could be achieved only through a re-establishment of ancient values – humaneness and equity (*ren*), filial respect (*xiao*), and attention to ritual (*li*): such values resonate more with the world of Virgil's Rome than that of Pythagoras, or even Lao Tzu.

A predominating concern both for harmony and reciprocity links Pythagoras and Confucius, but at the same time reveals the very different directions in which their thoughts were pointed. In a famous passage of the *Analects*, Confucius speaks of the so-called 'Golden Rule':

> Tsze-Kung asked, saying: "Is there one word which may serve as a rule of practice for all one's life?" The Master said, "Is not reciprocity (*shu*) such a word? What you do not want done to yourself, do not do to others." [3]

This brings to mind immediately the scene of Pythagoras and the man beating a dog. The moral consideration is the same in both instances. But there are two further implications in the case of Pythagoras which move the issue into different territory. First, the fact that the situation involves a dog and therefore implicates the whole breadth of creation through Pythagoras's central belief in the kinship of *all* living things. Second, the words of Pythagoras on this occasion are made in the context of the greater question of the reincarnation of our existence and the consequent part we play both as the 'hurter' and the 'hurt'. For Confucius the heavenly order, *tian*, is a given; its cosmic operation through time is not a matter that interests him.

In a similar way, harmony for Confucius is a more specific, worldly consideration and has less of the transcendent and spiritual breadth which Pythagoras attributes to it. In one section of the *Shang Shu* or 'Book of Documents' – one of those '*Five Classics*' or five great texts of ancient Chinese literature and thought mentioned above – the Emperor Shun, who has been designated by Emperor Yao to be his successor, is choosing and appointing his many officials and ministers to take care of the administrative and ritual affairs of the Empire:

And the Emperor said: "K'uei, I charge you to be Director of Music, to teach the descendant sons to be straight and yet mild, large-minded and yet careful, firm and yet not tyrannical, great and yet not arrogant. Poetry expresses the mind; the song is a drawing out of its words; the notes depend upon the chanting; the pitch-pipes harmonise the note. When the eight sounds [*the eight categories of instruments*] can be harmonised and not encroach upon each other, spirits and men will be brought into harmony."

If this last sentence resonates with the acoustic interests of Pythagoras, the reply of K'uei seems to come straight from the story of Orpheus:

K'uei said, "Ah, when I strike the stones, when I knock the stones, all the animals follow it and dance … all the governors become truly harmonious." [4]

In a later text (supposed by tradition to belong to the 3rd century BC but probably composed 'retrospectively' during the 3rd century AD as one sinologist, Yoav Ariel, has proposed), Confucius himself comments on this reply of K'uei, in a conversation with Duke Ai of Lu:

Confucius replied: "These words refer to the transforming influence of good government. When the Ancient Emperors and Kings had accomplished their deeds, they composed music. When their achievements were good, the music was harmonious. And if the music was truly harmonious, it seemed as if Heaven and Earth were resonating with it. How much more so was the reaction of the various kinds of animals? K'uei was the Director of Music in Emperor Shun's court. He was able to use music to bring the true essence of well-ordered principles of government to their full realisation." [5]

Aristotle's words on Celestial Harmony come to mind again: "melodious and poetical as [such a] theory is, it cannot be a true account of the facts". His pragmatism serves to remind us how much in our Western culture his perception of things has become our own, and has eclipsed our awareness of these more suggestive ideas which both Confucius and Pythagoras espoused. Confucius's perception of musical harmony as a moral force within the world overlaps with many aspects of the thinking of Pythagoras as it is related to us by the historians when they speak about his period of sojourn in Magna Graecia.

In the world-view of Confucius, harmony can, and must, be brought about by human agency – right choices, just discrimination, good manners and self-cultivation; it is to be engineered and nurtured. For the Taoist, on the other hand, this idea is a perverse illusion which leads to frustration and creates a dangerous separation between ourselves and the flow of nature. Letting go of the instinct to control, as Taoism suggests, helps us to feel, not so much accomplished, as content and at peace with all around us. The vocabulary used in these cursory definitions may seem quite different – the first positive and active, the second renunciatory and receptive; yet both these systems of belief share the same objective of bringing, through different routes, the earthly into harmony with the heavenly. For some, the one is the right way, for others, the other. For Pythagoras, however, the distinction between what was heavenly and what was earthly was not of primary significance. Harmony was ever-present and possessed a mathematical reality: it did not proceed from one thing to another, but existed, indifferent of precedence, in the fruitful relationship between things – in much the same way as an electric current exists only in the relationship between the poles of a battery once connection is made. The connections alone which we make, or are made for us, are what gives meaning to our existence.

[1] *Tao Te Ching*, Book I, 1-3, (translated D.C. Lau)

[2] Diogenes Laertius, *Vitae Philosophorum*, VIII. 1.3

[3] *Analects* of Confucius, 15.23, translated by James Legge

[4] *Book of Documents*, (Yao tien, 35 & Kao Yao mo, 19) translated by Bernhard Karlgren, *The Bulletin of the Museum of Far Eastern Antiquities*, Bulletin 22, Stockholm 1950.

[5] *K'ung-ts'ung-tzu: the K'ung Family Masters' Anthology*, translated by Yoav Ariel.

Qing Dynasty hanging scroll depicting an allegorical meeting,
in which Lao Tzu (left) and Confucius (right), give and receive the infant Buddha (centre),
symbolising, in unusual imagery, the complementarity of the three streams of thought.
(Pythagoras is not present... but sent his regrets.)

APPENDIX 3

Demonstration of the Pythagorean Theorem by Rearrangement

There are many different ways, geometric and algebraic, of proving the Theorem of Pythagoras – many of them highly ingenious. We do not know definitively which method Pythagoras may have used to demonstrate to others the validity of the theorem, but the following proof is one of the simplest and oldest methods, and the most likely one that he would have used. Because it involves the process of rearranging four identical triangles, it is referred to as 'Proof by Rearrangement'.

If the logic of its mathematics is accepted, this demonstration can of course be done with a simple rough drawing. But for some of his ancient interlocutors Pythagoras may have needed to use solid materials, as in the method described below. This physical demonstration uses pieces of wood and a piece of chalk.

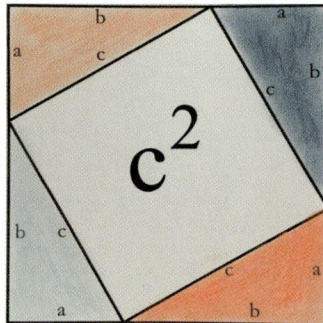

1. Cut two identical rectangles of wood of any size; then cut them both along the diagonal which joins their two opposite corners. This provides you with four right-angle triangles of identical size, each with two legs of length a and b, and a hypotenuse (the long side opposite the right-angle) of length c.

2. Arrange the four resulting triangles (two blue and two red), point to point, in a square. The perimeter of this outer square has four sides which are $a+b$ in length and an area therefore of $(a+b)^2$.

3. We have also created an inner empty space remaining between the triangles which is a perfect square whose perimeter is formed by the four hypotenuse lengths c, and whose area is c^2.

4. Mark round the perimeter of the whole design with chalk or a pen on the surface on which you are performing the demonstration.

5. Now dismantle and rearrange the triangles by reuniting them into the rectangles from which they were cut, and placing the two rectangles snugly into opposite corners of the chalk perimeter you have drawn, positioned with their axes perpendicular and in such a way that they just touch one another:

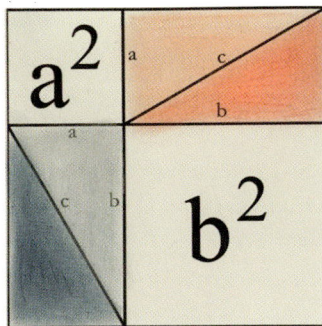

6. This has now created two new empty squares, rather than just one as previously. The small empty space is a square defined by sides of length of a, and has an area of a^2 , while the larger one is defined by sides of length b, and has an area of b^2.

7. Since the area occupied by the triangles remains the same throughout, and the overall area of the design remains constant at $(a+b)^2$, it follows that the sum of the two small red squares, $a^2 + b^2$, must be exactly equivalent to the square in the first arrangement with area c^2.

This shows that, for all right-angle triangles, $a^2 + b^2 = c^2$, or the sum of the squares on the two shorter sides, is equivalent to the square on the longest side.

THE MAPS & ILLUSTRATIONS

Notes, Acknowledgements & Credits

MAPS

p.30 The Aegean Sea: the 'frog pond' of Socrates.

p.33 The Eastern Mediterranean.

p.34 Greek and Phoenician colonisation in the Mediterranean area, from the 9th to 6th centuries BC.

p.40 The extent of the Persian Achaemenid Empire under Darius I (c. 500 BC)

p.50 Samos and Ionia

p.78 The Nile Valley

pp. 168 & 169 Anaximander's 'World Map'

p.188 Magna Graecia

All eight of these maps were drawn and designed by Nick Hill (Nick Hill Design, Devizes, UK.)

ILLUSTRATIONS

Where not otherwise stated, images are in the Public Domain for copyright purposes, or are reproduced here under pertinent Creative Commons (CCAA) licences.

Title Page: Silver *stater* of the 4th century BC from Knossos. Münzkabinett, Staatliche Museen zu Berlin. (Object no.18216476-rv).

p.v A fine, 1st century portrait of an older man, painted in encaustic on wooden panel, from the Fiayum oasis (Western Egypt). Its exact provenance is not known. The portrait was gifted to the Württembergisches Landesmuseum, Stuttgart, by the collector, antiquarian and amateur Egyptologist, Ernst von Sieglin (1848-1927). Image, kind courtesy of Landesmuseum Württemberg, P. Frankenstein / H. Zwietasch.

INTRODUCTION

Chapter 1

pp.4&5 The labyrinth at Fontanellato near Parma was planned and created by the publisher and collector, Franco Maria Ricci, during the first decade of this century. It is said to be the largest maze in existence, created from over 200,000 plants of different species of bamboo. It was in part inspired by Ricci's friendship with Jorge Luis Borges. Image by kind permission of *Labirinto della Masone;* photograph by Yann Monel.
p.7 The Maze of Villa Pisani, Strà. Photograph by Cristina Allegri.

ASIA, AFRICA & GREECE

p.8 The archaeologist, Austen Henry Layard – an important benefactor of paintings to the collection of the National Gallery in London – first excavated at the site of Nimrud in 1845. He published his findings in a two-volume work entitled *Nineveh and its Remains.* This was followed, after his second campaign at the site in 1849, by *The Monuments of Nineveh,* illustrated with engravings and lithographs of works by James Fergusson, an accomplished artist and recorder of oriental and Indian antiquities: this image was the frontispiece. Fergusson based his images on drawings made on site by Layard. (Collection of the Royal Academy of Arts.)

Chapter 2

p.11 Image of Orion in the sky; adapted from a photograph by manpuku7: Getty Images, Korea.
p.14 Table Mountain, Cape Town, South Africa. (Adobe Stock photograph, by Andrea).

Chapter 3

p.17 Song Dynasty, silk fan, painted in ink and colour. (National Palace Museum, Taipei, Taiwan.) The tree depicted appears to be an early predecessor of *Citrus x sinensis,* the Sweet Orange tree, a hybrid which was first created in Southern China. It followed the Bitter orange, *Citrus x aurantium* (brought by Arab settlers into Europe possibly as early as the 11th century), arriving into Spain and Portugal four centuries later. It is now one of the most widely cultivated trees in the world.
p.19 Marcus Julius Philippus, known as Philip the Arab, Emperor of Rome 244-249. Marble bust in the collection of The State Museum of the Hermitage, St. Petersburg since 1787; formerly in the John Lyde Brown Collection.
p.22 The *Moschophoros* or "Calf-bearer" in the Acropolis Museum, Athens. (Acr. 624 © Acropolis Museum, 2018, photo: Yiannis Koulelis.)
p.23 Monumental statue of Ramses II with his daughter, Bintanath, between his legs, from the Temple of Karnak. (Alamy Stock Images.)
p.24 Detail of the upper part of the the *Moschophoros* (see above, p.22).
p.25 The Parthenon and the Acropolis of Athens seen from the hill of the Pnyx. (Photograph by the author.)

p.26 A photograph from 1972 of the Temple of Apollo *'Epikourios'*, the 'Protector', at Bassae, high in the mountains of the Western Peloponnese. The roof of the temple, according to Pausanias, was also of stone, although its design was hypaethral, i.e. with its centre open to the sky, admitting light into the interior. The temple's frieze is now in the British Museum in London. Since 1987 the temple has been encased in a protective tent of PVC over a metallic structure.

p.27 Albumen silver-print photograph of the *Moschophoros* and the *Kritios Boy*, after they were exhumed on the Athenian Acropolis around 1865. (Photograph in the Gilman Collection of the Metropolitan Museum, New York – Gift of The Howard Gilman Foundation, 2005).

Chapter 4

p.28 Watercolour reconstruction of the façade of the 6th century BC, Ishtar Gate of Babylon, by the German Art Historian, Friedrich Wachtsmuth, c. 1912. Reproduced by kind permission of the Deutsche Orient-Gesellschaft. (Photograph by Olaf M. Teßmer.)

p.31 Minoan engraved seal in blue chalcedony from the 17th century BC. J. Paul Getty Villa, Malibu California. (Photograph courtesy of the Getty Museum).

p.43 Detail from Nebuchadnezzar's Inscription from the Ishtar Gate of Babylon: Pergamon Museum, Berlin. (Photograph by Osama S.M. Amin: CCAA licence.)

Chapter 5

pp.44 & 46 The *Kouros* of Samos, early 6th Century BC, carved in local limestone – full view, and detail of flank – in the Archaeological Museum, Vathí, Samos. (Photographs by the author.)

p.47 One of the inner Ionic capitals from the temple of Hera, carved in local limestone, showing the softness and flexibility evoked in the carving. Archaeological Museum, Vathí, Samos. (Photograph by the author.)

p.53 Remains of the stereobate of the Temple of Hera, designed and built by Rhoikos and Theodoros of Samos, c. 560 BC. The sanctuary was one of the most important in the Hellenic world and attracted visitors and votive gifts from all corners of the Mediterranean world and Near East. (Photograph by the author.)

p.55 A view down the hand-carved gallery of the Tunnel of Eupalinus in Ancient Samos. The water channel is below and to the left. (Photograph by the author.)

QUALITIES OF GREEKNESS

p.58 Mid 5th century BC Athenian silver tetradrachm, figuring the Little owl *(Athene noctua)*, emblem of the city and of Athena. (Private collection).

Chapter 6

p.61 Ink and wash drawing of the Eastern front of the Temple of Hephaistos, or 'Theseion', in Athens, from *The Antiquities of Athens measured and delineated by James Stuart, FRS & FSA, and Nicholas Revett, painters and architects;* London 1794. Courtesy of Architectural Watercolors, Michael Hampton Design Inc., Washington DC.

p.63 Madewood Plantation House, near Napoleonville, Louisiana, designed by Henry Howard, 1846. Photograph by Olivier Brei, New Orleans.

p.64 The Jain temples of Parshvanatha (left) and Adinatha (centre), of the 10th & 11th centuries respectively, in Khajuraho (Chhatarpur district of Madhya Pradesh). Anonymous photograph of 1885.

p.66 A drawn reconstruction of a transverse view of the Portico of the Temple of Artemis at Ephesus, from Fritz Krischen, *Die griechische Staat: Wiederherstellung*, Berlin 1930 (plate 33).

p.68 *(left)* Female face from decorations of the column-bases of the Archaic Temple of Apollo at Didyma, now in the Antikensammlung in Berlin. (Photograph by Merja Attia, Helsinki.)

(right) Female face from the Archaic Temple of Artemis at Ephesus, now in the British Museum, London. (© The Trustees of The British Museum.)

Chapter 7

p.71 The Ancient Theatre at Delphi. (Original colour photograph by 'KtrnDrta': CCAA Licence.)

Chapter 8

p.74 The strait between the islands of Kalymnos and Telendos, with the islet of Kalavrós in the foreground. (Author's photograph.)

p.78 The East bank of the Nile above Aswan. (Author's photograph.)

p 79 View from Karpathos towards Saria, across the bay of Vrykounda. (Author's photograph.)

p.81 View south towards the Cyclades from the Western tip of Ikaria, between Kalamos and Karkinagri. (Author's photograph.)

PYTHAGORAS DISTILLED

p.82 Detail from a fine, 1st century portrait of an older man, painted in encaustic on wooden panel, from the Fiayum oasis (Western Egypt). Württembergisches Landesmuseum, Stuttgart. (*See above p.270, credits for illustration on p.V*)

Chapter 9

p.85 *His Master's Voice:* painting (1898), by Francis Barraud, of 'Nipper' listening to his deceased master's voice registered on an early phonograph.

p.86 Detail of the central area of Michelangelo's fresco painting of *The Last Judgement* on the west wall of the Sistine Chapel, 1536-1541. (Because of their central theological importance, both Saint Peter's Basilica in Rome and the adjacent Sistine Chapel are oriented with their respective main altars placed in the West, contrary to the canonical orientation for places of Christian worship.)

p.91 A woman panning for gold in the Irrawaddy River: photograph by Werner Padarin ©.

Chapter 10

p.92 Detail of a relief, in Parian marble, on the grave-stele of a certain 'Stephanos', from Tanagra in Boeotia: 4th century BC. National Archaeological Museum of Athens. Photograph by the author.

p.98 Sketch in pen and ink by the author's mother of a dog sleeping (1973).

Chapter 11

p.99 *"Shepherd and Rocks"*, oil on board, by John Craxton (1943). Britten-Pears Foundation, Aldeburgh. © Estate of John Craxton. All rights reserved, DACS 2021.

Chapter 12

p.106 Oak tree at the site of the Oracle of Zeus at Dodona, in Epirus. Photograph by Damian Entwistle.

p.109 A modern monochord created by Michalis Georgiou, Cyprus – specialist maker of ancient instruments.

p.110 Drawing showing a possible reconstruction of a *cithara* or lyre incorporating an ivory human figure of the mid-7th century BC from the Archaeological Museum of Vathí, Samos. Image by kind permission of Professor Andrew F. Stewart, University of California at Berkeley, from *Greek Sculpture* (Yale University Press, 1990); original drawing from the *Athenische Mitteilungen*, vol. 74 (1959): 54, fig. 7, published by the German Archaeological Insitute in Athens.

p.114 Wood-cut made from a drawing by Andrea Palladio (published 1581) for the Villa Rotonda near Vicenza, taken from his *Quattro Libri dell'Archittetura* (Book II, page 19). Metropolitan Museum of New York, Bequest of W. Gedney Beatty, 1941.

p.115 Albert Einstein playing the violin made for him by Oscar Steger in 1933, at a charity recital in January 1941 for the Present Day Club, Princeton, NJ. The violin was sold at Bonhams in New York for over half a million US dollars in March of 2018. *(Every effort has been made to trace ownership of the copyright of this exact image, but has not resulted in any success to date. The author and publisher will be grateful for any information which can lead them to the copyright holder.)*

Chapter 13

p.116 *Le Silence:* plaster model by Antoine-Augustin Préault. Museum of Fine Arts Houston: purchase funded by Fayez Sarofim in memory of Maxwell Alexander Sarofim.

p.119 Banryutei garden at Kongobu-ji Monastery on Koyasan, Japan, created in 1983/4. (Photograph by Tatsuya Suzuki)

p.121 *"Counting the Stones at Ryoan-ji Temple"*, ink on paper.

Chapter 14

p.122 Painted terracotta *rhyton* in the shape of a dog's head, with decoration attributed to the Brygos Painter, Athens c. 490-47 BC, from the National Museum of Etruscan Civilisation at Villa Giulia, Rome. (Reproduced here by kind permission of Dott. Valentino Nizzo, Ministero della Cultura, Museo Nazionale Etrusco di Villa Giulia.)

p.126 4th century BC pebble mosaic figuring Dionysos riding on the back of a leopard, from the so-called 'House of Dionysos' at Pella, Macedon.

p.131 *(Upper image)* Sculpture in Parian marble of a Hunting Dog attributed to the so-called 'Rampin Master', c. 520 BC, in the Acropolis Museum, Athens. (Acr. 143 © Acropolis Museum, 2013, photo: Socratis Mavromatis.)

p.131 *(Lower image)* Late 6th century BC, Athenian, red-figure mixing cup, with tondo figuring a dog scratching its ear with its hind leg, attributed to the Euergides painter. (Image © Ashmolean Museum, University of Oxford.)

134. *The Dog*, painted in oil on plaster by Francisco de Goya, c. 1820, for the upper-floor reception room of his house in Madrid, referred to as the 'Quinta del Sordo'. (Prado Museum, Madrid. Bridgeman Images, London)

Chapter 15

p.135 Detail from an oil on panel painting entitled *Heracleitus, "The Weeping Philosopher"*, by Abraham Janssens, c. 1601, last sold at auction in New York in 2012.

p.138 Votive relief from Daskyleion (Dascylium: modern Ergili) in Phrygia close to the Propontis, now in the Achaeological Museum in Istanbul. Photograph by kind courtesy of Dr. Lloyd Llewellyn-Jones, Professor of Ancient History at the University of Cardiff.

p.143 11th Century, bronze image of Shiva in his manifestation as Nataraja – from Tamil Nadu, India. Art Institute of Chicago.

Chapter 16

p.146 Albrecht Dürer, *Das große Rasenstück*, or 'The Great Piece of Turf', 1503: watercolour, pen and ink. The Albertina Collection, Vienna. (Author's photograph.)

p.151 *(Upper image)* Plimpton 322: Babylonian clay tablet inscribed with mathematical text in cuneiform, c. 1800 BC, from Larsa, Mesopotamia. Columbia University, New York, NY.

p.151 *(Lower image)* The *Zhou Bi Suan Jing*, (Chou Pi Suan Ching), in a 17th century edition, showing a diagrammatic proof of the 3-4-5 Pythagorean triangle. Butler Library (Rare Books and Mansucripts), Columbia University, New York, NY.

p.159 YBC 7289. Babylonian clay tablet, showing a value for the square root of two; early 2nd millennium BC. The Yale University Babylonian Collection, New Haven, CT.

p.161 Albrecht Dürer, *Melencolia I*, 1514 (detail): engraving. Metropolitan Museum of Art, New York (Harris Brisbane Dick Fund, 1943)

p.163 (footnote 12) Magic square from the entrance to the temple of Parshvanatha at Khajuraho. (Photograph by Rattibha.)

Chapter 17

p.164 Detail from the large (5.8m x 4.3m) Nile Landscape mosaic from the Sanctuary of Fortuna Primigenia at Palestrina – Ancient *Praeneste*. (Author's photograph).

pp.168&169 Reconstruction of Anaximander's World Map, reproduced by kind permission of Prof. Dirk Couprie – re-drawn by Nick Hill, Nick Hill Design.

pp.170&171 Central section of the *Tabula Peutingeriana* in the Austrian National Library, Vienna. The tabula is a long parchment scroll, measuring 0.34m in height by 6.75m in length. It is based upon a Roman *itinerarium* of the known world, dating from the 1st

century, and re-copied in this form probably in the 12th or 13th century.
p.173 The early 6th century BC, Babylonian *Imago Mundi* clay tablet (inv. No. 92687) from Sippar. (© The Trustees of The British Museum.)
p.177 The Earth seen from outer space. (European Space Agency.)

Chapter 18

p.178 Ceiling fresco of a diver, from a tomb in the Necropolis of Paestum (Poseidonia), Italy – a rare survival of Greek painting from the early 5th Century BC. (Author's photograph.)

PROBLEMS WITH PYTHAGORAS

p.182 An Attic *kylix* of the late 6th century BC, decorated by the Euergides Painter. National Archaeological Museum of Spain, Madrid. (Photograph by Dorieo, CCAA 4.0 International licence)

Chapter 19

p.185 The single surviving Doric column from the early 5th century BC temple, dedicated to *Hera Lakínias*, at Cape Colonna, south of Croton, which probably replaced a preceding temple at the Sanctuary dating from the time of Pythagoras. What still remained of the temple in the 17th century was demolished to provide building material for the Episcopal Residence in Croton. (Photo by Nerolito, for *krotolando.it*).
p.190 An overview, in a photograph of the 1940s, of the alluvial plain of the Sybaris and Crathis rivers, where Ancient Sybaris was probably situated. Photo from *In Search of Sybaris* by Donald Freeman Brown, in *Expedition Magazine* 5.2 (1963), published by Penn Museum. Reproduced by persmission of Penn Museum.
p.194 Flower and leaves of the cultivated Fava Bean plant *(Vicia faba).*

Chapter 20

p.196 Fifth Century BC bronze Head "of a Philosopher" found in the sea-bed, off Porticello in Calabria. Museo Nazionale della Magna Graecia, Reggio in Calabria (no. 17096). (Photograph by Vincenzo Caroleo, Alamy Stock Photo.)
p.198 Author's collage of a fava bean and a drawing of a human child in the womb.
p.200 Mid-2nd century portrait of a young soldier from Ancient Philadelphia (Er Rubayat), in Faiyum, Egypt, painted in encaustic on panel. Staatliche Museen zu Berlin, Antikensammlung (inv. no. 31161,5)
p.202 The great *botafumeiro* censer, or thurible, of the Cathedral of Santiago de Compostela, which weighs more than 75 kilograms. (Photograph reproduced by kind permission of Ilona Fried.)

Chapter 21

p.207 The *Morpho peleides* blue butterfly, native to the tropical forests of Central and South America, is one of the largest butterflies of the natural world. Photograph by kind permission of Xavier Lobaina.

p.208 The philosopher, Benedetto Croce, photographed 1947. (Bridgeman Images, London.)

p.209 The ruins of the Ancient Library at Nysa on the Meander, a city of Asia Minor, about 30 miles inland to the east of Ephesus (near modern Sultanhisar in Turkey). The city was founded below the mountain which was believed to have been the birthplace of the god, Dionysos. Most of its buildings, including the library, date from the 2nd century AD. The city appears to have been a centre of considerable learning and culture in Antiquity. (Photo by Carole Raddato, CCAA 2.0)

p.213 Drawing by William Wallace Denslow for L. Frank Baum's story, *The Wonderful Wizard of Oz* (1900), depicting the wizard surprised behind his screen.

Chapter 22

p.218 Theran wall-painting of the 17th Century BC, recovered from Xeste 3 at the Bronze Age archaeological site of Akrotiri on Santorini, now in the Museum of Prehistoric Thera, in Firá.

p.220 *Aphrodite Pudica* of the 2nd century BC, of a form derived from the famous Aphrodite of Cnidos by Praxiteles. Possibly from the Temple of Aphrodite beside the Commercial Harbour of Rhodes, she was recovered from the sea-bed to the north of the harbour. Now in the Archaeological Museum of Rhodes. (Author's photograph.)

p.221 Detail from a portrait of a young man of the Hadrianic era (117-138) from Faiyum executed in the mixed tempera and wax encaustic technique, typical of the era and the location. Painted from life, and used during the sitter's lifetime in perhaps the same way as we would use a portrait photograph today, it was then later used as a funerary portrait fixed and bound over the face of the mummy of the deceased. Excavated at Hawara in 1892 by Richard von Kaufmann; now in the collection of the Staatliche Antikensammlungen, Munich, Germany (inventory no.15013).

p.223 Detail of a 1st century coloured stone, mosaic floor found in the *tablinum* of the House of the Faun in Pompeii. The scene depicts the defeat of Darius by Alexander at the Battle of Issus in 333 BC, and, according to Pliny, is based on a lost painting of the 4th century BC by Philoxenos of Eretria. National Archaeological Museum of Naples. (Author's photograph.)

p.223 Part of the face of a female divinity of the 'Daedalic type', in painted terracotta, dating from the 8th century BC. Paolo Orsi Archaeological Museum, Siracusa, Sicily. (Author's photograph.)

p.227 Fragment of a carved marble frieze from the area of the stadium in Ancient Tyre. (Author's photograph.)

PYTHAGORAS TODAY

p.228 The Hawai'i 'Ō'ō Bird (*Moho nobilis*); tinted lithograph by John Gerrard Keulemans, c. 1895. Keulemans (1842-1912) was a talented Dutch ornithological illustrator, who worked for much of his life in England. The 'Ō'ō Bird (depicted here) became extinct a little over thirty years ago: what is believed to be the last existing recording of the song of the closely related *Moho braccatus*, the Kaua'i 'Ō'ō Bird, was made by David Boynton in 1987. An edited version of this recording can be found on www.youtube.com.

Chapter 23

p.230 Image of the Standing Buddha from Gandhara, 1st century, now in the Musée Guimet, Paris. (Photograph by Rama: CCAA 3.0 FR).

p.236 A Weeping cherry-tree (*Prunus pendula*) in the park of the Castle of Matsumoto, Japan. (Author's photograph.)

Chapter 24

p.237 Carl Jung in 1950, aged 75. (Bridgeman Images, London.)

p.239 Image of the goddess Sekhmet, daughter of Ra, in polished Egyptian granite, early 14th Century BC, XVIIIth Dynasty. Sold at Sotheby's New York in December 2016.

p.238 *The Created Cosmos and Expulsion from the Garden of Eden*, Giovanni di Paolo, in tempera on wood panel – originally part of the predella of an altarpiece in the Church of San Domenico, Siena (1445). Now in the Robert Lehman Collection, Metropolitan Museum, New York. The trees seen behind the figures in this exquisite painting are almost certainly fantastical apple trees hung with golden apples, whose foliage here happens to look rather like that of the orange tree. 1445 would be an unusually early figuration for orange trees. The nudity of the angel here is also most unusual.

p.245 Sebastian, born 2nd August 2021. Photo by kind courtesy of Michael and Christopher.

EPILOGUE

p.248 Drawing, or tracing, made by John Keats of an image of the Sosibios Vase in the Louvre which Keats may have found either in a volume of engravings, entitled *Musée Napoléon* (the fomer name of the Louvre Museum) that he had likely seen at the house of the painter, Benjamin Haydon, or – according to Edmund Blunden – in a copy of *A Collection of Antique Vases, Altars, Paterae* by Henry Moses. The vase is a late Hellenistic marble *krater* by the artist Sosibios, who worked in Rome in the 1st century BC.

p.249 Sketch in pen and ink by Joseph Severn, who devotedly nursed Keats during his last days, made at the time of the poet's death which is recorded below the drawing as "28th January 1821 at 3 o'clock in the morning".

AFTER-THOUGHTS & APPENDICES

Appendix 1

p.234 A scene from the 2015 production of Handel's *L'Allegro, il Penseroso e il Moderato* (1740) by the Mark Morris Dance Group, Brooklyn, NY.

p.236 A detail from the combined text and musical notation of the *Delphic Paean to Apollo* of Athenaios Athenaiou. The lyrics are incised on two marble slabs visible from the Sacred Way at Delphi on the south side of the Treasury of the Athenians. The paean is believed to have been composed in 138/7 BC and carved maybe a decade later. It represents the earliest and most complete example of a Greek song recorded together with its musical notation. (Photo courtesy of Kelly Lambert, Harvard Kosmos Society.)

Appendix 2

p.238 *Lao Tzu, Mounted on an Ox,* by Zhang Lu, early 16th Century ink on paper hanging scroll, from the collection of the National Palace Museum, Taipei, Taiwan. (Image from WikiMedia Commons, Public Domain.)

p.245 *Lao Tzu, Confucius and the Infant Buddha:* hanging scroll of coloured ink on silk, probably by Wang Shugong (1649 – c.1733). British Museum, no. 1913, 0501,0.18 (© The Trustees of The British Museum.)

p.289 Painted terracotta rhyton in the shape of a dog's head, with decoration attributed to the Brygos Painter, Athens c. 490-47 BC, (see p.122). (Reproduced here by kind permission of Dott.re Valentino Nizzo, Ministero della Cultura, Museo Nazionale Etrusco di Villa Giulia.)

SOURCES & SELECT LITERATURE

1) Primary Ancient Literature:

Aeschylus, *Prometheus Bound*

Archilochus, poems: *Greek Lyric Poetry*, translated by M.L. West, Oxford, 1993

Aristotle, *Metaphysics*, Book I. Fragments in *Aristotelis Qui Ferebantur Librorum Fragmenta*, Valentin Rose.

Athenaeus of Naucratis, *Diepnosophistae*, Book XII

Baudhayana and the Sulba Sutras, in Plofker, Kim, *Mathematics in India*, 500BCE -1800 CE

Chou Pi Suan Ching / Zhou Bi Suan Jing, in *Astronomy and Mathematics in Ancient China*, Christopher Cullen, Cambridge 1996.

Clement of Alexandria, *Stromata*, Book I

Confucius, the *Analects* and the *Five Classics*, in *The Chinese Classics* (Five volumes), translated by James Legge, originally published in 1861.

Diodorus of Sicily, *Bibliotheca Historica*, Book X

Diogenes Laertius, *Lives of the Eminent Philosophers*, Book VIII

Euripides, *Hippolytus*

Eusebius of Caesarea, *Preparatio Evangelica*, XI

Fragmente der Vorsokratiker, compiled by H. Diels and W. Kranz, is the gold-standard for reference to the fragments of Pherecydes, Thales, Anaximander, Xenophanes, Heracleitus and the other Pre-Socratic thinkers. It is translated into English by Kathleen Freeman as *Ancilla to the Pre-Socratic Philosophers* (Harvard University Press, 1957)

Herodotus, *The Histories*, Books I, II, III, IV, V

Hesiod, *Theogony* and *Works and Days*

Homer, *Iliad*, Books II and XIV; *Odyssey*, Books V and XIII

Iamblichus, *De Vita Pitagorica* ('On the Pythagorean Life')

Lao Tzu, *Tao te Ching* (tr. into English by James Legge 1891, Arthur Waley 1934, D.C. Lau, 1989 inter al.)

Lucian of Samosata, *Erotes*

Pausanias, *Description of Greece*

Pindar, *Fourth Nemean Ode*

Plato, Dialogues: *Cratylus, Phaedo, Phaedrus* and *Timaeus*. Other: *VIIth Epistle*

Pliny, *Naturalis Historia*, Books XII and XXXV

Plutarch, *Life of Numa Pompilius* from *Parallel Lives*

Polybius, *The Histories*, Book II

Porphyry, *Vita Pithagorae* ('Life of Pythagoras')

Sappho, poems: *Greek Lyric Poetry*, translated by M.L. West, Oxford, 1993

Shang Shu, Volume III of *The Chinese Classics* (Five volumes), translated by James Legge, originally published in 1861.

Shiji, *Records of the Grand Historian of China, translated from the Shih chi of Ssu-ma Ch'ien*, tr. Burton Watson, 1961

Strabo, *Geographica*, Book VI

Zhou Bi Suan Jing / Chou Pi Suan Ching, in *Astronomy and Mathematics in Ancient China*, Christopher Cullen, Cambridge 1996.

2) Post-Antique literature:

Brewster, Sir David, *Memoirs of the Life, Writings and Discoveries of Sir Isaac Newton*, 1855

Butler, Samuel, *The Authoress of the Odyssey*, 1897

Cavafis, Constantine, *Collected Poems* (tr. Edmund Keeley & Philip Sherrard) 1992

Croce, Benedetto, *Teoria e Storia della Storiografia*, 1916

Eliot, T. S., *Dante* (in *Selected Essays* 1917-1932)

Keats, John, *Ode on a Grecian Urn*, written 1819, published, 1820

Kepler, Johannes, *Harmonice Mundi*, 1619

Keynes, John Maynard, *The general theory of Employment, Interest and Money*, 1936

Marco Polo (with Rustichello da Pisa), *The Travels of Marco Polo*

Masuno, Shunmyo, *Zen Garden Design, Mindful Spaces by Shunmyo Masuno*, co-author, Mira Locher, 2020

Nietzsche, Friedrich, T*wilight of the Idols: or How to Philosophise with a Hammer* (original title: *Götzen-Dämmerung, oder, Wie man mit dem Hammer philosophiert*), 1889

Ruskin, John, *St Mark's Rest: The History of Venice*, 1877

Ruskin, John, *Ruskin Today*, anthology of Ruskin's writings by Kenneth Clark, 1964

Russell, Bertrand, *A History of Western Philosophy*, 1945

Santillana, Giorgio de, and Hertha von Deschend, *Hamlet's Mill*, 1977

Schlipp, Paul A., *Albert Einstein: Philosopher-Scientist*, 1951

Whitehead, Alfred North, *Process and Reality*, 1927

3) *Related secondary literature:*

Ariel, Yoav, *K'ung-Ts'ung-Tzu – The K'ung Family Masters' Anthology.* Princeton University Press, 1989

Ball, Warwick, *Rome in the East: The Transformation of an Empire*. Routledge. London 2000

Braudel, Fernand, *Les Mémoires de la Méditerranée*. Editions de Fallois, Paris, 1998. (Now translated into English as *The Mediterranean in the Ancient World*, Allen Lane/Penguin Press, London 2001.)

Broodbank, Cyprian, *The Making of the Middle Sea*, Thames & Hudson, London 2013

Couprie, Dirk, *Heaven and Earth in Ancient Greek Cosmology: From Thales to Heracleides Ponticus*. Springer, New York 2011

Guthrie, W. K. C., *A History of Greek Philosophy*, Volumes I & II. Cambridge University Press, 1962

McEvilley, Thomas, *The Shape of Ancient Thought*. Allworth Press, New York, 2002

Neugebauer, Otto, *The Exact Sciences in Antiquity*. Brown University Press, 1957 (Now a Dover publication)

Plofker, Kim, *Mathematics in India*, 500 BCE -1800 CE, Princeton University Press 2009

Scully, Vincent, *The Earth, the Temple and the Gods: Greek Sacred Architecture*. Yale University Press 1962

Stewart, Andrew, *Greek Sculpture* (Two Volumes). Yale University Press 1990

INDEX

(Page numbers in bold type indicate a related illustration or map, in addition to text;
'n.' indicates a foot-note.)

The Author's Thanks

The saying of thank-yous is perhaps the happiest moment in the production of a book: it marks the end of a lot of pain and drudgery for the author, and is a chance to remember the many unsolicited kindnesses of others. Because the writing of this book has been a pretty solitary business, there are not that many people to thank – but my gratefulness to each one of them is immense:

- first, to my dog, Livia (not strictly a person, but almost…) for her quiet companionship throughout, her supportive cheerfulness, and for her suggestion and approval of the title: no-one could have taught me better about the souls that animals have, than she did through the quiet depth of her presence.

- Charles Foster, Janet Foyle, Pico Iyer, Alex Martin, John Wakefield, Andrew Wordsworth, and my brother, Iain, all selflessly offered to read an early version of the manuscript and made invaluable comments on it – some in meticulous detail – when they all had far better things to do with their time. Nearly every one of their suggestions has been willingly adopted and has helped to make this a less faulted book. I am humbled by the generosity of these friends who took the considerable time involved to read and to comment, and I am hugely grateful to each one of them.

- I could not have had a designer, page-setter and graphics guru, more congenial, attentive, and easy to work with, than David Gillingwater. David is a portraitist of great talent, and his innate artistic sense has helped to make this a beautiful book to the eye, if it is nothing else. I would never wish to work with a different designer.

- Other debts I owe are less obvious, but every bit as important: I am very grateful to Ivan de Jesus Tabares, whose quiet and continuous patience throughout the years of writing, kept the wheels of creation turning; and, for the inspiring conversations we have had together, I would also like to thank my former student, Enrique Espinosa, and Yiannis Kasimatis, the philosopher-blacksmith of Kythera.

- I am grateful also to Caterina Napoleone for her assistance with images for the book; to my kindly and long-suffering agent, Michael Alcock, of Johnson & Alcock, and to Alexander Fyjis-Walker, for their support, un-flappability and encouragement. Finally, (and not just because his name begins with the last letter of the alphabet) my sincere thanks to Antonis Zaglakoutis who valiantly attempted a Greek translation of the text at my instigation, and persevered in a difficult project which is still close to my heart. One day perhaps, this account of Pythagoras, may be read in the living language of his descendents.

These are, I think, the very last words I have to write. The rest is silence, as Hamlet says. And silence, as Pythagoras tells us, is the mind's most cherished rest.